Indoctrination 159F

PHILOSOPHERS
DISCUSS
EDUCATION

Also by S. C. Brown

Do Religious Claims Make Sense?
Linguistic Analysis and Phenomenology
  (*co-editor with Wolfe Mays*)
Philosophy of Psychology (*editor*)

PHILOSOPHERS DISCUSS EDUCATION

Edited by S. C. Brown

Senior Lecturer in Philosophy at the Open University and
Assistant Director of the Royal Institute of Philosophy

First published 1975 by
THE MACMILLAN PRESS LTD
London and Basingstoke
Associated companies in New York
Dublin Melbourne Johannesburg and Madras

SBN 333 18108 5

Typeset in Great Britain by
PREFACE LIMITED
Salisbury, Wilts
and printed in Great Britain by
UNWIN BROTHERS LTD
London and Woking

Contents

Conference/1973/1975

Published

Contents   vii

Preface

The five symposia which are included in this volume are devoted to separate and variously related topics in the philosophy of education. The papers are largely as presented at a Royal Institute of Philosophy Conference held at the University of Exeter in 1973. In each case there is a primary paper, a reply and a chairman's contribution. Postscripts have been added to three of the symposia.

In arranging the conference Professor Godfrey Vesey and I were advised by Professor David Hamlyn, Professor Paul Hirst and Professor Richard Peters, and I should like to record our gratitude to them.

S.C.B.

PART ONE:

AUTONOMY AS AN EDUCATIONAL IDEAL

1 Autonomy as an Educational Ideal I

R. F. DEARDEN

I

The concept of autonomy seems first to have been formed
and applied in a political rather than in an ethical or
educational context. According to Pohlenz, that context was
in fact the wars fought by the Greek cities to maintain their
independence from Persia.[1] But already in the Platonic
dialogues Socrates can be seen applying the concept, if not
the word, to the individual person. If the *Crito* is taken as
representative of this conceptual extension, then strong
political overtones are still retained through Socrates's
equation of part of the *nomos* in autonomy with the city's
own 'laws and institutions' as a 'man's most precious
possessions'.[2]

With Kant, the concept is of course applied primarily to
the individual person. Kant does in fact define autonomy as
'the property the will has of being a law to itself'.[3] The
Kantian autonomous man has to fight for his independence
on two fronts, defeat on either of which would be a triumph
for heteronomy. He has to submit the moral example of
others to his own judgement for testing, and he has to
struggle with his inclinations as 'alien causes' which constantly tempt him from his dignified noumenal eminence.
Kant's notion of a 'categorical imperative' serves to combine
personal autonomy with the logical autonomy of moral

[1] M. Pohlenz, *Freedom in Greek Life and Thought* (Dordrecht: Reidel, 1966) ch. 3.
[2] Plato, *Crito*, 53 c.
[3] Kant, *Groundwork*, p. 108 (Paton's edition).

discourse. For he thinks that moral discourse and moral imperatives are logically irreducible, while action according to such imperatives serves no further interest but is absolutely spontaneous. Such action has a causeless origin.

This tracing back of autonomy to some form of absolutely spontaneous activity is a feature also of Spinoza's concept of autonomy, or 'freedom' as he in fact calls it. According to Spinoza, 'that is free which exists by mere necessity of its own nature and is determined in its actions by itself alone'.[4] In spite of a man's continuity with the unified, single system of nature, Spinoza still thinks of rational nature as having a kind of spontaneity. Thus 'ideas which we form clear and distinct seem to follow from the mere necessity of our nature in such a manner that they seem to depend absolutely on our power; but the contrary is the case with confused ideas. They are often formed in us against our will'.[5]

But although there is thus a resemblance between Spinozistic and Kantian autonomous man in respect of spontaneity, in two other respects they are strikingly different. For Spinozistic autonomy is that of egoistic and not moral rationality, although the self-preservative endeavours of Spinoza's individual men are made compatible through the pursuit of a non-competitive good. And again, Spinoza finds autonomy supremely in the activities of theoretical rather than of practical reason.

On all these views autonomy is in one way or another an activity of man as a rational animal. Some contemporary versions of autonomy, however, break this connection. Professor Hare almost does this when he describes the point in justification at which a man 'has to decide whether to accept that way of life or not.'[6] But even at this point, apparently, there does remain the rational requirement of universalisability as a limit on such ultimate decisions. Yet Sartre, in spite of some Kantian things said in *Existentialism and Humanism*, surely does disconnect autonomy from reason. For there can be reasons and reasonings only after our fundamental projects have been chosen. 'When we

[4] Spinoza, *Ethics*, pt. 1, def. 7
[5] Spinoza, *Treatise on the Correction of the Understanding*, para. 108, item vi.
[6] R. M. Hare, *The Language of Morals* (O.U.P., 1952) sect. 4.4.

deliberate, the chips are down.'[7] The spontaneity thought to be at the heart of autonomy now takes a purely voluntaristic form which places it outside reason.

Yet surely at this point we no longer have autonomy. Put crudely, we may possibly have *autos*, but without any *nomos* as the price of authenticity. True, there are situations when we do choose criteria, and there are situations where being rational is one option. But the authentic criterionless choices of Sartre do not seem intelligible as choices; or if they are intelligible, then they are far from criterionless, assuming as they do whatever criteria make 'bad faith' bad, make inauthenticity something to be condemned, and make one's vast responsibility serious to the point of anguish. The Sartrean autonomous man is, after all, not just anomic man.

II

Does attributing autonomy to individuals presuppose some form of absolute spontaneity, then? The belief that there is such a presupposition is a very natural one; for if it is denied, must there not then be prior causes of what we do, in which case where is our autonomy? In a recent sustained attack on the concept of the autonomous man, B. F. Skinner evidently thinks that he has to attack this presupposition of spontaneity. Thus in lining up his target, Skinner says that:

> unable to understand how or why the person we see behaves as he does, we attribute his behaviour to a person we cannot see, whose behaviour we cannot explain either but about whom we are not inclined to ask questions ... The function of the inner man is to provide an explanation which will not be explained in turn ... he is a centre from which behaviour emanates ... we say that he is autonomous.[8]

But if the object of Skinner's attack here is misconceived, if we do not need to presuppose the exploits and adventures of some spontaneously self-active inner man, then much of his

---

[7] J. P. Sartre, *Being and Nothingness*, trans. H. Barnes (Methuen, 1957) p. 451.
[8] B. F. Skinner, *Beyond Freedom and Dignity* (Cape, 1972) p.14.

argument against autonomy will collapse through misdirection. Certainly introspection could not establish the existence of such an inward origin of action, since the feeling of having any such spontaneity is logically quite compatible with the existence of a variety of 'hidden persuaders' as the real explanation of why we act as we do. Kant himself had doubts about the actual existence of an autonomous will, as opposed to the theoretical necessity of the idea of it.

Is such an inner man supposed to be self-created *ex nihilo*? If he falls short of that godlike origin, then he will surely have come into existence endowed with various genetic characters, then to be influenced by a determinate physical and social environment. These will together have moulded his consciousness in all sorts of ways long before he begins, if he ever begins, to think of himself as autonomous. And if we look at the *nomoi* of the philosophers' autonomous man, they are far from having sprung from his rib, as it were, but are drawn from socially transmitted ideals and modes of thought as these had been developed at that particular point in history.

Better than directly to attack the presupposition of absolute spontaneity might be to show it to be unnecessary. Certainly we shall look in vain for such a spontaneity in the autonomous *state*, to return for a moment to the political origin of the concept. We may even be able to show just how a state was made autonomous: how a colonial power carefully prepared the way by educational programmes and institutional reforms, and how eventually the colony became autonomous in a symbolic act somewhat comparable to an individual's twenty-first birthday celebrations.

Philosophers may have been too apt to overlook or ignore the fact that men have childhoods. If we do attend to childhood, we may find there educational policies, comparable to political policies, aimed at 'making' children autonomous. Appropriate expectations, encouragements, praises, and modes of talk are addressed to children by parents and teachers, with varying degrees of success. The criteria which are to serve as the *nomoi* of thought and action may be similarly taught to the child. And with the acquisition of a socially transmitted concept of himself as autonomous, the child, like the ex-colony, may well then go on to think and act in ways unforeseen by his teachers, and doubtless also sometimes in ways that would not always be approved by them.

III   *Description of autonomous man*

What sorts of activities would mark out the person who had grown up, and doubtless also been brought up, to think of himself as autonomous? I suggest that the following would feature prominently in anyone with such a character: (i) wondering and asking, with a sense of the right to ask, what the justification is for various things which it would be quite natural to take for granted; (ii) refusing agreement or compliance with what others put to him when this seems critically unacceptable; (iii) defining what he really wants, or what is really in his interests, as distinct from what may be conventionally so regarded; (iv) conceiving of goals, policies and plans of his own, and forming purposes and intentions of his own independently of any pressure to do so from others; (v) choosing amongst alternatives in ways which could exhibit that choice as the deliberate outcome of his own ideas or purposes; (vi) forming his own opinion on a variety of topics that interest him; (vii) governing his actions and attitudes in the light of the previous sorts of activity. In short, the autonomous man has a mind of his own and acts according to it. And this 'mind of his own' will typically be no purely natural product, but the outcome of one sort of education.

At the centre of these activities, and common to them all, is the forming of one's own independent judgement, though the criteria and occasions of that judgement may be very various. Whether the criteria are rules, principles, values, desired goals, or standards, they will be general in their reference, applying to numerous instances and at different times. Through their application a distinct identity and style of life will in varying degree be revealed. And the resulting judgements will be adhered to or acted on with a firmness matched to the man's conviction of their rightness. Advice may be sought, persuasion may be listened to, authoritative utterance may be heard, yet there remains the man's own mind to be made up on whether he will agree or comply, or whether he will reject or resist.

Yet what he thinks and does certainly need not be very

original, so far as its appearance on the human scene is concerned. What is essential is not so much originality, in the sense of novelty, but origination, or how it came about that the views, wants, choices or opinions came to be his. Just conceivably, though highly improbably, a person could be autonomous yet outwardly rather conformist. For he might conform to certain conventions not just out of mindless habit, or because it had never occurred to him to do anything else, or from anxiety at being different, or through yielding to social pressures without resistance. He might conform because he genuinely wanted to act in that conventional way, or because it suited his purposes in a given context. As an educational ideal, therefore, autonomy might be open to the criticism that it did not include the additional value of creative imagination.

The autonomous man's mind is his own not necessarily because of its originality, then, but because of how his views, wants, choices and opinions are originated. He applies the relevant criteria for himself, without having to be told, shown or pushed. Benn and Weinstein try to state this motivational requirement a little more precisely by saying that for *B* to want *P* it must not be sufficient that *A* wants *B* to want *P*.[9] But while this is surely correct, as far as it goes, it still leaves open such possibilities as that *B*'s activities are compulsively determined by dissociated elements within himself. One recalls that Kant's autonomous man had to maintain his autonomy on two fronts, not just one. And David Riesman found it necessary to distinguish the autonomous man not only from the other-directed but also from the inner-directed man.[10]

Yet it seems hard to rule out the possibility of compulsive inner-direction without returning to the forming of one's own independent judgement. For why do we say that an activity is compulsive? Surely this is in part because it cannot be truly seen as stemming from the man's own judgement. In the compulsive case, the activity has escaped from, or never

[9] S. I. Benn and W. L. Weinstein, 'Being Free to Act and Being a Free Man', *Mind*, Vol. 80 (1971) p. 210.
[10] D. Riesman, *The Lonely Crowd* (New Haven: Yale University Press, 1963) ch. 14.

been brought under, such judgemental control, and may indeed bend or distort judgement to suit itself. Whether this was the case with someone we could test empirically by addressing ourselves to what would be the relevant judgements (views, choices, opinions, etc.) and seeing whether the man was prepared to modify his behaviour accordingly.

But is this 'making up one's own mind' enough? I have argued so far that central to the activities typical of the autonomous man is independent judgement. In this, criteria of various kinds are applied on his own initiative, without either social or psychological pressures or compulsions being sufficient to explain the making of the judgement. But consider someone who, quite on his own initiative, applies religious, moral, political or aesthetic criteria which he has in fact never once reflected on. Perhaps he acquired them unquestioningly from his parents, or they entered his mind through the hypnopaedic whisperings of a bedroom dicta-phone. Would he then be autonomous?

To be regarded as autonomous, I suggest that a man must not only make judgements on his own initiative, but that the doubt must have entered his mind at some point that the criteria he employs in judgement might not, on reflection, be such as he would wish to acknowledge as his own. But then, in reflectively reviewing some area of judgement, the second-order judgement he now makes may in turn be similarly open to doubt. And clearly such a process of reconstruction of his mind and action is in principle impossible to complete. For wherever such a review may come to rest, the last judgement made will not itself have been reviewed. Indoctrination tries paternalistically to prejudge where such reflection will in fact come to rest. Hence the 'search and destroy' operation in education directed against indoctrination by those who favour autonomy as an educational ideal.

To be autonomous, therefore, is very much a matter of degree. Unlike being six feet tall, married, or a British citizen, whether a man is quite simply autonomous or not is something which we will often quite rightly refuse to say. And our hesitation will be related to at least three dimensions of variability: the extent to which he shows initiative in forming judgements of his own, the firmness with which he then adheres to those judgements, and finally the depth of ramifying reflection which lies behind the criteria which he employs in making those judgements. And such a character in a man can now be seen to have its own inner logic of development, as it were, implying as an ideal its own growth towards completeness and integrity. It represents one out of many forms of the perfectibility of man.

I am not trying to set out here the criteria of responsibility for an action, though autonomy is closely connected with being a responsible person. Autonomous action would be only a sub-class of those actions for which someone is responsible. The wider class would include the actions of anomic and of heteronomous men. Nevertheless, our ascriptions of responsibility may be related to autonomy in that they presuppose this, not as what a person is, but as what he could be in some 'reasonable' degree. He may still be judged by reference to autonomy, granted that he did have certain capacities and opportunities for developing in this way. This is the case when we refuse to accept being under orders as a valid excuse for doing something evil.

Responsibility could be ascribed, and by some people sometimes is ascribed, on bases quite other than that of autonomy. Responsibility may be vicarious, as when parents are held responsible for their children's actions. It may be collective, as when a whole class is punished for what an undiscoverable few actually did. It may be based on 'strict liability', as with some of our laws, and with our impulsive tendency to blame for upshots without any preliminary inquiry into motive, intention, or state of mind in acting. Relating ascriptions of responsibility to personal autonomy is therefore only one possible basis for such ascription, but it is one deeply embedded in our ordinary ways of apportioning credit and blame. Whether it should continue to be that basis will no doubt depend on how we think of autonomy and what value we accord to it. Skinner, at least, would like to see changes here. Curiously, he tries to persuade us to accept them.

IV

What does autonomy presuppose in the way of freedom? If we define freedom as being the absence of constraints on

what a man wants, or might want, to do, then certainly
autonomy could not be equated with freedom. Both the
anomic and the heteronomous man may be 'free' in this
negative sense. A young child in a 'free school', an ex-
prisoner whose autonomous powers have been atrophied by
institutional life, or even Winston Smith released by his
interrogator in Orwell's *1984*, could all be said to be free,
though none of them is autonomous. Again, in the Aristo-
telian sense in which we may possess a virtue while asleep, a
man might have the virtue of autonomy yet be denied the
freedom of its outward exercise, for instance by imprison-
ment, or by military conscription as a private in the Guards.

The relation between freedom and the outward *exercise* of
autonomy is therefore to be seen, not as one of identity, but
as one in which freedom is a necessary condition. Attempts
to identify the two more closely lead to a version of 'positive'
freedom which may make a kind of sense but which is
ill-advised. For when autonomy has as yet no psychological
reality in a person, coercion may then be passed off as
liberation, as being what he 'really' wants or wills, and thus as
needing no further justification. Discussion of different positive ideals of character, or worthwhile exercises of freedom,
will also be confused by each view claiming that it alone gives
a true account of what freedom is.

What is more interesting from the point of view of
autonomy as an educational ideal is the question of whether
freedom is a necessary condition for the development, as
opposed to the exercise, of autonomy. Being a necessary
condition for the latter by no means logically implies being a
necessary condition for the former. Logically, it could be the
case that a rather strict and tightly controlled upbringing best
developed an autonomous character, partly through the
ingredient disciplines which it taught and partly through the
inward rebellion which it engendered. A. S. Neill was not
himself brought up at Summerhill. But it has been commonly
assumed by child-centred educationalists, and more recently
and more extremely by the de-schoolers, that freedom is a
necessary condition for the development of autonomy. Thus
the Plowden Report[11] stresses that children should be free to

---

[11] Central Advisory Council for Education (England), *Children and Their Primary Schools*, Vol. 1: Report (H.M.S.O., 1967) ch. 15, 16.

be themselves, to be choosers and to be the agents of their own learning. Neill went so far as to allow one pupil at Summerhill to be absent from all lessons from the age of five to seventeen.[12] De-schoolers such as Illich want not just freedom at school, but freedom from school altogether, and very much in the interests of autonomy.[13]

This last extreme is surely too extreme. As is usual with advocates of extreme freedom, to gain this freedom increased compulsion would paradoxically be necessary. For as things are, the great majority of parents would certainly oppose de-schooling, so that it would be necessary to de-family society as well. Again, why should the area of freedom left by the dissolution of the school be filled by autonomous activity? A principal historical reason for compulsory school attendance has been to protect children from pressures that would otherwise decisively bear on them: from parents who would use them to supplement the family income, and from employers in search of cheap labour. The 'youth market' increasingly attracts commercial interests which would doubtless wish to manipulate the wants that create their market, as well as to supply those created wants with the products and services being marketed.

The de-schoolers assume autonomy to be a natural development, whereas what seems altogether more natural is to act on impulse and to yield to group pressure. Dewey amongst the child-centred educationists saw this most clearly. 'The crucial educational problem', he wrote,[14] 'is that of procuring the postponement of immediate action upon desire until observation and judgement have intervened. Unless I am mistaken, this point is definitely relevant to the conduct of progressive schools. Overemphasis upon activity as an end, instead of upon *intelligent* activity, leads to identification of freedom (sc. autonomy) with immediate execution of impulses and desires.' Dewey was not, of course, the first philosopher to be embarrassed by some of his friends. But referring back to the previous section, one might say that

---

[12] A. S. Neill, *Summerhill* (Hart: New York, 1960) p. 29.
[13] I. Illich, *De-schooling Society* (Calder and Boyars, 1971).
[14] J. Dewey, *Experience and Education* (Collier, 1963) p. 69.

those who champion freedom in education see clearly enough that autonomy calls for allowing initiatives to the child. What they do not so readily see is that judgement, the search for criteria to acknowledge as one's own, and adherence to these with corresponding integrity, are rather less obviously the fruits of a generous freedom.

The general point here is that the de-schoolers, and indeed the more moderate child-centred theorists, assume without either evidence or even reasonable expectation that children are already autonomous before their education begins. Children are assumed already to be discriminating choosers and consumers who may even be given, under the name of 'educredit', a kind of bank account to operate consisting of credit exchangeable for personally selected educational resources. The young child is to approach his education in the manner of a wary adult selectively seeking out a driving school or evening class.

That someone wants to do something is *a* reason for letting him do it, quite apart from what it is that he wants to do. Often what he wants, even if he is a child, will be unexceptionable, and his wanting it will therefore properly be allowed to prevail. There are, too, educationally instrumental reasons for allowing freedom to children, as well as *prima facie* reasons for non-interference. Children who act freely reveal their interests more, and these the teacher can observe with a view to their intrinsic development, or with a view to their employment in effecting some intrinsically rather uninteresting but nevertheless very useful piece of learning.

From the more specific standpoint of developing autonomy, it is hardly to be supposed that this will be achieved all at once, like getting married or arriving at Euston Station. It will be progressively achieved and correspondingly exercised, this exercise in turn requiring relevant freedoms as its necessary condition. This corresponding exercise may be viewed as practice, or more importantly, as the strengthening of a certain self-concept. Friends of autonomy will no doubt bear more patiently with poor choices, wrong decisions and misjudgements, if the longer-term interest is nevertheless served thereby.

Difficult problems of judgement, familiar to Mill, will be raised if a young person growing in autonomy exercises it in ways which are destructive of that autonomy itself, for example through taking heroin. Again, someone may prefer passively not to use such autonomous abilities as he has, preferring without any deliberate choice simply to be carried along by the mood of the group. Since autonomy increases responsibilities, and does not necessarily make us happier, it would not be unintelligible for it to fall into such disuse and thus to atrophy. We have to educate children to an understanding of what we honestly think valuable, but if that includes autonomy then it would be insolubly paradoxical to leave them with no choice but to be autonomous, once they had some understanding of what this was.

V

Why, then, should anyone value autonomy, having come to some understanding of what it is? The usual context of justification in which autonomy features is that of elevating into rights the social freedoms which are a necessary condition of its outward exercise. In our educational institutions, this is currently the case with demands for participation in decision-making, and with resistance to authoritarianism of any kind. But in such a context of justification others are assumed already to have those rights and the argument is for their wider distribution. The appeal is directly to justice, and rests on the value of autonomy as something taken for granted rather than explained. But why are these rights worth having at all? Justice would equally be satisfied if no one had such rights. Indeed, B. F. Skinner's arguments, though apparently directed to the unreality of autonomy, are really a misconceived attack on the value of it. It awkwardly stands in the way of controlling human behaviour, by operant conditioning, in such a manner as to produce the smoothly integrated and efficiently functioning happiness of a *Walden Two*, or a *Brave New World*.

According to Berlin, autonomy is part of a search for security.[15] Historically, this appears to have been the case

---

[15] Sir Isaiah Berlin, *Two Concepts of Liberty* (O.U.P., 1958) p. 21.

with the Stoics, who stressed the value of not being subject to external changes of fortune, and of not being caught up in strife with other men. Through being self-determining, a man can achieve command over his desires and emotions, redirecting them towards a more secure, stable and rewarding object.

Another, less withdrawing side to the security value of autonomy would be that it makes us less vulnerable to exploitation. This is not to assume that no one can be trusted, but only that not everyone can be trusted. Political deception, commercial exploitation and personal manipulation are not utterly rare features in human life, and a certain wariness shown in submitting what others say and do to our own independent judgement is therefore doubtless valuable as a safeguard.

Some large features of our contemporary mode of social life doubtless also help create a climate that favours autonomy. Amongst these features are rapid social change and the expansion in consumer choice. People have to change their jobs, or to change in their jobs, thus constantly having to face new decisions and to relearn what they are to do. Not only do jobs change, but so also do all our major institutions and the opportunities open to consumer choice and leisure activity. The role of chooser is not just offered to individuals but is positively thrust before them. And social and geographical mobility make frequently inappropriate the clothing of custom that may once have lasted a lifetime. Thus wants and attitudes have constantly to be redefined and choices and decisions have constantly to be re-opened. Of everything, and certainly not least in education, it becomes true to say that there will be a new one along in a minute, thus posing a fresh problem on which to make up our minds.

But coupled with this situation of kaleidoscopic change is thought to go an enlargement of the sovereignty of preference, and at the expense of any credible belief in the objectivity of value-judgements. Some things will clearly still have a demonstrable utilitarian value related to the needs created by a changing situation. And some moral values will still be needed to regulate, preferably with the force of law, the sovereign consumers in their experiments in living. But beyond this basic, rather formal, and certainly widely permissive framework, the individual can reign autonomously. Our contemporary mode of social life therefore strongly favours autonomy as a value.

But if this were all that could be said, then surely so-called 'autonomy' would turn out to be no more than ideological. 'Life' would indeed determine consciousness, rather than consciousness life. So we have to ask how real are the choices of these sovereign consumers. For if choosing is to be real, it is not sufficient that various alternatives are open to us, and known to be open. Those alternatives must also be independently judged by reference to criteria. This, however, is as yet only one of the conditions that I earlier suggested for autonomy. I also suggested as a necessary condition that there should be some alertness to the possibility of disclaiming the criteria thus employed. Furthermore, there should be some firmness in adhering to the judgements and criteria which one does acknowledge as one's own. Illich, like Benn and Weinstein, has seen that 'choosing' in our form of social life may be appearance only, the reality being the not always very subtle or hidden manipulative persuasions of advertisement, fashion, trendiness, or majority feeling, together engendering a compulsive competitiveness in consuming.

But independent judgement can itself become a source of intrinsic satisfaction and pride, and the right to it may be claimed from a sense of its dignity. A man is thus engaged in shaping his own life, and to do so in all matters importantly concerning himself can acquire the power and infinite perfectibility of an ideal. The unexamined life may come to seem not worth living. But our susceptibility to this as an ideal, like our susceptibility to any ideal, must in the end be a fact of human nature. Justification has to stop somewhere. However, it can be said that if we do try deliberately to choose between different ideals, then that choosing will itself reinforce our commitment to autonomy.

I mentioned a moment ago the pride, satisfaction and sense of dignity of which autonomy can be the source. But, as such an ideal, autonomy may also be felt to have a certain necessity in its claims upon us. In certain circumstances it may be felt, less agreeably, as a duty, though a 'duty to oneself'. The notion of 'duties to oneself' has rather fallen from favour, or at least from attention, in recent moral philosophy, perhaps through concentration on interpersonal conduct. But it seems an indispensable notion in connection with personal ideals. The notion of a 'duty' belongs to situations in which there is something which we ought to do, in which there is a tendency not to do it, and in which what we ought to do then claims a counteracting necessity for action. 'Duties to oneself' are such counteracting necessities of action when we are inclined to fall short of, or fall away from, some personal ideal. Thus a person might, intelligibly at least, be said to owe it to himself to develop his talents, to make the best of himself, to keep his integrity, to be true to himself, or to defend his honour. In connection with the present ideal, a person might feel he owed it to himself not to experiment with drugs which would impair his autonomy, strongly tempted by curiosity though he might be.

There may be respects in which a 'duty to oneself' is not fully parallel to a duty to others, for instance in locating the owner of a corresponding right who could release us from the duty. But if I have a duty to myself, then there must at least be corresponding rights against others in respect of being able to fulfil that duty. Furthermore, a duty can properly be overridden only by another duty, but a duty to others may properly be overridden by a care for ourselves, which must therefore be a duty, too (and not just a duty in respect of ourselves, though still to others, as sometimes is the case with our health or safety).

Traditionally in our own society entering into full possession of the corresponding rights has been ritually recognised with the celebration of one's twenty-first birthday, now presumably to be moved to eighteen. Public legitimation is then given to resistance to any parental reluctance yet to recognise independence. The ritual is not one of gratitude for any good done to others, though in fact autonomy may have all sorts of social instrumental value. Nor is the occasion one of teaching any new duties towards others. It simply recognises the right to be self-determining as something suited to the dignity of an individual to possess, though no doubt the free exercise of that right is conditional on the recognition of a similar right in others.

VI

Of the many problems which I have not adequately faced in this paper, a perplexing one is to know what to say about the value of autonomy as it may be diminished or enhanced according to the different directions which it can take. Morality is only one such direction, since clearly theoretical and aesthetic judgement represent others, and there are many less exalted examples, too. And what are we to say of autonomy as it may be manifested in criminal planning, the capitalist entrepreneur with his wage-slaves, or the activities of a Clockwork Orange?

One thing which this problem serves to make clear is that autonomy cannot be the whole of an adequate educational ideal. It centrally involves independent judgement, but judgement of what, and according to what criteria? A selection on these two latter points has to be made at the very start in any education aimed at developing autonomy. And it does not seem possible that criteria of much educational interest, other perhaps than those of formal logic, could be shown to be necessarily amongst any selection that might be made. Such a selection will rather reflect what have honestly come to be thought of as important spheres of judgement in their own right (and no doubt spheres of much else besides judgement) in human culture. As Matthew Arnold so persuasively argued, the Puritan must be Hellenised. Rather than just 'one thing being needful', we need also some 'sweetness and light'.

But when, in the face of a modish subjectivism, some such selection has been made, and a more comprehensive and altogether ampler educational ideal has been formed, there may well be some implications to be drawn for the manner of educating which will be compatible with developing auto-nomy. It must not, for example, close the mind to doubt on the criteria of judgement which we employ. It may even turn out that the learner has to be an embryonic philosopher.

2 Autonomy as an Educational Ideal II

ELIZABETH TELFER

Dr Dearden's paper can be summarised in seven propositions: (i) Historically, even in the thought of Sartre, the concept of autonomy has involved, not only independent activity of the self, but also recognition of principles: (ii) Spontaneity, in the sense of uncaused choice, is not a necessary condition of autonomy, because we can explain how people can be *made* autonomous: (iii) The essence of autonomy is forming one's own independent judgement on the basis of criteria which are themselves made subject to continous reassessment: (iv) Freedom, in the sense of 'absence of restraints', is neither necessary nor sufficient for the existence? of autonomy, though it is necessary for its exercise: (v) Freedom is *not* a necessary condition for the development of autonomy: (vi) Autonomy can be seen as having an intrinsic value: (vii) It varies in value according to the sphere in which it is exercised, and hence cannot be sufficient as a specification of an educational ideal, although it is necessary.

Space forbids my considering all these themes in my paper. I therefore propose to concentrate on Dearden's account of what autonomy is and on the question of its place as an educational ideal. On the first of these topics I shall try to supplement, rather than contest Dearden's conclusions: on the second, I aim not only to supplement but also to raise a doubt or two.

Before I come to these two topics, however, I should like to take issue with Dr Dearden's argument that Sartre's authentic choices, if they are intelligible at all, are far from criterionless since they assume the badness of bad faith, the

19

reprehensible nature of inauthenticity and the seriousness of the responsibility involved. It is true that Sartre's position assumes these values. But this does not make the choices any more comprehensible, since none of these values can be appealed to in making the choice itself, as considerations favouring one alternative rather than another. Without criteria which can be used in making the choice, the idea of choosing is still unintelligible. In fact we might say that, rather than the basic values making the Sartrean choice intelligible, the Sartrean choice makes at least one of the basic values unintelligible; for why should one be anguished about a kind of choice which, unlike choice in general, affords no possibility of making the wrong decision?

Dearden introduces his own account of autonomy *via* a discussion of the connexion between autonomy and spontaneity. This discussion seems to me to embody a *non-sequitur*. To account for the origin of an autonomous personality, in terms of a certain kind of environment and upbringing, is not to deny that autonomy itself requires the notion of a causeless choice. Why should we not say that it is only by means of a certain kind of early training that a person learns to rise above the heteronomy of causes? How far the notion of autonomy does require such choice depends, not on its origin, but on its nature. But a prior question is the place of choice of any kind in the notion of autonomy. I propose now to examine the notion of autonomy by attempting an answer to this question, leaving on one side the thorny problem of whether such choice must be in some sense causeless.

Dearden lists seven types of activity as characterising the person who 'thinks of himself as autonomous'. (We may ask incidentally whether this formula is strong enough for Dearden's purposes; presumably a person can think of himself as autonomous without really being so, though perhaps the converse does not hold.) These activities can be divided into three groups, according to the ways in which they involve choice. I shall call them discovery, forming of opinions and wants, and overt action; I shall say a little on discovery and then discuss the other types of autonomous activity at more length.

The activity of discovery is that described as 'defining what one really wants'. Here, I take it, the agent is making clear to himself what is there all the time but may have become overlaid by such things as confusion, convention and self-deception. There is obviously no choice as to the outcome of the discovering activity: the wants are there to be discovered, not created. But the agent has the choice of whether or not to unearth them by self-examination, a choice which may take courage. An analogous process, not mentioned by Dearden, is clearly possible in the case of opinions. At any given time one already possesses views on various matters, some of which may be awkward to acknowledge, and whereas one has the choice whether or not to bring the views to the surface, one has no choice as to what view will be unearthed. These activities of discovery are necessary for autonomy, in that his basis for further thought and action is his own wants for further thoughts and action is his own wants and beliefs and no one else's. But the distinguishing mark of the autonomous man is the nature of the process whereby his opinions and wants become his, and this brings me to the second type of autonomous activity, the forming of wants and opinions.

For our present purposes we may group together the forming of an opinion and the appraisal and criticism of our actual opinions as discovered and of possible opinions as suggested by others, by convention etc. In all these cases we proceed by marshalling evidence or grounds and weighing up conflicting claims. This activity seems at first sight to allow for choice to a greater degree than the discovery type of case: the phrase 'forming an opinion' suggests we can make it take what shape we like. But is this really so? We can often decide whether to reflect about an issue or to shelve it: 'I must sit down and make up my mind about the importance of Picasso', or, 'the justification of capital punishment.' But we cannot choose what to think about it, because we cannot choose the outcome of our reflections. Either a conclusion emerges which *is* what we think on the topic — whether we like it or not — or we find we cannot come to a conclusion. It does not make any sense to say, 'I decided to think that such-and-such is the case'.

Among the opinions which may be formed in this way are

opinions about the agent's own interests: he forms these by reviewing what he wants already, what he believes to be conducive to achieving such wants, the possible by-products of achieving them and so on. A new want, as well as a new opinion, may form as a result. As before, although the agent embarks on the initial deliberation by choice, he has no choice as to the outcome — one cannot say 'In view of my desire for such-and-such, I choose to want so-and-so.' On the other hand, a want may not emerge even where it is the natural outcome of the deliberation; an agent may form the opinion that such-and-such is really in his interests but still find that he does not want it.

The wants and opinions that are formed in these ways belong to their possessor in a stronger sense than those which are merely discovered. It is true that he has not the choice as to what they turn out to be, but he has chosen to practise the reflection which gives rise to them and this is what makes them autonomous.

I wish now to consider three objections to my picture of autonomous wants and beliefs as formed but not chosen. The first is an appeal to ordinary language: it might be pointed out that we can say, 'I don't choose to believe that'. But what do we mean when we say this? I suggest we mean one of three things: either, 'Despite the evidence, I *find* I don't believe that' or 'I don't choose to think about that at all' or 'I do believe that, but I refuse to acknowledge it to myself.' In any case, idiom just as often suggests that we do not have this choice: 'I am forced to conclude' and so on. Of course there can be and in most cases is a *logical* gap between grounds and conclusion, such that it is not self-contradictory to assert the premises and deny the conclusion. But it does not follow that any particular thinker is in fact able, while acknowledging the premises, to choose to deny the conclusion.

The second objection is that my picture of unchosen beliefs, while perhaps adequate for 'factual' beliefs, cannot apply to *evaluations* of various kinds (perhaps what Dearden calls 'views' as distinct from 'opinions'). Such an objector grants that I cannot, having surveyed the evidence, choose whether or not to believe that Richard III killed the Princes in the Tower, but insists that I must be able to choose whether or not to hold that capital punishment is wrong. The ground given for this insistence is that the latter kind of view has implications for action. It is thought to follow from this that saying that I cannot choose my evaluations entails saying that I cannot choose my actions — and since this conclusion is unacceptable, the objector rejects the premise which is thought to give rise to it.

But in fact this conclusion can be avoided without saying that we can choose our moral and other evaluative views. The more plausible alternative is to say that we hold certain views which we have not chosen, but we can choose whether or not to act on them. Moral views have implications for action in the sense that often a particular course of action is prescribed by them, not in the sense that he who holds them is bound actually to act accordingly. Of course he may feel a pressure to do so: precisely what this is held to consist in will vary with one's theory of moral judgement.

Now I am quite aware that many people will deny the existence of this logical gap between moral judgement and action. They might do this in one of two ways, not always (I think) sharply distinguished. Firstly, they might agree with me on the phenomena but differ verbally on their most appropriate description: that is, they might agree that there are unchosen belief-like moral positions and logically separate chosen commitments to try to act in the ways prescribed by the positions, but attach the name 'Moral judgement' to the latter phenomenon rather than the former. I am not particularly concerned about this verbal disagreement, though I might point out in passing that it makes such apparently meaningful admonitions as 'Act in accordance with your moral convictions' turn into tautologies. But secondly, and more importantly for our present topic, they might disagree on the phenomena themselves: they might deny that there is ever such a thing as a moral conviction or position or insight which is borne in on us without our choosing it. Here I can only say that this isn't how it seems to be. Suppose I think that abortion is wrong, or for that matter that Braque is a greater artist than Picasso or poetry more valuable than pushpin: could I choose, or have chosen to think otherwise? It is true that we have the power to form our own opinions on these matters. But, as we have seen, this is the power to conduct a deliberation process whereby our own opinion emerges, not to choose what our opinion is to be.

The third objection to my view, which applies equally to evaluative and non-evaluative judgements, is that I ignore the fact that choice enters not only into the initiation but also into the conducting of reflection. After all, reflecting is not something like sliding down a shute, which simply happens once initiated: it is something which I *do*, as shown by the fact that I can be blamed for doing it *badly*: 'You didn't think out your position properly.' Now this is of course true. But it does not follow that I can choose what the outcome of my reflection is to be. The position is rather that I can in various ways choose whether to conduct the reflection in accordance with my actual beliefs or to distort it to suit my wishes. If I adopt the latter policy, I have in a sense chosen *a* conclusion; but it is in precisely these cases that we would say that I don't really believe in the conclusion, that I am not genuinely convinced, that it is not my true view. Let me briefly illustrate these possibilities of distortion.

There seem to be four such possibilities. Firstly, I can choose what factors to take into consideration, and in so doing can either choose all and only those factors which actually seem relevant, or choose a set which if I were honest I would acknowledge to be partly irrelevant or incomplete. Secondly I can to some extent choose how much weight to give a particular factor, and this choice can be either in accordance with or contrary to the weight I actually think it carries. Thirdly, I can choose whether to rest content with the factors that have already suggested themselves as relevant or to cast around for others, and this choice may or may not tally with my true opinion as to whether I have thought of everything. Fourthly, I can choose whether to take a conclusion which emerges as settled or to go over the ground again, and this choice may or may not reflect my true opinion as to whether further thought is needed.

It is probably clear from this account that various qualities of character are necessary in order to safeguard the autonomous formation of judgements. Honesty with oneself is the most obvious of these, but it is not the only one; courage to face unpleasant truths, patience and thoroughness are others. How far these qualities are the same when shown in thinking and in overt action is a knotty problem which I prefer to leave on one side.

I have now dealt with the three objections to my view of autonomous wants and desires as formed but not chosen. Before I turn to autonomy of overt action let me mention the process of reviewing criteria of judgement. Dearden mentions this as a separate activity from that of forming judgements; but while this is clearly true in some sense, the process will involve choice in the same way as forming judgements, so I shall mention it at this stage. I agree with Dearden that the autonomous man not only forms his own views in accordance with criteria but also subjects the criteria to review. But I think Dearden's account of this is too voluntaristic: he says the criteria 'might not, on reflection, be such as he would *wish* to call his own'. I should say rather that he might on reflection come to the conclusion *that* they were not after all valid, relevant or sound criteria, in the light of further criteria which remain unquestioned for the moment. The agent can choose whether or not to embark on this reflection, and this choice can come about in two ways: either doubts may assail him which he can choose either to examine or to repress; or, in the absence of actual doubt, he can choose either to test his assumptions or to rest on them. We need not insist, I think, that the autonomous man must always *feel* doubt, as distinct from acknowledging that there is always room for doubt and thinking accordingly.

I now come to consider autonomy in action, or perhaps I should say 'in overt action' since, as we have seen, forming judgements and wants is also an activity. From the items in Dearden's list I would distinguish three stages in this: forming purposes, deciding how to act and acting. In all these activities, unlike those of forming judgements and wants, the outcome of the autonomous activity seems to be under the control of the agent, and it is therefore in the sphere of overt action that the notion of choice is bound up most closely with that of autonomy.

I have two problems about the connexion between autonomous thought and autonomous action. Firstly, there *obj* may be a conflict between the action recommended by an autonomous conviction of self-interest and that recommended by an autonomous conviction of what is morally right. Would both actions be autonomous in this case? The Kantian would say that the self-interested action is heteronomous, albeit rational in a way in which action on impulse is not, whereas the moral action is autonomous. But the Kantian distinction rests on a notion which I have contested: that moral principles are chosen whereas wants are imposed on the agent without his choice. On my view, therefore, both these actions may be equally autonomous (though not of course equally good morally speaking). I take it that Dearden would agree with this conclusion, since he never makes a distinction between the hypothetical and the categorical imperative in respect of their autonomy.

oly My second problem about autonomous action concerns the firmness with which an agent adheres to autonomous judgements. Dearden says that the firmness will be 'matched to the man's conviction of their rightness'. I am not clear whether it is held to be analytic that firmness of action matches strength of conviction. But in any case, is conviction of their rightness a characteristic of autonomous judgements? On the contrary, the autonomous man is one who is always ready to question even the criteria employed in the making of the judgement, let alone the calculation by which it was arrived at. Presumably then he will tend not to have a conviction of its rightness at all. Will he be able to act with resolution? One has come across people whose intellectual integrity is so extreme that it leads to a kind of paralysis in action. But if a man is to act autonomously he must be able to avoid this paralysis, and to act at any given time in accordance with his beliefs at that time, while acknowledging that these beliefs are in a sense provisional and subject to constant revision. This would seem a difficult psychological position to maintain, but it is not unintelligible. But of course a man may fail to live up to his beliefs, not because they are not firm enough, but because of various weaknesses in his character such as cowardice, impatience, lack of self-contol. Autonomous action, then, requires not only the ability to act on provisional beliefs but also the same qualities of self-mastery as, or similar qualities to, autonomous thinking.

I am now in a position to sum up my account of the nature of autonomy. While agreeing with Dearden on the phenomena characteristic of the autonomous man, I think his account suggests more scope for choice than is in fact the case and hence perhaps suggests that the autonomous man is self-governing in a stronger sense than actually applies. I also disagreed with the basis proposed for autonomy of action — namely, the alleged firmness of the autonomous man's convictions — and suggested instead an ability to act on beliefs regarded as provisional, together with possession of those self-mastery virtues which are in any case needed in some form for autonomy of judgement.

I turn now to a discussion of my other main theme: autonomy in the context of education. Dearden's most important thesis on this topic is that we cannot assume that, because freedom is a necessary condition of the exercise of autonomy, it is also a necessary condition of its development. I agree with the main tenor of his argument here — that the progressive schools and the de-schoolers may be mistaken if their assumption is that maximum freedom in childhood promotes maximum autonomy later. This is presumably partly an empirical question. But one should note that the de-schoolers need not espouse the view attributed to them by Dearden that children are already autonomous before their education begins. They might equally well hold the weaker view, which he also mentions, that autonomy naturally *develops* if not inhibited by pressures from above.

Now Dearden's main discussion here does not make clear how widely he is taking the concept of 'education'. There is a tendency nowadays to use the word very widely indeed, to cover any kind of desirable development in a child, whether intellectual, moral, emotional, aesthetic or whatever. According to this usage people say things like, 'True education is learning to care for others'. But the more traditional conception is narrower and concerns intellectual development only. It is this latter conception which is linked with an equally traditional notion of an educated man; in fact we may say that the aim of education in this narrower sense is to produce

educated people. This narrower sense, though more specific
in content than the fashionable one, is still to some extent
evaluative, meaning something like 'desirable development in
the intellectual sphere'. There can thus be room for debate
and disagreement about what constitutes desirable development in the intellectual sphere. But I think we can assume a
rough consensus, and I shall expound this shortly.

I am in favour of keeping the use of the word 'education'
narrow, if only because the wider use seems to render
vacuous questions which we at present ask and which do
seem to have a meaning, such as 'Should parents play a part
in their children's education?' or 'Is education or character
more important in adult life?' or 'Does a high degree of
education inhibit personal relationships?' But if we adopt this
narrower usage, as I propose to do for the remainder of this
paper, it seems clear that the picture of autonomy which we
have been considering includes some things which fall outside
the scope of education. For example, the autonomous man
was described as one who regularly acts in accordance with
his judgement. But a man would not be thought of as any the
less *educated* if he did not live up to his principles. Again, the
autonomous man is one who makes his own plans, defines
what he wants and so on. But absence of these features
would not normally be thought to show a man to be any the
less educated.

The aspect of autonomy which does fall within the scope
of education is what we may call intellectual autonomy: that
concerned with the formation of one's own judgements and
the criticism of those of others. Indeed, it is natural to think
of the point of education as getting people to think for
themselves and so forth. On the other hand, intellectual
autonomy constitutes only a small part of educatedness: as
Dearden says, 'Autonomy centrally involves independent
judgement, but judgement of what, and according to what
criteria?' I shall spend the last part of my paper in exploring
the part intellectual autonomy might play within educatedness.

Before I do so, however, I must guard against two
misunderstandings. Firstly, I am not maintaining that no
qualities of character are required for intellectual autonomy

itself. As we saw earlier, it requires moral virtues just as much as the autonomy of action. We shall return to this point. Secondly, I am not asserting that schools should concern themselves only with intellectual development, ignoring character training except insofar as intellectual development in any case entails it. How far they should follow this policy is one of the questions which tend to be blurred by the wide use of the term 'education'. Personally I would say that schools should be concerned with character training as well as with education in my narrow sense.

To return then to the concept of educatedness and the place of intellectual autonomy within it. I suggest that the educated person possesses three things which the intellectually autonomous person does not necessarily have: a large fund of knowledge *that* of a particular kind, knowledge by acquaintance of some works of art, and knowledge of how to think. I shall say a little about each of these requirements.

Firstly, the educated man's knowledge *that*. By this I do not mean that he possesses an encyclopaedic general knowledge of isolated bits of information, but rather that he possesses sufficient and integrated knowledge in various spheres to understand something of the world he lives in, and his place in it. For example, he knows enough history to understand why Britain has the position in world politics which she has, and enough science to appreciate man's unique biological position as a rational animal, and so on. There will of course be some room for selection here, by teacher or by pupils if they are of an age to understand the selection. But there are not infinite possibilities, if the knowledge *that* is to be both structured and 'relevant' to our situation; some things just are basic, in the sense that they are necessary before one can understand other things. This need not necessarily be construed as a defence of the contents of a traditional school curriculum, although this makes a *prima facie* claim precisely because it is traditional and hence part of the culture within which pupils find themselves.

Secondly, the educated man has a knowledge by acquaintance of some of the great works of art. He does not know merely that they exist and that they have certain features, he knows them firsthand. The difficulty again is: what works of

art must he know? I am not prepared to give a list such that
the educated person must know all the items on the list. But
one can proceed negatively to some extent: in our culture a
person who knows no Shakespeare play is not educated, a
person who knows no music by Bach is not educated, and so
on. Nor need these stipulations represent simply the taste of
the teacher. Doubtless the main point of presenting one piece
rather than another is that knowledge of them furnishes the
mind with what are thought to be treasures, but the teacher
can defend a classic choice on more objective grounds by
pointing to the part such works have played in our culture.

Thirdly, the educated man knows how to think. This
phrase covers a multitude of different capacities, but we may
pick out three kinds. The first kind is that which is connected
with various kinds of knowledge *that*: he knows how to think
historically, scientifically, mathematically and so on. He has a
command of the intellectual methods whereby various kinds
of knowledge are arrived at and can therefore assess claims to
such knowledge and seek it for himself. The second kind of
thinking is what we may call appraisal; it links with the
knowledge by acquaintance though also with other things. It
is the capacity to make reasoned judgements in spheres where
it is appropriate to speak, not of truth or correctness, but
rather of reasonableness: aesthetic appreciation, moral judgement, evaluative questions in general. The third kind has no
special subject-matter or sphere: it is the capacity to be
logical, in a more formal sense. It is learnt in the course of
learning other forms of thinking, but is also sometimes
studied separately.

In learning all these kinds of thinking there is a two-way
traffic between the academic sphere and that of real life. The
hope is that the capacities, once acquired, can be applied in
non-academic spheres as well: that the ability to criticize a
historical argument in a historian's work will enable its
possessor to assess a similar argument in a leader column, the
ability to assess an artist's picture will help in the choice of
an attractive environment. But conversely real-life thinking
can be used as a demonstration of the techniques required
academically: for example, one can show how to assess

historical evidence by considering how we would go about investigating the facts concerning a contemporary political incident.

Now it might be maintained that my educated man's three kinds of knowledge can after all be subsumed under intellectual autonomy. Such an argument would attempt to show, first, that knowledge *that* and knowledge by acquaintance are of importance only as means to knowledge how to think; and second, that knowing how to think is the same as intellectual autonomy. But both of these theses are mistaken, in my view. The first is of course an evaluative thesis and as such cannot be refuted, only disputed. My disputation would maintain, firstly, that most people would in practice expect far more knowledge *that* from a person they deemed educated than is required for the development of knowing how to think; and secondly, that the knowing-*that* and knowing-by-acquaintance components provide a continuous understanding of life which knowing how to think cannot by itself provide. For example, knowing how to appraise a work of art is no substitute for seeing the world with sharpened eyes because one knows certain works of art.

The second thesis, that knowing how to think can be equated with intellectual autonomy, is a conceptual thesis which needs discussion at greater length. Broadly my view is that knowing how to think is a skill, or set of skills, enabling a man to think well if he chooses to think, whereas intellectual autonomy is a disposition or habit which makes a man choose to think, though not necessarily well. This distinction can be illustrated by consideration of the cases of autonomous thinkers who lack knowledge of how to think, and *vice versa*. For example, a piece of research by a schoolchild into some historical problem might well be autonomous, in that he refused to accept the established conclusions without questioning them for himself, and so on. But it might at the same time be full of non-sequiturs, confused between historical investigation and moral evaluation, riddled with unsupported and implausible surmise, and in general show that he does not know how to think historically. Conversely, a person may know how to think (in a particular sphere or in general) but nevertheless on some occasions, perhaps through laziness or bias, accept uncritically implausible views from others, produce half-baked arguments, and so on. I suggest then that knowing how to think is neither a necessary nor a sufficient condition of intellectual autonomy.

Now the latter possibility, of a man's knowing how to think and yet not implementing this knowledge, is denied by some writers, who point out that knowing how to think is not like knowing how to tie a reef knot. It is an evaluative notion, implying, as I have already said, the idea of thinking *well*. The man who knows how to think, therefore, understands what constitutes excellence in different spheres of thinking: cogency, rigour, elegance, plausibility and so on. How (it is asked) can anyone understand these values and not pursue them?

This would-be rhetorical question, however, arises from a particular view of the relationship between knowledge of the good and action upon it — the action in this case being a kind of thinking. Most people would hold that I am not logically committed to action by my evaluation, even in the sphere of morals; it seems possible to allow that I may fail to live up to my convictions through various weaknesses of character. Moreover, in the sphere of intellectual activity the evaluator is at a further remove from action than in the moral sphere; for whereas in the latter sphere, even if he does not act, he is presumably committed to an acknowledgement of the importance of so acting or at least to some kind of wish to do so, in the intellectual sphere he can always without self-contradiction say 'That's good thinking of that particular kind, and were I trying to think I would try to think like that, but I don't think that thinking is important (or 'I don't want to think') in any case'.

What further is needed, then, to ensure that the man who knows how to think does actually think accordingly? Firstly, a basic conviction that thinking is important or a basic desire to think about things, or a combination of these (what may be called 'intellectual motivation'); and secondly, those qualities of character which enable the conviction or desire to

be implemented whatever the difficulties: honesty, per-
severance, carefulness, courage. And since these two kinds of
things are necessary if knowledge how to think is to be used
in life and not remain merely an unactualised potential,
developing them can reasonably be considered part of
education — perhaps as vital a part as the acquisition of the
kinds of knowledge, though whether they can in any sense be
taught is another matter.

Here it might be said that, although I have resisted the
equation of knowing *how* with intellectual autonomy, I have
in effect just shown that intellectual autonomy is no less a
necessary part of what it is to be educated than the forms of
knowledge, since the qualities I have just enumerated are all
aspects of intellectual autonomy. But this is not obviously
the case. It is true that the autonomous man must possess
some of the same qualities of character as the educated man,
but it is far from clear that his basic motivation must be the
same. So far nothing much has been said about the
motivation which makes a man try to be autonomous, as
distinct from the behaviour which constitutes his autonomy.
But it is perfectly consistent with the nature of autonomy as
so far described, and is often the case, that the autonomous
man's basic motivation is rather more self-referring than that
I have assigned to the educated man.

I shall illustrate this distinction, which may however be
one of emphasis more than of substance, in terms of a
possible case. Suppose some new novel is widely acclaimed
on both sides of the Atlantic as something quite out of the
ordinary. The educated man and the autonomous man will
both be unwilling to accept the general verdict unquestioned,
and will want to form an opinion for themselves. But whereas
the autonomous man's main concern is that he should form
his own opinion, the educated man's main concern is that he
should form a reasonable opinion. In practice this may well
come to the same thing, since both will be eager to weigh up
and question the views and criteria of others, and to sift out
irrelevant emotional factors such as liking for the author as a
person or dislike of books printed on yellow paper. But the
motivation will be different, rather in the same way that the

motivation of someone who behaves well out of self-respect (a determination that *he* at least shall maintain proper standards) is different from that of someone who behaves well out of a sense of duty (a concern for the standards themselves).

Now Dr Dearden would no doubt challenge this last point, on the ground that the 'self' which rules in the autonomous man is not merely the individual self of self-respect, Jones rather than Smith, but also the 'true self' or 'rational self' which transcends the individual. The autonomous man, therefore, can and should see the exercise of autonomy, not chiefly as the assertion of himself as an individual, but as the duty of fostering in himself an impersonal standard of true personhood or selfhood. I agree that the exercise of autonomy can be seen in this light. But this still seems to leave a possible divergence from the ideal of the educated man: should not the educated man's ideal be seen as a devotion to truth and beauty as such, rather than to personhood in himself or whatever? As before, this difference may be merely one of emphasis. But it may all the same have practical implications. If the educated man sees his task as the pursuit of truth, he may be committed to a careful consideration of the views and criteria of others in the field to a degree which the intellectually autonomous man is not. The latter wishes to form his own judgements, to question what seems unconvincing, to re-examine his criteria to make sure he still finds them adequate; but if this process is for the sake of exercising his own personhood, might it not still permit an arrogantly solipsistic approach? It is true that the educated man also, like the autonomous man, must make up his own mind. But unlike the autonomous man he must, not merely may, take account of the views of others in doing so; for that is the safest route to the truth and reasonableness which he seeks.

I conclude, then, with a note of caution about intellectual autonomy as an educational ideal — a note I sound with diffidence, because modern trends are all against impersonal ideals. Perhaps I can say that thinking for oneself can be seen as important, not only because it is part of one's own self-mastery, but also because truth is most likely to be attained thereby, and stress on autonomy, while it is very useful in providing motivation, may obscure this objective and transcendent aspect of the educational exercise.

3 Chairman's Remarks

R. M. HARE

I am going to be as brief and as clear as I can, and in the attempt to do so may seem provocative, though that is not my main intention. Besides commenting on certain issues raised by Mr Dearden's and Miss Telfer's papers, I shall say some things which are relevant to Mrs Warnock's and Mr Norman's; for it is thought by many people (perhaps rightly) that autonomy and neutrality are two sides of the same coin. And indeed I shall be saying things which have a bearing on a lot of the other topics of the conference.

It may have occurred to you to ask, when reading Mr Dearden's paper, what the connexion is between the psychological state, state of mind, state of character, or whatever, which is called 'autonomy', and what Mr Dearden, speaking of Kant, calls 'the *logical* autonomy of moral *discourse*' (p. 3f.). We are accustomed in philosophy to slip back and forth between logical and psychological ways of speaking; but all the same the transitions need to be explained. I am going to try to do this, and shall maintain in the course of my explanation that at least one of the issues about autonomy is an issue in philosophical logic.

Autonomy, as an educational ideal, seems most often to mean a disposition to think in a certain way. Even when it is action that is called autonomous, it is called that because of the nature of the thinking which has led up to it. By 'thinking in a certain way', I mean of course, not 'thinking certain things' but 'doing one's thinking in a certain manner'. The manner is characterised, as Mr Dearden has brought out, by two features corresponding to the two parts of the word 'autonomy': the thinking has to be done by a man for himself (*autos*); and he has to do it in accordance with some regular procedure (*nomos*). I should not be thinking autonomously *as a mathematician* either if, instead of calculating for myself, I looked up the answer at the end of the book, or if, instead of employing arithmetical procedures, I picked the answer by jabbing a pin into the table of logarithms. However, we must not exaggerate the second point into requirements which are *not* part of autonomy. As Miss Telfer rightly says (p. 24) it is not a necessary part of autonomy that the thinking should be done correctly. A man may be thinking autonomously (for himself and applying a regular procedure), but he may not have mastered the procedure, and so may get the answer wrong. Nor do I like Mr Dearden's use (which Miss Telfer takes over) of the word 'criterion'; regular procedures do not involve the matching of results against criteria; in mathematics, again, we do not tell whether someone is really doing the sums for himself autonomously by seeing whether he checks his results against criteria, but by seeing whether he arrives at them by certain procedures which he himself follows.

Next (and this is important when considering Mrs Warnock's paper) the procedures will differ with the subject matter. I was therefore a bit suspicious of the slide which she seemed to be trying to institute from Latin, French and mathematics via science and history to morals. If the procedures of these kinds of thinking are all different, it may be that some of them do, and some of them do not, require submission to the discipline of (for example) empirical facts. Empirical science does require this — and in empirical science we must perhaps include linguistics and therefore Latin and French; so if the teacher knows that this is not the way native speakers of French would express a certain thought, of course he can tell his pupils so, and invite them if they disbelieve him to ask a Frenchman. All of these procedures are subject to the discipline of logic — and mathematics to that alone. Art, which is also taught in schools, is not subject even to logic, but perhaps has its own disciplines. We have therefore to ask separately in each case in what autonomy, and therefore in what neutrality, will consist.

Professor Elliott may disagree with this; for he thinks that the same 'powers of the mind' fit us for engaging in *all*

disciplines, and therefore, presumably, for engaging autonomously in them all; and so differences in subject matter will
not make the sort of difference that I am going to claim. But
since he does not mention the empirical work that has been
done on the particularity or generality of mental powers, and
does not produce any at all solid conceptual arguments
either, I do not know what his grounds are for being so sure
of what he says.

In any case, the procedures of the different disciplines *are*
different in fundamental respects. The problem therefore
arises of how the procedures are to be determined in each
case. Mr Dearden rightly says of his 'criteria', and I would say
the same of the 'procedures' I have been speaking of, that the
autonomous thinker has to be able to review or even reject
them in favour of others (p. 9). But within what limits? I
think that this is the basic issue. We have to determine, in the
case of each discipline separately, the ways in which the
liberties of the thinker are restricted by the nature of the
subject. Of course, as we shall see, even though there are
these restrictions, the thinker can escape them by no longer
studying *that* subject — for example, the historical novelist or
playwright can take liberties with the facts; but then he is not
doing history, and it is part of the education of a historian to
learn to tell the difference between this sort of thing and
genuine history, and also between the latter and political
propaganda.

However, having said this, we must admit that the
autonomous thinker cannot be confined within the strait
jackets of subjects as currently delimited, nor even of
education as currently understood. That is what is wrong
with what might otherwise seem a short way of solving our
problem about how the procedures are determined — that of
saying that they are determined, of conceptual necessity, by
the subject, whatever it is, that is being studied. For example,
if one claims to be doing *mathematics*, one is not allowed to
make logically invalid inferences, just as, if one is learning to
ride a bicycle, one cannot claim success if one falls off. If one
does not know this (we are tempted to say) one does not
know what mathematics or bicycle-riding is, or what the
words mean. The problem remains, however, even on this

view, of how to extend this idea to the more difficult cases.

There are two opposite dangers to be avoided here. Take history, for example. If someone occupying a position in a department of history gave lectures which were more like historical novels or like political pamphlets than like attempts to determine the facts most relevant to his topic, however repugnant to his own views, then I should think him worthy of censure and even, in extreme cases, of expulsion, irrespective of the complexion of the politics or novel-writing in which he was indulging; and bogus appeals to academic freedom would not move me. I hope that we shall discuss this aspect of the matter when we come to Mr Stuart Brown's and Professor Griffiths' papers. I am not saying that historians are not allowed to make political or moral judgements about the facts, once established; it is a good thing if they sometimes do. But the two activities can be kept distinct, and so can that of selecting the field of inquiry; and we should not allow ourselves to be persuaded of the opposite view just because it is repeated so often — if there are solid arguments for it, I do not know what they are. It seems to me that the same principle should be applied here as lay behind the Trade Descriptions Act and the prohibition on people practising as doctors when what they are doing is not medicine as usually understood.

On the other hand, we do not want professors to be able to say to junior colleagues 'What you are doing in your lectures is not history as *I* understand the word, so I shall see to it that your appointment is not renewed'. Is there any middle ground between these two objectionable positions, one of which would allow anything whatever to be taught under the name of history, and the other of which would allow various 'authorities' to impose their definition of what history is on unwilling colleagues? If there is, it can best be found by means of democratic decisions (for *somebody* has to do the deciding) between clearly understood alternatives. The clarity is at least as important as the democracy. We shall achieve it only if we distinguish carefully between two questions, the confusion between which can easily lead to acrimonious muddle. The first is, 'What are the limits of what is to be described as, for example, history?'. The second is

'How much of the academic cake ought each of the subjects, as so delimited, to be given?'. I offer this as an example of the utility of separating questions of definition from normative questions, which I dare say Mr Norman thinks impossible.

The utility is doubly apparent in cases like psychology and, I regret to say, philosophy, in which agreement is lacking as to the limits of the subject. Even there, by separating the questions, we can *first* allow that there are different and mutually compossible answers to the first one — that there are, for example, different things that are called psychology or called philosophy, one of which demands, as the case may be, controlled experiment or logical rigour in argument, and the other does not, but is perhaps more exciting to immature minds (which is undoubtedly a virtue) — and only then go on to the inevitable political infighting about the extent to which these various sorts of philosophy or of psychology are to be studied in a given place, or how much money they are to get. If these decisions are made by reasonably democratic procedures and accepted, by and large, within a given institution, then we shall have a regime in which those of us who are seriously interested in our subjects (which does not include all academics) can get on with our work and teaching, and so exert whatever good influence on the world is made possible by the nature of our subjects and our own abilities.

But the main point for my argument is that subjects are different, and therefore what constitutes thinking autonomously or teaching neutrally in them will be different too. When we come to moral and other evaluative questions we have to ask afresh whether, here too, there is a subject called, say, 'art' and another called 'morals', which, of conceptual necessity, impose certain disciplines which the teacher can know just as he knows Latin or mathematics. Mrs Warnock's good husband thinks, if I am not getting him wrong, that in the case of morals there is.[1] And so do I; but I think we differ about what restrictions the discipline imposes upon autonomous thinking. Obviously on this will depend what a

[1] *Contemporary Moral Philosophy.*

teacher can legitimately do when professing to discuss a *moral* question (as classes should certainly be encouraged to do).

And this is where the issue in philosophical logic emerges which I mentioned at the beginning. Those who believe, as I do, in a viable distinction between analytic and synthetic propositions will be able to state this issue clearly; those who reject the distinction will not. But I do not want to argue with this second sort of people, because they are committed by their view to saying the same about the closely related concept of entailment as they do about analyticity; so they are implicitly claiming that it is impossible to distinguish cases in which '*q*' follows from '*p*' from cases in which it does not (where '*p*' and '*q*' are statements in ordinary discourse); so obviously it is no use arguing with them.

However, for those who understand what a conceptually valid argument is, and what is the difference between things which we cannot deny without self-contradiction and things which we can, the issue can be stated as follows: when children are learning moral language from their parents, teachers and others (and the best way of doing this is by hearing the language *used* in discussing questions they think important) does the learning of the language, by itself, (for example the learning of the use of the word 'ought' as it is used in moral discourse) entail the adoption of certain moral opinions? Or can children learn the language *without* thereby being committed, on pain of self-contradiction, to embracing certain moral opinions (those of the people from whom they are learning it)? If they can, then the teacher can be neutral about moral questions, though he can, and ought to, be *not* neutral about the language itself and its logic — which means that he ought not to be easy-going about sloppy thinking in morals any more than he ought to be in mathematics. Miss Telfer is right when she says (p. 33) that intellectual autonomy requires moral virtues — honesty, courage, patience and thoroughness, and I would add clarity and rigour, which, though not themselves moral virtues, are such that the failure to strive for them is a sign of moral defect.

It is the teacher's task, in morals as in mathematics, to help the children to learn the language so that *they* can do the sums; his job is not to teach them answers but to raise questions, and at the same time to initiate them into the logic, which is an inherent property of the language, in accordance with whose rules those questions have to be discussed. So the question arises crucially: '*What are* the logical properties of the moral words, and what restrictions do they place on what we can or cannot consistently say?'. I hope that we philosophers, when we discuss moral education, will not allow ourselves, in the pursuit of relevance, to be diverted from this, the most relevant question of all.

PART TWO:

EDUCATION AND THE DEVELOPMENT OF THE UNDERSTANDING

4 Education and Human Being I

R. K. ELLIOTT

In his paper 'Education and the Educated Man'[1] Richard
Peters asks how the pursuit of knowledge can be justified for
those who are not committed to it and who do not find it of
absorbing interest. He asks also for a justification of the
pursuit of 'breadth' of knowledge. In this paper I accept
Peters' view of education as involving the development of
knowledge and understanding and try to provide the begin-
nings of answers to the questions raised by him, stressing the
element of vitality in intellectual enquiry, which he tends
perhaps to neglect. I shall maintain also that a criterion of the
educational value of a branch of study is that it concerns
matters which it is important for human beings to know
about and understand. These two moves will bring me into
collision with Paul Hirst's well-known doctrine concerning
the curriculum, the first because it involves a notion of
mental development which is different from his, the second
because it is incompatible with an account of the curriculum
based entirely on formal considerations. Though my chief
concern is with the justification of education as the pursuit
of knowledge and understanding, it is hoped that the paper as
a whole will give an indication of the kind of shift of
emphasis which would occur if education were understood in
relation to a concept of human being in which the element of
nature is allowed to assert itself rather more freely against the
element of convention.

---

[1] In *Education and the Development of Reason* (Routledge and Kegan Paul, 1972)
pp. 3–18.

Both Peters and Hirst connect education very closely with the development of mind, and understand intellectual development as development of knowledge and understanding. I adopt this view provisionally, leaving open the question whether education is also concerned with states of mind other than knowledge and understanding. But the concept of development is ambiguous. Applied to knowledge and understanding it means either merely additive increase or change of a more 'organic' kind. In the latter sense, development of knowledge and development of understanding are the same. An additive concept of development is our ordinary educational notion of 'breadth', i.e., understanding in a number of separate fields, such as history, geography, mathematics. The additive concept of development of knowledge is applicable when one gains an acquaintance with some new part of a topic or knowledge of some new item of a relatively superficial and presently inert kind belonging to some part of a topic with which one is already acquainted. Such items can form new material which is organised, and the relations and further significances of which are discovered, by the process by which we gain a fuller understanding both of the topic and the items. This is development of understanding in the 'organic' sense, which I shall consider more fully below. But first additional ambiguities of 'development' need to be considered.

Development in the understanding of something may be conceived as the attainment of a progress towards an understanding of that thing as it truly is; but the achievement of some further way of conceiving the object under study may be regarded as a development of the understanding of it, even if it leads the enquirer away from rather than nearer to the truth. At first sight this looks like a simple conflict between two criteria of understanding, *viz.* truth and comprehensiveness. Some disciplines, philosophy and literary criticism for example, are as much concerned with considering every plausible mode of understanding a topic as with achieving a true understanding of it. Others are much less concerned with this type of comprehensiveness but seek to build solidly truth on truth. Nevertheless, in many spheres we are inclined to talk of development when a series of changes can be seen as each arising out of the antecedent state according to an internal principle or something sufficiently analogous: the change from acorn into oak, for example, or the progressive movement from realism to abstraction in an art style; or when the antecedent state is, or seems sufficiently like, a logically necessary condition of the subsequent one, e.g. Kohlberg's account of the development of moral understanding. When we use 'development' in this way we are employing a concept of development which appeals to no value but the movement of the developmental change itself, whether or not there is thought to be a final state towards which the development is directed. If there is a final state it is valued simply because it is the final stage of the development; in general, subsequent states are valued because they are subsequent; and the only possible disvalues are the cessation or arrest of the developmental movement, and movement back along stages already traversed (regression). This notion of development can be said to have only an internal norm. In contrast, development thought of as a movement towards truth, or the value of whose stages is justified in some other way independently of the developmental process, can be said to have an external norm. This distinction will be invoked later, in considering the justification of the educational transition from the acquisition of common knowledge to the pursuit of knowledge within the systematic disciplines.

There is a further ambiguity, between development of the understanding of something and development of the Understanding, i.e. of a person's power of understanding. For Peters and Hirst the criterion of the development of a person's Understanding is his degree of mastery of the seven Forms of Knowledge, but since this mastery is shown in the understanding of particular topics it seems that the key to the notion of development of Understanding lies in the notion of the understanding of a particular topic, to which I now return.

There are a number of criteria for a person's having a fully developed understanding of a complex topic, e.g. Wittgenstein's philosophy. First, for an understanding to be perfect it must be a true or correct or valid understanding rather than a

misunderstanding. Secondly, it must be a profound understanding — one which goes deep to fundamental principles,
presuppositions and motivations. Thirdly, it must be comprehensive, not ignoring anything of significance. Fourthly, it
must be synoptic, getting a view of the thing as a whole.
Ideally, it will also relate this whole to ever broader
backgrounds. Fifthly, it must be sensitive to hidden significances, delicate shifts of emphasis and nuances of expression.
Sixthly, it must be critical: a person does not fully
understand Wittgenstein's philosophy if he is blind to its
errors, weaknesses and omissions, and to the possibility of
alternative descriptions or explanations. Seventhly, it must be
steady, not insecure or intermittent. Eighthly, it must be
fertile or creative: a person does not really understand
Wittgenstein's philosophy if he cannot begin to apply its
principles to any topic unexamined by Wittgenstein. Appropriate evaluative response may be a further, ninth, criterion,
since we might be reluctant to allow that anyone fully
understood Wittgenstein's philosophy if he did not have even
a grudging admiration for Wittgenstein's achievement. An
understanding which is true, comprehensive, profound,
synoptic, sensitive, fertile, critical, firm and justly appreciative would be a fully developed or excellent one. The
characteristics named in this list are more or less separate
virtues or excellences of understanding. In particular cases
some may be present to a much higher degree than others.

As Peters recognises, those who achieve an excellent
understanding of a complex and difficult topic typically
exhibit certain moral or quasi-moral traits or determinations
of attitude, e.g. integrity, lucidity and courage. These, and
other similar traits, are associated with imperatives which
together constitute intellectual conscience. But understanding
cannot be achieved without the exercise of many psychical
powers which are nothing like moral traits and which depend
not on intellectual conscience but on intellectual *eros,* a
composite of energy and desire which calls them into play for
the sake of achieving understanding. Such powers are
exercised, for example, in retention and anticipation; in
synthesis and synopsis; in the reduction of wholes to parts; in
the discernment of relations and discovery of structures; in

'bracketing' properties and aspects; in discovering the objects of feelings and impressions; in guesswork; in pushing ideas to their limits; in shifts of perspective of many kinds; in weighing pros and cons and sensing the balance; and so on. The virtues especially characteristic of this vital domain of intellectual activity are *eros* itself, involvement, ambition, adventurousness, tenacity, endurance, hope and faith. These, together with the necessary skills and knowledge, constitute 'intellectual power', the successful putting forth of which in great endeavour is a kind of victory, an expression of vitality which is no doubt as satisfying as victory in battle or at the Games, though hardly a satisfactory means of obtaining a favourable balance of pleasures over pains.

This sketch of an analysis of what is involved in achieving understanding is relevant both to the problem of justifying introducing children to intellectual enquiry within established 'disciplines', and to the question whether the development of mind is adequately conceived in terms of acquiring a degree of mastery in each of a number of separate Forms of Knowledge. I shall consider first its bearing on the notion of mental development.

According to Hirst, in 'Liberal Education and the Nature of Knowledge'[2] there is a 'radical difference of kind' between the seven Forms of Knowledge, which are so many separate ways in which experience is structured and made meaningful. Coming to have one's experience structured and organised in these ways is acquisition of knowledge and development of the mind in its most fundamental sense. Hirst rejects any attempt to understand the development of mind in purely psychological terms. Mental powers and all other forms of consciousness have 'no independent intelligible structure', and it is only when psychical abilities are divided out into the various public domains that we can see what would be involved in developing them. He writes: 'It is vitally important to realize the very real objective differences that there are in forms of knowledge, and therefore of our understanding of mental powers that are related to these', and goes on to say that the unfortunate desire to characterise

[2] Op. cit., pp. 391–415.

mental development in terms of psychological unifying concepts is perhaps a relic of the times when all Forms of Knowledge were thought to be similar. Hirst's own opinion is that the structure of the mind itself is constituted by the logical structures of the Forms; and that since these structures are radically different the powers which operate within any one Form are radically different from the powers which operate within any other Form.

In the same article he admits that skills used in the different Forms of Knowledge may perhaps have something in common, but asserts that this is a matter of no importance since the rules of the Forms are different. In *The Logic of Education* Hirst and Peters seem to hold this latter position. I hope it is not unfair to read Hirst as maintaining that no power operative in one Form is the same as any power operative in any other Form, and Hirst and Peters as maintaining that even if every power were operative in every Form, still the most fundamental development of mind is the acquisition of the several Forms.

The first of these positions is based on a decision to use the expression 'the same' in a certain way. The second expresses the closely related belief that the public/objective must play a very much more fundamental part in the development of mind than the private/subjective. Hirst's doctrine of liberal education is grounded on a further decision to understand 'development of mind' additively across the Forms. His reason for this decision is the intimate connexion which he believes to exist between the Forms and our experience, which they are said to structure and organise. I shall argue against each of these positions in turn, in support of a notion of mental development as development of the mental powers. I shall not be maintaining that there can be satisfactory development of mind without the learning of language, but that since the same powers are operative in all the Forms then if the Forms are systematic disciplines development of mind can be achieved within one Form only or outside the Forms altogether. If they are not systematic disciplines but include all forms of discourse, then although development of mind cannot be accomplished outside any

Form, it can still be accomplished outside any systematic discipline. I shall suggest that the Forms of Knowledge owe their origin, character and achievements to the nature and operations of the mental powers, and that this is a reason for understanding the development of the mental powers as the most fundamental development of mind. Finally I shall maintain that because of the very general character of the notion of a 'Form of Knowledge' Hirst and Peters by-pass the problem of justifying education in the systematic disciplines.

An objection to the view that the sets of powers operative in each Form of Knowledge are radically different is that the same criteria of understanding are applicable in all the Forms, and that there are grounds for believing that in each Form satisfying these criteria involves the operation of the same powers. The philosopher comprehensively surveys Wittgenstein's *Tractatus* as the literary critic surveys *Hamlet*, and both refer the work surveyed to the capacity for appreciative response, putting out of operation certain possible determinants of that response. Both modes of appreciation, philosophical and aesthetic, have the same psychical structure; they differ in the principles which determine what is relevant in the content of the object appreciated. These principles are not external logical objects but expressions of mental life and directions to the mind, and have to be made effective in the life of the enquirer. This is done as described above, by a complex direction and suspension of attention and by calling upon a spontaneity. Even where it seems that very different powers are being referred to by the same name often the difference is illusory. For example, we tend to think that moral judgement is radically different from aesthetic judgement, but we also tend to compare the aesthetic evaluative judgement of a work as a whole with the moral judgement of the obligatoriness of an action. If instead we compare it with the moral estimation of a person the similarity becomes very much more striking than the difference. In Hirst's view the 'disciplines' (i.e. Forms of Knowledge) are each concerned to validate one logically distinct form of expression. Yet the estimation of persons, works of art, scientific achievements (e.g. Einstein's or Darwin's), religious achievements, histories, etc., are justly attributed to the same faculty — an indication of the value of psychological concepts for preserving a sense of the unity of mind. One need hardly labour the ubiquity of such powers as retention/anticipation; aspect-seeing, etc. Yet these are the powers by which one arrives at a degree of understanding which makes a just estimation possible. Whether it is Wittgenstein's *Philosophical Investigations* or the French Revolution which I fully understand, my understanding must be synoptic, and I could not accomplish the synopsis except by a psychical process of gathering parts into the whole. My understanding could not be profound, except through the discovery of fundamental structures by an analytical process which I live as a 'putting aside and seizing upon' according to an idea of ground, the operation of which again depends on the putting into play of a complex system of powers. If each psychical power operative in understanding belonged exclusively to some one Form of Knowledge it would be impossible to specify any power relative to an object in general rather than to the objects of some one particular Form, or to illustrate any power now by reference to one Form, now to another. It is difficult to regard a psychical power used in two different disciplines as two entirely different powers when introspective analysis reveals an identity or close similarity of structure. When we think of understanding in terms of psychical powers it seems that it is the same Understanding which is active in each domain, and that the logical differences between the domains spring from differences in the nature of objects towards which the one Understanding is turned, or from differences in what we are interested in in the same objects. There is no good reason for thinking that logical difference must override psychological sameness, or for supposing that differences between the Forms generate seven separate sets of unique mental powers. On the contrary, in an inter-subjective context, the same psychical powers generate the logical differences.

One could insist that our criteria for the sameness of psychical powers are too easy-going, and that we ought to change them so that powers used in different Forms count as different powers. But nothing is to be gained by this, not if we have any interest in understanding the unity of mind, the development of mind, or the nature of an adequate education; for the total subordination of the psychical powers and structures of the mind to the logical structures of the public Forms of Knowledge makes all these things impossible. According to Hirst and Peters the powers of the mind presuppose and can only be exercised in the 'modes of experience' and cannot be conceived in separation from them. It is true that they cannot be conceived separately from experience. It is also true that they cannot be conceived without at least an indirect reference to some object towards which they are directed or with which they are concerned. It is not true that the notion of 'general' powers (e.g. 'Understanding') presupposes the seven Forms of Knowledge, unless one writes the seven Forms into the notion of generality, which Hirst and Peters do, but which we ordinarily do not. Whether all instances of understanding can be classified in Hirst's manner, and whether that manner of classification is especially apposite to development of mind, are further questions. Hirst's and Peters' terminology, in which 'modes of experience' is synonymous with 'Forms of Knowledge' makes their contention that the powers of the mind 'can only be exercised in the modes of experience' both truistic and heavy with presuppositions.

The essence of Hirst's and Peters' position is the idea that understanding presupposes public standards: therefore the public Forms of Knowledge are logically prior to the powers of the mind. But the public standards are, or ought to be, indications of ends presupposed by the psyche in its relation to the world. People have to be taught to think more clearly, for example, but clarity can be recognised as desirable independently of its being demanded of us by others. It is something we are already implicitly seeking. Language cannot determine what understanding shall be, irrespective of the psyche. The public standards reflect the nature of the mental powers on which they themselves depend, and which make possible their development and correction. If, in this matter, logical priority is read as if it determined primacy in the order of reality, the originative powers are transformed into epiphenomena of their own achievements, and nothing is comprehensible any longer.

According to Hirst, not only the contents of experience but the mental powers themselves are wholly indefinite until they receive a structure from the Forms of Knowledge. It is difficult to see how a wholly indefinite mind could begin to receive a structure from the public Forms. For the acquisition of forms of knowledge we have to presuppose definite mental powers, as we have to do if we wish to construct a plausible notion of the genesis of the Forms. These powers would have had an intelligible structure even when they had not yet brought into being the means for their own discovery and description, and so were not yet intelligible to us. Hirst conceives Understanding as a sort of self-created Plotinian One, whose emanated Forms of Understanding are logically constituent parts of it; and mental development as the individual's being invaded and taken over by this public authority. This picture is not altogether false, but if we think more in terms of the genesis and development of the Forms, instead of in terms of a rigorous conventional education, we catch a glimpse of a different picture, in which the relation of the mental powers to the Forms appears more like that which exists between a pre-existent god and the works which abundantly reveal but do not constitute him. (For an understanding of man, nature and convention must both be given exactly their due.)

Public Forms of Knowledge cannot provide any new psychical power but only occasions and motives for using existing powers, perhaps in new combinations. It seems unlikely that these powers are in any way changed by the Forms, but rather that the Forms depend on them for their development. Free enquiry developed in historical times but its emergence was not necessitated or even encouraged by the existing arts and sciences. It came into being through individual insight or creativity, involving the falling away or putting into abeyance of practical ends as regulative for Understanding, and a subsequent pushing on to the limit in the application of the new *noesis*. But the capacity for renunciation of practical ends must already have been extremely ancient. A captured warrior, for example, gave up his heroic ends and came to see himself as no longer having practical ends of his own. The free enquirer did a similar thing, only in a different context and spirit. The capacity or tendency to push a procedure on to the limit must also have been very ancient, but was applied only to finite sets. Thus the operation of powers already possessed by all normal persons resulted in the emergence of a concept of 'things as they are in themselves'. The concept of works of art as pure forms, though now part of the aesthetic form of discourse, emerged surprisingly late in time on the basis of capacities for seeing perceptual aspects and for directing attention in such a manner as to induce the seeing of an aspect of the desired type. It is incredible that these powers should have originated in the nineteenth century.

If we can assume that the same powers are employed in the different Forms, and that the Forms came into existence through the exercise of the mental powers and for the purpose of understanding, the criterion of development of mind in its most fundamental sense will be the flexible and effective use of the mental powers for the purpose of understanding, and this can be achieved in a single Form, or perhaps outside the Forms altogether. Whether one ought to take a serious interest in each of the seven main areas with which man has historically concerned himself would be a separate question.

It is not difficult to imagine a brilliant chess-master who since his boyhood has been seriously interested in nothing but chess, and who by early manhood has achieved supreme eminence in the game. He possesses to a very high degree excellences of the kinds that all thinkers strive to develop: synoptic power, analytical power, profundity, creativity, etc. Everyone recognises him as a man of formidable intellect. There is something absurd in the idea that his mind has not been developed, yet he is proficient only in a single 'discipline', namely chess.

The view which I have outlined of the development of mind as development of the mental powers is a version of a common notion: 'development of the mental powers' is an accepted synonym of 'development of mind'. When we speak of 'development of mind', however, we do not always mean development of the mental powers, or not this primarily, but rather the application of these powers in a number of different areas of knowledge or 'subjects'. Hirst's view is a modified version of this other common notion. But the two notions are not exactly on par. The justification of education as development of mind in the sense 'development of the mental powers' is that this development is necessary for a human being to live as a human being. The exercise of these powers is constitutive of human life. But why, if someone's intellectual powers find ever more demanding employment and his intellectual vitality ever more satisfying expression in chess, should he bother to achieve a mastery of the seven Forms of Knowledge? To say, simply, that the acquisition of the Forms is development of mind in its most fundamental sense is to beg the question of the nature of mental development, and that of the nature of a liberal education.

Hirst claims that the Forms of Knowledge structure and organise experience. It might be said, therefore that because the chess-master has not acquired the seven Forms of Knowledge his experience is structured and organised only when he is playing chess. That would suggest that during the remainder of his waking hours he lives in a sort of delirium. This indicates a pervasive ambiguity in Hirst's doctrine. Hirst does not adequately distinguish between forms taken by our direct experience of the world (empirical, aesthetic, religious, etc.) and modes of symbolic operation. Presumably he believes that we organise experience when we calculate because if we can operate with a certain class of symbols appropriately, symbols of that class must derive their meaning from reference to experience. In 'Liberal Education and the Nature of Knowledge' Hirst presupposes a 'common area of everyday knowledge where the various disciplines can be seen in embryo and from which they branch out as distinct units'. Here he is clearly regarding the Forms of Knowledge as systematic disciplines. In *The Logic of Education*, however, he suggests that every concept belongs to some one of the seven areas of knowledge. He classifies ordinary empirical knowledge or experience under 'science', maintaining that an appeal to 'observable features of an event' in support of a religious interpretation, or to 'empirical facts' in justifying a moral principle, means that there is a scientific prerequisite for religious and moral understanding in these cases. No room is left for a separate 'common area of everyday knowledge', which the Forms of Knowledge have been extended to cover. The Form 'science' includes both common empirical experience discourse and knowledge, and the systematic sciences. The same criteria distinguish all these together from the other Forms of Knowledge.

Now, if the Forms of Knowledge were regarded as systematic disciplines the suggestion that when the chess-master is not playing chess he is living in a delirium would be false. His ordinary knowledge and experience of the world would be structured as any other normal person's is. All he would lack would be organised knowledge in any systematic discipline other than chess. If, on the other hand, the Forms of Knowledge are taken to cover common knowledge and experience, the chess-master would begin to learn the Forms of Knowledge at a very early age. By early manhood he would, no doubt, have a fair mastery of them, even if he had had no formal education, and since he has plenty of depth in chess, whose concepts must belong to some Form or Forms of Knowledge, he would seem to qualify as an educated man, according to Hirst's and Peters' criteria of an educated man.

That we could accept him as an educated man according to our common criteria is more dubious. The fact that his mental powers are developed counts towards his being educated, but something else counts against it. This is not lack of mastery of the seven Forms of Knowledge, however, for it is no more evident that someone who has mastered all seven Forms would be any better educated than the chess-master would be if he mastered six more, logically separate, games. What we have against the chess-master, from the educational point of view, is not so much that his understanding is narrow but that he understands nothing of importance. But Hirst makes no attempt to show that any of the Forms of Knowledge provides understanding of anything of importance. It does not matter what they are about or whether they are about anything at all. It does not even matter whether or not they organise experience. Concerning 'fields' of knowledge, Hirst writes: '. . . these organisations are not concerned, as the disciplines are, to validate one logically distinct form of expression'. Thus, at least in

'Liberal Education and the Nature of Knowledge'[3], the foundation of Hirst's doctrine is a logical classification of judgements by reference to their mode of validation. It does not matter, therefore, whether mathematics is derived from experience or not, or whether it is or is not applicable to experience. It is sufficient that it validates a logically distinct form of expression. That is considered a sufficient reason why children should study mathematics throughout their school career. It need not even be a Form of objective Knowledge, since Hirst admits that there are doubts about the objectivity of the characteristic judgements of three of the seven Forms, yet recommends the inclusion of these Forms in the curriculum all the same.

Despite Hirst's sustained attempt to establish the nature of the development of mind and the content of the curriculum on a purely formal, logical basis, the task seems an impossible one.[4] He has not succeeded in justifying his scheme of liberal education, or the inclusion in or exclusion from the curriculum of anything whatever. To show that a subject has an educational value we need to show either that it is a good means of developing the powers of the mind, or that it concerns things which it is important for a human being to know about, or both.

---

[3] In Chapter 4 of *The Logic of Education*, Hirst says that the differentiation of the seven areas of experience and knowledge '. . . is based on the claim that in the last analysis, all our concepts seem to belong to one of the number of distinct, if related, categories. . .' For each of these categories there are certain ultimate concepts which the other concepts presuppose. The doctrine is not worked out in detail, but although the Forms are said to be fundamentally different the concepts considered ultimate for the category 'Knowledge of Persons', e.g. 'wanting', presuppose a concept which is considered ultimate for the category, 'Science', *viz*. 'time'. The chapter induces doubt concerning the identification of the Forms.

[4] It is perilous to make curricular recommendations on the basis of irreducibility alone. If it turns out, or, if philosophers come to believe, that moral judgements are reducible in some complex manner to judgements concerning matters of fact, morality will fall under science, and Hirst recommends that Physics should be taught as a paradigm of science. Similarly, things which we do not want to teach may have to be taught. It might be argued, for example, that the Fancy (cat Fancy, dog Fancy, etc.) is a Form of Knowledge, since although its judgements have aesthetic and scientific prerequisites it is nevertheless concerned entirely with the validation of one logically peculiar expression ('prize dog', etc.).

It seems obvious that rigorous and systematic disciplines — Mathematics, Physics, History and Philosophy, for example — provide great scope for the exercise of the powers of understanding, and are about things that matter; and it seems obvious, therefore, that at an appropriate age children should be introduced to disciplines of this kind, and that it would be good for those who show promise in a discipline to be encouraged, in due course, to enter upon a special study of it. The matter calls for closer examination, however, first because a 'discipline' has a complex character which may have educational drawbacks, and secondly because, in some cases at least, it may be possible to approach the objects which the discipline studies without learning the discipline, and that could be the better way.

Hirst and Peters do not properly face the problem of justifying the educational transition from common non-theoretical understanding to understanding within the systematic disciplines. Although they both refer frequently to the pursuit of knowledge and truth they locate the criteria of knowledge and truth within the disciplines and do not ask whether these criteria might be in any way inadequate. In effect, they operate with a notion of development which employs only an internal norm. It is presupposed that since the disciplines are logically subsequent to common unsystematic understanding transition to the disciplines is desirable. Combined with this attitude towards the disciplines, the ambiguity in the conception of the 'Forms of Knowledge, Experience or Understanding' creates the illusion of a justification of the educational transition from common knowledge to the disciplines, for it would be absurd to ask whether a child who has no form of empirical experience should be given educational assistance, if that could possibly help him. But it is not absurd to ask whether children should be taught Physics. Similarly, a child who had no aesthetic experience would stand in obvious need of aesthetic education, but it does not follow that he should be taught Literary Criticism.

The various disciplines are very differently related to their corresponding areas of common knowledge, and the transition to the relevant discipline requires consideration and justification in each particular case. Hirst and Peters write: 'A budding specialist needs a detailed knowledge of all the relevant concepts, skills and tests for truth that will progressively provide him with a comprehensive understanding within a given domain', but one needs a realistic idea of what the budding specialist may be letting himself in for.

In *The Crisis of the European Sciences* Husserl suggests that since Galileo the motivation of Physics has undergone a gradual but massive change, chiefly owing to progressive idealisation; that the science no longer provides an understanding of the reality with which it was originally concerned; and that its own practitioners proceed for the most part technically and have only a technical understanding of what they are doing. In *Identity and Difference* Heidegger maintains that the sciences have come to embody a fundamentally manipulative orientation which no increase of moral responsibility on the part of scientists could do anything to alleviate. Peters' view, expressed in 'Subjectivity and Standards', seems over-optimistic in comparison: 'Science is the supreme example of reason in action not just because of opportunities for criticism which it provides, but also because of the agreement in judgements which it permits by means of its testing procedures. These guarantee objectivity and the escape from arbitrariness'. So far as science is concerned I do not know where the truth of the issue lies, but it is far from inconceivable that a discipline should go on using its criteria effectively and all its practitioners be satisfied with it, yet no one know exactly how it is 'organizing experience' or exactly what it is that they are understanding in depth.

Objectivity, agreement in judgements, and the explicit intention to eliminate arbitrariness are insufficient to guarantee the rightness of a discipline. When, in the earlier half of the century, Aesthetic Formalism dominated philosophical Aesthetics and deeply influenced aesthetic criticism, Aesthetics remained as objective as it had ever been, and there was a great deal of agreement in judgements. How could the Formalists possibly see any degree of arbitrariness in their insight that Form was the essence of Art and Beauty? No doubt philosophical Aesthetics and aesthetic criticism emerged from common experience and understanding of Art, but the Formalists could not find anything which was aesthetically relevant in this common knowledge, and took to referring to ordinary art-lovers as 'the uninitiated'. If the domain studied in these disciplines was that 'given' by common experience, then the discipline reduced it almost to nothing. Representation, expression, imaginative stimulation, truth, communication, historical and technical considerations all were declared to be aesthetically irrelevant. But the practitioners of the disciplines sincerely believed that what they had excluded did not properly belong to the domain. Art was defined in terms of Form, and to criticise the Formalist doctrine was to place oneself among the uninitiated. 'Understanding' a work of art became entirely a matter of discriminating abstract formal relations. There was no conspiracy, though if any of the millions of 'philistines' created by Aesthetic Formalism thought there was, their error was pardonable. Disciplines should enable us to have life more abundantly, not cramp and distort our life.

It is not clear what Hirst and Peters intend to include in the Form of Knowledge they call 'Knowledge of Persons', but if it is thought that common understanding of persons develops into the various branches of systematic Psychology, Psychoanalysis, Sociology, etc., and that knowledge achieved in these disciplines surpasses and supersedes common knowledge, educational transition from common to systematic knowledge of persons would have far-reaching consequences for our interpersonal life. One such consequence would be that the unsystematic understanding of persons obtainable in imaginative literature would be depreciated in favour of types of understanding which are unlikely to be more sensitive, more catholic in their attitudes, more innocent in their purposes, or less prone to error.

These considerations suggest a task which properly belongs to Philosophy of Education, namely enquiry into the character of the disciplines with a view to assessing their educational value. It is less than just to give a student an education which encourages him to take enthusiastically to a discipline whose true character is not what it is proclaimed to be. In an extreme case he might be like a person who trains as a soldier in order to free the Holy Land, and, through nobody's fault, finds himself sacking Constantinople instead.

Nor is it profitable for him to spend years of his life in arduous study when he would have been better advised to approach the objects studied, or supposedly studied, by the discipline not through the discipline itself but through common understanding.

In order to proceed further, a clearer idea is needed of the difference between 'common' or 'pre-theoretical' understanding and understanding through the disciplines. Unlike understanding within the disciplines, common understanding does not limit itself to any special area of being, but concerns itself with anything which will yield to it. It is not necessarily undisciplined, for discipline, as the following of rules counter to immediate inclination, may be exercised whenever a person is tempted to resort to arbitrariness in thinking. Common understanding is largely embodied in practical capabilities and mastery of language, both of which are acquired largely pre-reflectively, but there is also a considerable truistic common lore concerning human being and the world. Considered as a whole, this area of common knowledge is rich in content and subtle in distinctions but, compared with theoretical knowledge, lacking in depth and systematic organisation. In addition there is a large body of more or less explicit opinions, not universally accepted, concerning the same matters. Everyone comes into contact with a large number of these opinions in conversation, through literature, or during the ordinary business of life. Some of these opinions are expressions of profound insight, but they are not adequately criticised nor are their consequences fully explored, so that they fail to establish themselves intellectually against contradictory opinions. Criticism is vigorously practised within the domain of common understanding but its scope is limited, for, when pressed, the man of common understanding tends comparatively early to present his positions as unshakeable beliefs. If a writer, he may express his many insights and communicate his view of life as a whole, and it may be possible to discover the principles underlying his view from the fiction itself, whereupon their uncriticised character becomes apparent. Compared with theoretical understanding, this domain of common understanding is rich and free, but lacks objectivity, and in consequence its depth is insecure.

Common understanding, as so far described, is the kind of understanding possessed in large measure by Shakespeare, for example, which does not depend on rigorous education. It might appropriately be called 'natural' understanding. However, a group of persons in regular discourse together might make a more extensive use of criticism, answering objections to their opinions beyond the usual point of refusal, reformulating their views and obtaining a clearer and deeper understanding of the matter with which they are concerned. Such persons would differ from the rest in being more disciplined in their thinking, but one would hesitate to regard them as practitioners of a special discipline. Everyone attaches importance to criticism to some degree; these men attach rather more importance to it than the others, and use it more effectively as a means to knowledge and understanding. One might call their understanding 'natural-objective' understanding. We can imagine a group of such persons accumulating natural-objective knowledge, organising it upon the basis of such principles as they had discovered, building upon it in subsequent enquiries, and subjecting it to critical re-examination and reorganisation when the principles were modified. There would then seem to be a difference in kind between the discipline involved in the practice of the group and that which is customary within the domain of common understanding. If special teaching were provided to transmit the accumulated knowledge and the standards of the group to persons who wished to join it, we would have a 'discipline' in the developed institutional sense. Further typical features or stages in the development of a discipline are: limitation of interest to some particular area or aspect of being; invention of special methods of enquiry, some of which may become technicised; exclusive use of certain accepted modes or styles of communication; construction of concepts not used, or not used with full understanding, by persons who are not followers of the discipline, and the substitution of these concepts, often without change of name, for the concepts of ordinary discourse; and the transmission not only of knowledge, methods, etc., but also of past projects in so far as they influence present attitudes and orientations of enquiry.

If this outline is tenable, the following points can perhaps profitably be made. First, an adequate account of the means of validating the characteristic judgements of a discipline cannot be given in the manner suggested by Hirst, which serves also to distinguish a corresponding area of common understanding. Reference would have to be made to all the overt and tacit historically determined conventions of the discipline which are relevant to verification. Furthermore, an account of the Form of Knowledge as a whole would involve an account of the relation of each developed discipline not simply to experience as determined or appealed to by the discipline, but to the corresponding area of common understanding and common experience, and any such account would raise the question of the legitimacy and desirability of the departures embodied in the discipline, including changes in purpose or motivation. So long as we did not presuppose the superiority of the more highly developed, the task of evaluating the discipline would be forced upon us.

Secondly, the ambiguity in the concept of a Form of Knowledge prevents Hirst and Peters from fully understanding the aims of progressive educationalists, creativists, self-expressionists and other similar enthusiasts. The authors argue that these people make creativeness and criticism their educational aims, but that unless there were Forms of Knowledge there would be no content with which to be creative or critical. They say that without training in public Forms of Knowledge the aims of creativeness and critical thought are 'empty uplift'. Either they are saying that one has to acquire a mastery of language and a degree of common knowledge and understanding if one is to be creative and critical; or that one has to be trained in a particular discipline in order to be creative and critical with reference to that discipline. If the former, they are correct, but what they say does not constitute a criticism of the progressives, whose method is neither that of doing nothing whatever, nor that of educating surreptitiously in the traditional manner. If the latter, what the authors are saying is either tautologous or probably false. Suppose that someone — Nietzsche for example — not having been trained in philosophy or having mastered any body of philosophical knowledge, began to think on matters traditionally regarded as philosophical and immediately displayed extraordinary creativeness and very powerful critical ability. If it is argued that he must have trained himself in philosophical techniques as he went along, and mastered the necessary body of knowledge in the same way, the thesis becomes tautologous. If, on the other hand, it is said that as a matter of fact no one could possibly be a creative or critical philosopher without prior philosophical training and education, the thesis is probably false. I do not know how much philosophical training Nietzsche and Wittgenstein had had before they wrote their first philosophical books but I see no reason why either needed any philosophical training at all, since both were persons of formidable intellect whose intellectual powers were already highly developed. They simply thought about matters which we call 'philosophical'.

It may be that Hirst and Peters believe that no one can do anything really worthwhile in any area of intellectual concern unless he has had a suitably rigorous training in whatever discipline or disciplines are especially appropriate to that area. For them, creativity is necessarily 'creativity within the discipline'. This belief is justified, if at all, only if and where achievement absolutely depends on learning a special language. There are indeed special languages for the contemporary disciplines called 'Philosophy' and 'Aesthetic Criticism', for example, but one can also approach the objects traditionally studied by these forms of enquiry directly on the basis of ordinary language and natural understanding, and what one says about these objects may contribute to and even upset the disciplines one has not learned.

The progressives, etc., need not be regarded as extreme subjectivists, but as proclaiming the fertility of natural understanding, and protesting against the view that public 'Forms of Knowledge' can take objects out of the scope of natural understanding and make serious access to them possible only through established disciplines. In some cases, at least, it is possible to understand these objects outside the disciplines, and there are advantages in not approaching them through the disciplines. The learner does not inherit the errors of the discipline, does not have to adopt contemporary attitudes or concern himself with fashionable problems to the exclusion of possibly more important matters, does not have to follow accidental conventions as if they were essential means to understanding, etc. The advocates of 'self-expression' and 'doing one's own thing' are not necessarily vulgar or arrogant, but express the Understanding's need to live with intellectual *eros* in close contact with the object of its interest.

A more general problem is that of deciding how far the education of the young should be carried on through the disciplines, and how far it should continue at the level of natural understanding. One could attain the level of understanding achieved by many great writers without undergoing an education in the disciplines, for though it has a craft tradition, Literature, so far as content is concerned, belongs entirely to common understanding. Writers do not seek to validate any one logically distinct form of expression but express their attitudes towards and opinions about anything whatever, though most particularly man and his situation. There is no reason why education of the natural understanding should be reserved in secondary schools for 'unacademic' children, while the others go into the disciplines. On the contrary, there is good reason why education of the natural understanding should be carried on seriously in secondary schools of every type, and a wide variety of courses devised for the purpose, concerning things that matter. It seems a good means of fostering the life of the mind, since the students have to think more for themselves, yet when they express their views would not run immediately into an entanglement of ready-to-hand disciplinary criticism. With good teaching they could penetrate deeply into fields which supposedly belong to the disciplines, and develop points of view of their own without first having to confront the intimidating power of orthodoxy.

Some approach can now be made to questions of justification. I consider first the justification of education in general, still limiting the notion of education provisionally to the development of knowledge and understanding. What makes it fitting that a person should be educated is the importance of the things he comes to know, and the fact that the pursuit of understanding is constitutive of and an expression of the life of the mind, which is an essential aspect of the life of a human being. But understanding is not the only activity constitutive of mental life, since people commonly enjoy fantasies; and it is possible for a person to attach supreme importance to chariot-racing or football, rather than to 'the things that matter'. Why should anyone be persuaded, against his inclination, to seek understanding of things that matter, rather than watch football and enjoy fantasies about it? The immediate answer is two-fold. First, football is a poor and limited thing compared with the things that matter, and fantasy is a poor and limited thing in comparison with the pursuit of understanding. The rich and unlimited is to be preferred to the poor and limited, because through it the mind obtains life more abundantly. (It does not follow, however, that football should not be watched or fantasies not enjoyed.) Secondly, importance is not attributed to the 'things that matter' arbitrarily. If still it is objected that those who do not want to know about the things that matter or to have intellectual life more abundantly should be left in peace, the educator's only proper answer is that he cares for children too much simply to leave them to follow their own inclinations.

For our Western civilisation at least, as Peters recognises in 'Subjectivity and Standards', the things considered most important for a human being to know about and understand are Nature, Man — including his works, situation and history — and God, or the Transcendent. A person does not become a full member of the human race by the age of three, by which time, he has achieved an understanding of himself as a being separate from the others. He needs next to look around his environment, to take possession, as it were, of what belongs to him. By 'Nature' is meant the encounterable natural world, not the physical world of the sciences. Our justification for making even unwilling children aware of the world around them, and bringing them to a common understanding of it, is that they will live more abundantly if they allow themselves to take an interest in it. It is their dwelling-place, fit to stimulate their minds, and it would be unkindness on our part if we did not get them to open their eyes to it — almost as bad as neglecting to slap a new-born baby to get it to start breathing.

The justification for teaching children about the Transcendent is similar since the Transcendent is, in a sense, the furthest reach of the human environment and is capable of greatly enriching the lives of those who are attuned to it. Again, it seems to be part of a child's birthright to learn about this domain, and we would be wronging him if we kept it hidden from him, irrespective of whether it is real or only a product of the Imagination.

As for Man, a child needs to think himself into the human race, and begins to do so spontaneously, almost as soon as he is born. A person whose sense of his own being is imperfectly developed, or who cannot feel he 'belongs' among other people, or who cannot take an interest in others, is pitiable. We would be depriving a child of what properly belongs to him, and hopelessly impoverishing his life, if we did not help him to get an understanding of his own nature as a human being in the world together with the others, who include the men of the Past as well as those of the Present. It is hardly necessary for me to write at length on Man as an object of interest.

If all goes well, in due course the child will arrive at naive concepts of the natural world as whole; of history as reaching up to the Present; of Man as such, and as a totality to which he himself belongs; and, let us suppose, at some concept of the Transcedent as related to all these. He holds them all together in a primitive synoptic unity, and is at home within the totality. As the Romantic poets recognised, he has become a person with someting to lose.

The justification of education in general seems a comparatively easy matter, but we cannot justify education in the disciplines on the ground that transition to them is a straightforward development of the common understanding provided by early education. Nor is this transition inevitable if education is to proceed after, say, the age of eleven. The world is rich enough to go on rewarding understanding without demanding initiation into any systematic discipline as a condition.

A common objection against education in the disciplines is that it tends to result in a loss of the primitive sense of being within the whole, and in estrangement from natural understanding. Instead of understanding life and the world through deepening his experience of them, the educated man depends upon theoretical and scholarly explanations which, at least for the most part, he neither originates nor fully understands. He thinks he has gained from his initiation into the disciplines, whereas in fact he has lost genuineness as a human being. He is supposed to be able to make use of common knowledge for the enrichment of his systematic enquiry, but he cannot actually do so, either because he is no longer interested in anything which common understanding could possibly help him with, or he cannot see the world except through the eyes of his discipline, which teaches him to despise common understanding. But the explanations in which he puts so much faith have already been superseded. Although this is a caricature, unfortunately it is a recognisable one.

To justify education in any particular discipline it is necessary, first, to be reasonably sure that it is not likely to be detrimental to the life of the individuals who participate in it, or wasteful of their time. If many of those who have studied it have become disillusioned with the discipline itself, and perhaps have even turned away from the objects which the discipline studies, educators need to consider whether they are justified in recruiting for that discipline. A clear understanding is required of the nature of each discipline, including the objects it studies, the motivations which contemporarily inspire it, and its relation to common understanding. Secondly, we need to be able to teach or otherwise communicate some manner or method by which a person can recall himself from his discipline, once more adopt the relatively naive attitudes of common understanding even towards the objects of his discipline, and regain his capacity for the primitive synopsis. Obtaining breadth within the disciplines is of little value to the individual if this primitive sense of unity is lost, for no such unity is either available or possible within the disciplines. Without it, and

estranged from common understanding, the man who possesses breadth within the disciplines is merely possessed by
seven disciplines instead of one.

Granted these two conditions are met, the justification of
education in a particular discipline would be, first, the general
one that, taught well to persons interested in it, it is a good
means for the development of the mental powers and a good
medium for the expression of intellectual vitality both at the
level at which it can be taught in schools and thereafter; and
that it provides knowledge and and understanding of things
that matter. Secondly, there is the special justification that at
least in some regions disciplines may be essential if we are to
hope for secure depth of understanding. I assume both that
disciplines can in principle be corrected and that, in some
cases at least, we shall be willing to continue to risk the errors
to which they are susceptible, for the sake of the depth of
understanding which they alone can provide. Naturally, we
shall try to take the young along with us in the adventure to
which we are committed. As time passes, however, our
justification for making individual children persist with
disciplines which they dislike, and for which they have little
talent, diminishes to nothing. So far as study in the
disciplines is concerned, the taste of intellectual victory is all
important, and the acquisition of *quasi*-moral virtues a poor
consolation if this is lacking. Since the development of mind
does not depend on the attainment of a mastery of any
particular   discipline — mathematics   or   physics,   for
example — teachers have a continuous obligation to assess
whether an unhappy child's continuing with a particular
discipline is worth the price it is exacting. Education has
other means of developing the mind, and there are other
interesting aspects and departments of the things that matter.

'Breadth' of understanding, as understanding within two or
more disciplines, is of value because each discipline tends to
develop some powers more than others: because proficiency
in more than one discipline makes possible depth of
understanding of a wider range of important matters; and
because some disciplines can be used together for the better
understanding of certain particular matters. But these
grounds of value are not a sufficient reason for making the

attainment of 'some degree of mastery' of several disciplines the chief educational aim for children in secondary schools, and this multiple attainment is not identical with the development of mind. A case could be made for providing a variety of courses in the secondary school, some in which enquiry is comparatively systematic, others which depend on and develop common understanding; some in traditional school subjects, some in other subjects, some involving combinations of subjects; some in narrow fields, some broad surveys; some rich in information, others more in the nature of intellectual exercises. Hopefully, children would have a choice as to which courses to follow. The primary criteria for assessing a course would be its suitability for developing the powers of the mind, and the value of its content; and whether a course is likely to arouse and sustain interest is relevant to its suitability for developing the mind. A curriculum of this sort would limit the extent of the injustice perpetrated on unwilling learners, avoid any sudden compartmentalisation of knowledge, and allow for frequent shifting of perspective from systematic to natural understanding. No doubt it would be as good a method as any for discovering the special potentialities of individual children, and those who specialise might come fresher to their chosen disciplines at the appropriate time. Whatever one's views on these matters, it is worth remembering that more than one interpretation can be given to the notion of a 'balanced' curriculum, and to the notion of educational 'breadth'.

Philosophical analysis can be strangely misleading when applied to educational issues, chiefly because of its tendency to create and exaggerate emphases. If one over-stresses the importance of public rules and standards enquiry begins to look like something a child has to acquire a taste for if he can, rather than something he takes to naturally. If one makes too much of the value of knowledge, enquiry takes on an aspect of acquisitiveness which may be repugnant to a generous spirit. Exclusive emphasis on the exercise of the intellectual powers, without reference to what they are concerned with, makes enquiry seem a pointless expenditure of energy. All these aspects need to be reintegrated in a notion of the pursuit of understanding as an activity and receptivity which is natural to man, in which he finds fulfilment. But Understanding is itself only an aspect of human being, and needs to be considered in the context of personal development as a whole, a wider perspective which for the most part I have failed to attain in this paper.

5 Education and Human Being II

GLENN LANGFORD

Mr Elliott begins by accepting Professors Hirst and Peters' view that education is connected with the development of mind; but differs from them in the account which he offers of the development of mind. He rejects the view, associated particularly with Professor Hirst, that mental development can be understood only by reference to seven officially designated forms of knowledge. His primary purpose, however, is not critical but constructive; and Hirst's account is criticised primarily to point the constrast between it and his own. According to Mr Elliott, the most fundamental development of mind is the development of the mental powers; and this may occur without any study of the systematic disciplines. A person becomes educated, therefore, not by becoming acquainted with Forms of Knowledge but by developing his mental powers. He justifies this preference by reference to a criterion of educational value; i.e. by reference to what "is necessary for a human being to live as a human being." (p. 56) Although study of the systematic disciplines is not necessary to becoming educated, a person may become educated through the study of them provided the criterion of educational value is satisfied. It may be satisfied directly if it concerns matters which it is important for a human being to know about and understand (p. 59); or indirectly if the study develops his mental powers. The topics in Mr Elliott's account which seem to me to most merit attention are: first, his account of the development of mind; secondly, his incidental criticism of Hirst's Forms of Knowledge which I will deal with only incidentally; and thirdly, his criterion of educational value.

First, then, Mr Elliott's account of the development of mind. His view, insofar as I understand it, is that the exercise of the mental powers, if exercised in accordance with the excellence proper to them, leads, by an 'organic' process of development possessing its own internal norms, to understanding; understanding, in turn, is thought of as the culmination of that process and is to be judged by the standards internal to it. No reference is made to the objects on which the mental powers are exercised; this is intentional and is, indeed, the crux of the difference between Elliott and Hirst. They must, as a matter of logic, be exercised on something and lead to understanding of something. But what that something is is not in itself important so far as the development of mind is concerned; although some things will, as a matter of fact, provide better exercise for the mental powers than others. Mr Elliott offers, therefore, what may be called a wall-bar theory of the curriculum.

In offering this synopsis of Mr Elliott's position, I have assumed that what he calls criteria of understanding are internally related to the mental powers (which he also refers to as psychic powers). I have taken it, that is, that the criteria of understanding to which he refers are criteria of the successful application of mental powers. A person's understanding of a topic is 'fully developed', 'perfect' (p. 48) or 'excellent' (p. 48) if it is true, profound, comprehensive, synoptic, sensitive, critical, firm, fertile and justly appreciative. Mental powers are those of retention and anticipation, synthesis and synopsis, analysis, discernment of relations and discovery of structures, 'bracketing' properties and aspects, discovering the objects of feelings and impressions, guesswork, pushing ideas to their limits, shifts of perspect and aspect-seeing, weighing pros and cons and, I think, capacity for appreciative response (p. 52) and capacity for renunciation of practical ends (i.e. for free enquiry.) (p. 54) The two lists do not correlate neatly; but neither is intended to be comprehensive and there is some degeee of correlation. For example, a person will achieve a profound understanding if he uses his power to discern relations, discover basic structures and see aspects; his understanding will be fertile if he is successful in pushing ideas to their limits, synoptic if he makes proper use of his powers of synopsis, firm if he makes proper use of his powers of retention, and so on. The alternative to interpreting Mr Elliott in this way is to think of the criteria of understanding as being dictated by the content of what is understood; and this is the position which he wishes to reject.

This interpretation of Mr Elliott's position gains support from his sympathetic account of what he calls 'organic' development in which change takes place according to its own internal rhythm rather than towards some external goal. He gives the explicitly organic example of the change of an acorn into an oak. Moreover, the mental powers are said to possess a structure which is independent of public forms of knowledge (see, e.g., p. 50); the public forms cannot, therefore, 'provide any new psychical power but only occasions and motives for using existing powers, perhaps in new combinations.' (p. 54) 'The relation of the mental powers to the Forms appears ... like that which exists between a pre-existent god and the works which reveal but do not constitute him.' (p. 54) Elsewhere Mr Elliott distinguishes between systematic disciplines and what he calls 'common' or 'pre-theoretical' understanding (p. 62); but there is no reason to suppose that common understanding can do for the mental powers what the Forms of Knowledge (equated with the systematic disciplines) cannot. These remarks suggest that the mental powers are thought of as natural, in a sense opposed to conventional; and, although Mr Elliott does not use these terms, as innate as opposed to learnt. What he does say is that he is trying to understand education 'in relation to a concept of human being in which the element of nature is allowed to assert itself rather more freely against the element of convention.' (p. 45) No account, however, is offered of the psychic structure which mental powers are said to possess except, perhaps, for the remark that synopsis is 'a psychical process of gathering parts into the whole' (p. 52); and this is merely a definition. Nor is any attempt made to clarify the sense in which the words 'natural' and 'conventional' are used. It seems at times, indeed, as if the words 'natural' and 'psychological' are used as synonyms; if so this is certainly mistaken.

In my view Mr Elliott's account goes wrong from the beginning in relying on the notion of development. It is true that in doing so he has the authority of Professors Hirst and Peters; although they, in *The Logic of Education,* handle it gingerly and with reservations. Mr Elliott, on the other hand, takes it very seriously, as I have tried to show. There is of course no objection to speaking of development of mind if this means no more than that someone has changed for the better as a person, just as changes which increase the market value of property are called developments; but attempts to use it in a stricter sense are simply inappropriate. They suggest that change occurs according to a fixed pattern and in the direction of a predetermined end. This may be true of the changes which occur in plant and animal bodies; and it may be true of the behaviour patterns of some animals. People, on the other hand, possess the ability to learn; moreover, in contrast with most other animals, their ability to learn is open-ended; they can learn to do, and can learn about, an almost infinite variety of things. It is because people can learn that they are also able to form themselves into groups of people, each group having its own traditions transmitted from generation to generation and its own history of change. If people could not learn, and therefore could not form themselves into social groups, there would be neither the scope nor the need for education. That people can do these things is, of course, an empirical matter; and my basic objection to the introduction of the notion of 'development' into the account of education is that it draws attention away from it.

There is, moreover, a certain ambiguity in Mr Elliott's use of the notion of development. He says, on several occasions, that the most fundamental development of mind is the development of the mental powers; but he also refers, on one occasion, to 'the flexible and effective use of the mental powers for the purpose of understanding.' (p. 55) 'Developing' and 'putting to effective use' need not amount to the same thing. Muscles, for example, may develop in becoming bigger and more powerful without being put to any effective use. A body-builder may use his muscles in order to develop them, for example by weight-lifting; but in doing so he need

not be developing them to use them in any further way. On
the other hand, one may learn to use existing muscles in new
ways, for example in acquiring new skills such as wrestling; in
this case the muscles may incidentally grow stronger but they
need not do so. Perhaps, therefore, Mr Elliott really does
mean, what he frequently says, *development* of the mental
powers. Indeed, since he is thinking of the mental powers as
natural not only in the sense of independent of convention
but also in the sense of unlearnt — to use his colourful
phrase, 'like a pre-existent god' (p. 54) — about the only
constructive thing they can do is develop. Unfortunately this
has the consequence, as I have already argued, of ruling out
both the scope and need for education.

It would be more plausible, therefore, to think of
education as coming to make effective use of the mental
powers; and coming to do so, not by a process of
development but by a process of learning. But if what you
are interested in is the effective use of mental powers — or
muscles — you must say what you want to use them for. It is
no longer a question of simply needing some subject-matter;
the subject matter is now important in its own right because
without it you cannot guarantee being able to use your
mental powers effectively. Transfer of training cannot be
taken for granted; if you develop your muscles by weight-
lifting you may be no better, or even worse, at wrestling. If,
therefore, Mr Elliott's concern is not with the development of
mental powers but with their effective use, the difference
between his own position and that of Professor Hirst is
reduced, as perhaps he realises. For only a little later he
contrasts two interpretations of 'development of mind' —
'development of mental powers', and 'the application of
those powers in a number of different areas of knowledge or
'subjects' (p. 55f.); and attributes the latter position to
Professor Hirst. The difference which remained between
them would then be that between the view of development
of mind as use of the mental powers *per se* and their use in
the different Forms of Knowledge.

There is, however, a further disagreement, or possible
disagreement, between them as to whether all knowledge
which it is possible to have is included in the Forms of

Knowledge or whether a distinction needs to be made between commonsense knowledge and what Mr Elliott calls the 'systematic disciplines'. Professor Hirst, according to Mr Elliott, is ambiguous as between these two positions but inclined, in the *Logic of Education*, to settle for the former. Ordinary empirical knowledge is then, for example, classified as science. Mr Elliott holds the latter view; and in this I am quite sure he is right. I cannot see how, on any view of science, statements like 'this is a table' can count as scientific statements. More generally, the notions of 'physical object' and 'cause' are philosophers' abstractions from a common-sense view of the world which preceded by a very long time anything remotely like what we now call science. Similarly. the indefinite article 'a' cannot be identified with the figure 1; arithmetical operations can be performed only with the latter, not with the former.

I accept, then, Mr Elliott's distinction between what he calls common understanding and the systematic disciplines; and also the consequence which he takes that the inclusion of the latter in the school curriculum requires justification independently of the inclusion of the former. Even if Professor Hirst were prepared to agree that first thoughts were best, however, this would not eliminate the difference between them. For the crux of the matter is whether, as Mr Elliott claims, one can make sense of the idea of the effective use of the mental powers, i.e. that use which leads to understanding, without reference to public standards; whether, that is, 'understanding' can be elucidated wholly in psychological terms. And on this central issue I agree wholeheartedly with Professor Hirst.

In view of my agreement with Professor Hirst on this central point, I would like to emphasise that I am not in agreement with him on all points. In particular, I find disturbing the claim that there are neither more nor less than seven Forms of Knowledge. Whatever criteria are adopted to demarcate and enumerate forms of knowledge, the upshot is bound to be controversial. According to one of the most powerful philosophical movements of the twentieth century, for example, all knowledge is scientific knowledge and science forms a unity; and the term 'knowledge' is misapplied in speaking of moral, aesthetic or religious knowledge. And if regard is paid to controversy, for example as to whether social science and physical science are both, in the same sense, sciences, then Professor Hirst's position is difficult to defend. Mr Elliott is, I think, aware of this sort of objection to Professor Hirst's views but does not press it because it is not directly relevant to the thesis he wishes to develop; and I will follow him in this.

An objection which is relevant is that speaking, in Platonic manner, of 'Forms of Knowledge' — complete with capital letters — leads to a tendency to reify things which people do. What you have is not any sort of thing but people applying various standards and looking at reality in different ways. Science, religion, mathematics and so on are better thought of as strictly regulated activities than as things such as books or depositaries. Professor Hirst may share this view; but if so the terminology of Forms of Knowledge, neatly counted and labelled, is misleading; and may, indeed, have lead Mr Elliott to exaggerating the difference between them. For he also has an inclination for the more dramatic form of expression and prefers to talk of the mental powers, the psychic powers or even 'the one Understanding' (p. 52) rather than of the things which people can do in order to achieve some knowledge of the world in which they live. And the difference between mental powers and Forms of Knowledge seems far starker than that between the things which people can do and the things which people do.

The main point, however, is whether one can make sense of the idea of the effective use of the mental powers *per se*, without any reference to public standards. Mr Elliott admits that the mental powers cannot be conceived without at least an indirect reference to some subject matter. (p. 53) And even if the subject matter on which the mental powers are exercised comes, not from systematic disciplines but from common understanding, it still brings with it public standards. Mr Elliott says that 'compared with theoretical understanding, this domain of common understanding is rich and free, but lacks objectivity.' (p. 62) But since it provides us, in the perception of physical objects, with our paradigm of objectivity, this is hardly true.

In order to develop this point I would like to return to Mr Elliott's list of the mental powers, which I reproduced earlier.

This seems to have been drawn up, rather grandly, with an eye to the systematic disciplines which he later argues are inessential to education rather than to our ordinary common-sense knowledge of the world which he refers to as common understanding. The most obvious omissions, from this point of view, are the ability to perceive and to make judgements and inferences. I will say a little about only the first and last of these.

Seeing is surely one of the things which we can do, well or badly, in order to gain knowledge and understanding of the world we live in; yet only what looks like a sophisticated development of it, aspect-seeing, is included in Mr Elliott's list. And it is surely unnecessary to argue that seeing involves a reference to public or, as I would prefer to call them, social or inter-personal, standards. This might be obscured by the fact that the notion of seeing, as of other perceptual modalities, involves a reference to the process which occurs when a part of an organic body,— an organ of sense — interacts physically with part of the world external to it. But as soon as we think of the eye as having a function, which may be performed well or badly, we have introduced a reference to standards, even if covert. The functioning of an organ is judged by its contribution to the survival of the system constituted by the whole body of which it is a part. Organs of perception make their contribution by informing the organism of the situation in which it is placed. Eyes which perform well, therefore, tell you what is there. And what is there can be decided not by any examination of the physical process which occurs in perception but by reference to the public world which exists independently of those processes.

One can make the same point in a slightly different way. Mr Elliott includes aspect-seeing in his list of mental powers, as I have said; and aspect-seeing suggests seeing things from angles which others have, perhaps, neglected. Jones, for example, may see the remains of a stone-age village where Smith sees only a collection of rocks. Jones is able to see the rocks in this way only if he knows what a stone-age village is; if, that is, he possesses the concept of a stone-age village. But, equally, Smith can see a collection of rocks only if he knows what a collection of rocks is; if, that is, he possesses the concept of a collection of rocks. Their seeing, therefore, is more than a physical process; it involves also the mental power of applying concepts. And, again, in general they exercise that ability well only when what they see as the remains of a stone-age village or a collection of rocks is in fact what they take it to be. Moreover, they can see the same thing only insofar as they possess the same concepts; and they possess the concepts only insofar as they share the same — public or social — criteria for their application.

Inference, also, is surely a means of achieving understanding and counts, therefore, as a mental power. Its use can be illustrated irrespective of subject matter; this is what makes its formalisation in logic possible. It illustrates very clearly, therefore, one of the features of mental powers to which Mr Elliott attaches importance. (for example on p. 51) A person who makes an inference in history and in philosophy does the same thing (i.e. makes an inference) in two different contexts. But the criteria for 'the same' are provided by logic; they are not established empirically by investigating the structure of the mind. There is, also, an excellence proper to inference thought of as a mental power; one arrives at understanding only if valid, rather than invalid, inferences are made. And it is a power which can be exercised within common understanding. The ability to make inferences is of course not the same as the ability to do logic; it is a familiar point that Aristotle invented logic, not inference. Finally, making inferences is something which people do; in that sense they have a psychological aspect. Nevertheless the standards by which the inferences a person makes are judged are public standards. Attempts to 'psychologise' inference — to understand logic as the science of the mind — belong very definitely to the history of logic; and I do not believe that Mr Elliott really wishes to revive them. If he does he is in a minority; the very terminology of modern philosophy, for example the substitution of terms like 'proposition' or 'statement' for 'judgement', reflects the unanimity of philosophical agreement on this point.

I agree with Mr Elliott, therefore, on the need to distinguish between what he calls common understanding and the systematic disciplines; but do not agree that sense can be made of the idea of the effective use of mental powers without any reference to public standards. I have argued also that if the notion of development is taken seriously it leaves no scope for education; while if it is used metaphorically it is misleading; and that it would be better, therefore, to abandon it altogether and rely instead on the notion of learning.

Finally I want to look briefly at Mr Elliott's suggested criterion of educational value. When first introduced this is offered only as 'a criterion of the educational value of a branch of study', i.e. 'that it concerns matters which it is important for human beings to know about and understand.' (p. 45) Later however Mr Elliott says that 'the justification of education as development of mind in the sense of 'development of the mental powers' is that this development is necessary for a human being to live as a human being. The exercise of these powers is constitutive of human life.' (p. 56) And, finally, he says, that 'what makes it fitting that a person should be educated is the importance of the things he comes to know, and the fact that the pursuit of understanding is constitutive of and an expression of the life of the mind, which is an essential aspect of the life of a human being.' (p. 66f.) In each case, therefore, Mr Elliott is combining a statement of his criterion with an application of it. In his view the criterion is best satisfied by development of the mental powers and, indirectly, by those branches of study which develop mental powers. Aspects of common understanding and the various branches of study or systematic disciplines have to be considered on their individual merits.

The criterion of educational value itself appears to be what 'is important for human beings' or what 'is necessary for a human being to live as a human being.' It takes for granted, therefore, the connection between the concept of education and that of a human being or person; and relies on the values built into the latter. This is a view which I have expressed myself; but it is not free from difficulties, and I would like to draw attention to some of them. First, we need to distinguish between the biological species, man, and persons; only the latter concept is evaluative. Mr Elliott's flirtation with the natural man is a little worrying in this connection. Secondly, clarification of the sense in which the word 'necessary' is to be taken is needed. Is what is necessary for a human being to live as a human being thought of as a question of natural fact, as a matter for decision or as dictated by a social tradition? I suspect Mr Elliott of favouring the first of these possibilities; I favour the latter, with perhaps a pinch of decision thrown in. Thirdly, there is the notion of importance; it is not difficult to agree to favour what is important or, indeed, 'things that matter' (p. 67), which allow us 'to live more abundantly' (p. 67) or which enrich our lives (p. 68) But this leaves us as free as before to disagree about what is important or enriches our lives, as, indeed, Mr Elliott and Professor Hirst do. In other words, 'importance', like 'good', itself needs criteria before it can be applied; by itself the advice 'Do good and avoid evil' is of no practical use. Fourthly, not everything which is important from the point of view of becoming a person is connected, at least in any obvious way, with knowledge and understanding, to which Mr Elliott confines himself. Perhaps what is most important for a person is to learn to live in a particular society; without this he is without roots or a proper sense of identity. And this is not just, or even primarily, a question of developing mental powers but of acquiring attitudes and coming to internalise social rules. This draws attention, also, to the fact that ideals of what a person should be differ from society to society and, to a lesser extent, within the same society; and so, too, will criteria of educational importance. Finally, in setting up a criterion of educational value at all Mr Elliott might be accused of adopting an instrumental view of education. Some instrumental views are objectional in that they tend to trivialise education; according to them, men are educated not in order to turn them into persons but to change them into economic or military cannon fodder. But this need not be so; on the contrary there is every reason to think of education as one aspect of social life among others, contributing to them as well as receiving support from them, rather than as wholly self-contained.

Despite the difficulties, I think that Mr Elliott's suggested criterion of educational value is worth serious attention and hope it will receive it at the meeting.

6 Chairman's Remarks

PAUL H. HIRST

Both Professor Elliott's paper and Mr Langford's reply focus on three related areas of philosophical problems of educational significance and my comments will therefore be organised around these. I shall look first at what is meant by 'the development of mind' and the place of education in mental development; secondly, at the nature of systematic disciplines and their significance for both mental development and education; and thirdly, and very briefly, at the question of the justification of education in general.

I

Like Mr Langford, I have some difficulty in being sure just how Professor Elliott views the overall character of the development of mind. If I have understood him correctly, basic to mind, at least where understanding is concerned, is a form of energy and desire, an intellectual *eros* which calls into play many psychical or mental powers. These are described as exercised in, for example, retention, synthesis and synopsis, reduction of parts to wholes, weighing pros and cons and sensing the balance. The virtues of these activities are *eros* itself 'involvment, ambition, adventurousness, tenacity, endurance, hope and faith'. It is these virtues which together with the necessary skills and knowledge constitute 'intellectual power'. Like Mr Langford I take it that Professor Elliott considers both what he calls *eros* and also the mental power which it calls into play, to be what they are as natural 'givens', and understanding to be what it is as a result of their characters. The view objected to by Professor Elliott is that the powers of the mind have a structure determined by publicly shared forms of knowledge and understanding, it being the case rather that such forms of knowledge and understanding as we have 'owe their origin, character and achievements to the nature and operations of the mental powers'. For this reason he regards 'the development of the mental powers as the most fundamental development of mind'.

For all his forceful assertion of disagreement with the view that I, and to some extent Professor Peters, have expressed on this subject, Professor Elliott and I are not I think quite as disagreed as he suggests. Setting on one side the question of development, my concern has been with the character of a person's understanding and the particular abilities it necessitates, and not with the character of the powers of understanding, or mental powers, that so concern Professor Elliott. To this extent we have been looking at the structure of different aspects or levels of mind, and therefore some of the things Professor Elliott has said about mental powers are not necessarily incompatible with points I have argued. That an adequate account of mind must presuppose some fundamental dynamic, that is in one sense the source of all our understanding, could well be. That however it *naturally* takes the form of certain particular powers is not so clear. Any fundamental dynamic is necessarily expressed in or on something and in a context, and even at the most general level, its character can only be indicated in terms of that content and context. Professor Elliott does not dissent from the view that we can only identify his powers of the mind with at least some indirect reference to some object with which they are concerned. Indeed, what other form of identification could there be? But if so, then we must begin by examining the objects of states of mind and mental activities, and it is from these alone that we can come to understand what powers there are. I have suggested that by examining the objects of understanding there seem to be a number of different types of understanding e.g. empirical, moral, religious, involving the exercise of different types of judgement. A type of understanding can I take it be picked out only by the use of certain criteria of 'sameness' for demarcating a class of the objects of understanding, which I have taken to be true propositions. Whether there are such types of understanding, is manifestly a matter of considerable dispute. But if we can make such distinctions, we do I think have reason to speak of abilities to understand and to judge in these different areas. Certainly we speak colloquially of such types of understanding. But if one is asked what general abilities there are, it seems to me we can only either look to see if the same patterns of conceptual and propositional relations exist in different areas of understanding, or test empirically to see what abilities correlate highly. In other words, the structure of abilities can I think only be determined by starting with the public character of the achievements in which we are interested, determining 'sameness' by reference to these.

What then of Professor Elliott's mental powers? How are these recognised and by what criteria is the same power said to be exercised on two different occasions? Only by showing that behind the abilities of the different forms of understanding there exist certain common powers can I see this to be possible. But Professor Elliott never shows this, for he does not argue from the objects and their use. We are offered instead a number of assertions. He asserts that in different forms of understanding the same criteria of understanding are applicable, but that is very far from obvious when the objects of understanding and their relations are manifestly different in so many respects. Why also should we accept without argument that satisfying these criteria in different areas involves the operation of the same powers? That philosophical and aesthetic appreciation have the same psychical structure I find an elusive claim. Again these forms of appreciation are said to differ in the principles which determine what is relevant in the content of the object appreciated; these principles being not external logical objects but expressions of mental life and directions to the mind. That they are expressions of mental life and directions to the mind may be, but are they not necessarily also logical objects? And again, do we in fact, as we are assured, attribute estimations of persons, works of art, scientific achievements, religious achievements, histories, to the same faculty, and even if that is so, with what justification? Introspection is said to be a basis, but can that function in ways which attention to the public expression of the logical objects of understanding can not? Professor Elliott suggests that it is the same understanding which is active in each domain and that logical differences between these domains spring from differences in the nature of the objects to which 'the one Understanding' is turned. True the differences do spring from the objects, but the question is how, other than by attention to these, and the differences of use these demand, can we distinguish any different powers of the mind there might be. Mr Langford seems to me absolutely right in his comment that certainly in both aspect-seeing and inference the criteria of sameness of mental power are publicly shared matters of logic. If Professor Elliott thinks there are any other ways of distinguishing such powers so that we can see their sameness without examining the public elements and their use, then it would help to know what precisely these are. If there are only these means, then Professor Elliott's assertions about these powers need a defence he seems very loathe to give.

Mr Langford's analogy of physical powers is I think helpful here though it has its limitations. There are many different physical achievements which are accomplished by the exercise of different skills. They all involve a number of muscular powers of one sort or another that are in a clear sense 'given'. In the mental case, I am most interested in the structure of the achievements and the skills and abilities they necessitate. Professor Elliott seems to be interested in the equivalent of the structure of muscular powers that lie behind the exercise of such skills. In physical matters we do however have ways of distinguishing muscular powers by direct examination, whereas in the case of the mind we can only understand the structure of skills or powers from an examination of performances and achievements. I am not wanting to deny the possible existence of general powers of the kind Professor Elliott instances, indeed I think there are likely to be such, but I do consider that we need logical or empirical arguments for them, which to my mind are available only from the investigation of the logical objects and their use in understanding. Otherwise I think we can be only too readily deceived by the use of merely general terms and the force of analogies. At the same time, however, for all that Professor

Elliott says, I see good reasons of a logical and empirical kind to think that in such areas as say those of artistic and philosophical appreciation different mental abilities are involved.

Whilst agreeing with Professor Elliott that there may indeed be certain general powers of the mind, I am not at all committing myself to the view that any structure they have is a natural given. It is this assertion that is to my mind the most disputable part of his account. How does he know that their structure, if it is to be identified through attention to the public objects of understanding, is natural and not in any way determined by the public objects themselves? This is the old nature-nurture issue again. Only if there is some other means of access to these powers of the mind do I think we can have a categorical answer to this question. But why does Professor Elliott want to argue the natural case? Mr Langford's analogy can I think be used to bring out well that there is no need for this where educational interests are concerned and to emphasise certain features of mind that Professor Elliott seems unwilling to recognise. Mental powers may in one sense be the source of all understanding, contribute to the character of understanding, and also contribute to the character of the public standards which it necessitates. So do muscular powers relate to physical skills and achievements. But these are not the only factors that are relevant in each case and it is therefore a mistake to suggest that they alone determine the character of the achievements. Physical skills are determined partly by the circumstances in which the muscular powers are exercised. So too do mental abilities depend on the circumstances in which they are exercised. Understanding and the intellectual abilities through which it is attained are surely constructs that have a character in part developed by the natural and social context. Physical skills are acquired only by appropriate exercises in the appropriate context in which the pattern of desired muscular co-ordination can be learnt. Is there not abundant evidence that in a very similar way a pattern of mental ability has to be acquired by appropriate exercise of mental powers in an appropriate context? Of course the skills can be extended progressively via successive generations, but only via the appropriate prior training that is necessary for the presup-posed skills. If this is so, then surely the mental abilities we are interested in in education are those structured to achieve understanding, not any 'given' mental powers. The develop-ment of the latter in their natural terms seems to me as irrelevant in education as the development of natural muscular powers is in the development of physical skills. Develop the skills and the development of the muscular powers, in an appropriate form, will thereby follow.

But these considerations suggest that even the structure of muscular powers we want is not a natural given, but must be seen as determined in part by the activities to which everything is directed. Just the same I suspect is true of mental powers, for all Professor Elliott's assertions to the contrary. I am certainly inclined to the view that the structure of mind as we can discern it at all levels, is a product of the interaction of whatever energy or desire is given and the context in which it operates. And incidentally I see no reason to think that anything in this situation is immutable or absolute in character, be this the given energy or the physical and social context. Professor Elliott sees the criteria of understanding as ends presupposed by the psyche in its relation to the world. Yet I think Mr Langford absolutely right to protest that the criteria that make understanding understanding, are the external demands of logic, not implicit natural norms. There is of course the pre-existent possibility for the creation of these standards. but that does not mean that the standards are themselves presupposed. They could instead be the progressive outcome of accidental achievements which prove adaptively successful to man in some way. The structured teleological drive Professor Elliott sees in the mind is, I suggest, not at all necessary to an account of the achievement of understanding any more than it is in the evolution of particular biological species. If I had to settle for a picture as to how forms of understanding come about, I think I would go for Professor Toulmin's view of them as evolving like new species rather than Professor Elliott's view of them as like the works of a pre-existent god.

If Professor Elliott is to sustain his case, it seems to me he

must give a fuller account of the criteria for the sameness of
his different powers of the mind, answer Mr Langford's point
that as the notion of effective use of the mental powers
necessitates a reference to public standards, understanding
cannot be characterised in terms of wholly psychologically
given notions, argue why these powers are thought to be
naturally given and show why they are an important concern
of education.

Granted his view of the mind, Professor Elliott's view of
its development in the individual is a matter of developing
both the mental powers and their effective use. As Mr
Langford points out, the development of the powers does not
necessarily imply their effective use indeed it can militate
against it in some cases. But I am not clear why Mr Langford
considers this to rule out either the scope or the need for
education, for presumably education could on Professor
Elliott's view be defined as at least in part concerned with
developing the mental muscles, provided this does not inhibit
their effective use. To my mind however it is in terms of
developing the abilities that effectively use the powers,
whatever these may be, that education in the area of
understanding should be characterised. We need to spell out
the achievements we want and the abilities to be acquired
both particular and general in character. As I have no concern
in this for whatever may be naturally given, and see the
structuring involved as available from outside the individual, I
approve very much Mr Langford's desire to talk about
education as a matter of 'learning' rather than 'developing'.
Learning too has its ambiguities of course and in particular it
is sometimes taken to imply too passive a process. It might
too be criticised by some, may-be Professor Elliott, for
implying that education is concerned with individuals coming
to understand what is in fact already understood by others
(including the development of understanding) and is not
concerned directly with individuals attaining any understanding that is totally new. The acquisition of understanding
new to the individual but which already exists, is not at all to
be equated with the discovery of new understanding, though
the processes may overlap, and to equate them is to
mischaracterise what education involves. If the use of the

term learning helps to assert that point, and I think it does, I am certainly with Mr Langford.

II

In his comments on systematic disciplines, and I shall stick to his use of the term discipline throughout, Professor Elliott seems to think he is attacking a thesis of mine which asserts the necessary significance of the disciplines in education or at least in liberal education. This is however not the case. What I have suggested is that man has achieved a number of different forms of knowledge and understanding which are the fundamental concern of education, but I do not hold these forms to be equatable with systematic disciplines as these exist in universities and schools. Some systematic disciplines are indeed developments of particular forms of knowledge and understanding at sophisticated levels, but others are certainly not that, being complex organisations of different types of knowledge composed for varying education, research and practical purposes. The diverse factors that Professor Elliott suggests do indeed lie behind the development of many disciplines and some of these have become on occasion domains marked as much by error and prejudice as by understanding. How far any existing discipline is therefore suitable as an educational instrument is, I agree with Professor Elliott, a matter of judgement in each particular case. Because certain disciplines are in fact expressions at sophisticated levels of particular forms of understanding, as is the case in the sciences, and because these seem above all other cases to be paradigm cases of systematic disciplines, I have occasionally perhaps unwisely used the term discipline for a particular form of knowledge. Nevertheless I have only done so in contexts where I have explicitly sought to dissociate that use of the term from its use for any well established organisation of knowledge in universities and schools. I can only apologise to Professor Elliott in so far as I have failed to make my meaning clear.

The distinctions I have been concerned with are those logical distinctions within our understanding and knowledge which mean that different kinds of judgement are involved. As I have already agreed, whether for example our understanding of the physical world, our understanding of persons and our understanding of art are indeed different in this way is manifestly a matter of serious disagreement amongst philosophers. I would certainly not argue either that there is some universally agreed number of such forms of understanding neither more nor less, or that any distinctions we may make between forms of understanding have any absolute or Platonic 'form' status. All that I have sought to do is to take seriously the differences in kinds of understanding that have been most clearly articulated and widely defended. Such differences as there are do seem to me of major educational importance. But if our understanding of the physical world is distinct in character from say our understanding of persons and also our artistic appreciation, there is surely within it both understanding at the level of everyday concerns, at the level of common understanding in Professor Elliott's terms, and also understanding at the level expressed in the systematic disciplines of the physical sciences. Clearly in some areas, as in this case, there are certain fairly clear differences between understanding at these two levels. The entities of the physical world differ sharply from the theoretical and idealised entities of the sciences. But I am not at all happy with the radical divorce Professor Elliott seeks to establish between these two levels. In the case of some disciplines, for example history and literary criticism, there are few if any theoretical or technical concepts. The boundary between the disciplines and common understanding seems to me to be not one of any formal kind, but rather a socially determined demarcation based on what as a matter of fact is at any given time commonly understood. Even in the sciences, whose features Professor Elliott and Mr Langford seem to think make them necessarily outside common understanding, there is surely a vital logical continuity with that part of common understanding which is concerned with the observable world. Do the sciences not explain events in the physical world that are parts of common understanding? Is this not of their very nature? Precisely what the basis of the distinction between these two levels of understanding is for Professor Elliott or Mr Langford I am not clear, but manifestly for Professor Elliott it is of considerable educational importance. To my mind the differences between the levels is far less important than the fact that the disciplines contain all the sophisticated developments of the forms of understanding we have within common understanding. The different forms of understanding we have seem to me to be discernable at both levels, though, I repeat, the disciplines are not by any means simply neatly allocatable extensions of areas of common understanding. Where a sharp line can be drawn between common understanding and certain disciplines, say by virtue of theoretical constructions, it seems to me a misunderstanding and corruption of the nature of the disciplines to see them as dissociated from common understanding. From this point of view, education in an understanding of the physical world can progress without any necessary dichotomy from elements of common understanding to theoretical constructs that add to that common understanding and correct it. Similarly aesthetic appreciation of the novel can proceed from elementary common judgements to their refinement through a study of literary criticism. The question of the place of the disciplines in education is then to my mind simply a question of their value in the progressive development of understanding in its different forms. Some disciplines will be valuable, but others, because of peculiarities in them of the kinds instanced by Professor Elliott, may be totally unhelpful. Some disciplines may be degenerate and now dissociated from common understanding. Some may have become more concerned with fashion and prejudice than with truth. Disciplines that might superficially seem helpful might in fact be irrelevant and certainly some aspects of our understanding of persons will not be increased by the study of the existing disciplines of psychology and sociology. Even when they could be valuable, disciplines may be so aridly studied that no development of understanding takes place, pupils' fertility of mind and creativity being inhibited into the bargain. On all this Professor Elliott and I agree.

We do however disagree about certain features of common understanding which result in his regarding the disciplines as educationally suspect even when carefully and critically used. In particular, he sees common understanding of nature, man and God as producing a sense of being within a whole, a primitive synopsis or sense or unity which he regards as of great value. To my mind this is nothing but a romantic vision that bears little relation to most people's common understanding, understanding which seems to me to be rather a body of beliefs, true and false, that are loosely and patchily related, in part because of their diverse characters. I see nothing particularly cohesive about common understanding and much in it that is of little value. Of course the immediacy of the everyday world and its demands is there and academic concerns in the disciplines lack this immediacy. One can pursue understanding that is only remotely related to what is immediate, and doing so can get in the way of immediate things of importance. Being not only remote but narrow in significance too much involvement in the disciplines may limit a person's involvement with the common concerns of men. If this is undesirable, and I think it can be, general education for all in matters of common understanding may be very important. I think it is, and there is something very odd about an education that leaves people totally lacking in say a common understanding of men whilst teaching them a great deal of mathematical physics. But the development of understanding in any area must if it is to reach any depth progress into the disciplines, for there is nothing else as Professor Elliott agrees. That those disciplines be used so that they retain their connections with common understanding is precisely what we want in general or liberal education and I see no reason why with suitable teaching it should not be achieved. But I cannot see the disciplines as breaking any valuable unity to common understanding. Nor do I see general education which progresses into the disciplines as producing an involvement from which a person must learn to recall himself to the relatively naive attitudes of common understanding, to regain his capacity for the primitive synopsis. Rightly used, it seems to me the disciplines can contribute to a continuous development and sophistication of understanding that thereby moves out of what can be loosely identified as common understanding. If thereby unsatisfactory elements of common understanding and false synopses within it become despised, so much the better. One feature of Professor Elliott's common understanding I must confess I do not understand, but I suspect it has something to do with his interest in the primitive synopsis. Common understanding he does, on the odd occasion, refer to as natural understanding. Is it to be seen as in some sense a natural product of the natural mental powers whereas the disciplines are seen as removing objects from the scope of natural understanding, making access to them difficult and esoteric? I simply raise the matter for clarification.

To Professor Elliott one of the major roles of the disciplines in education is that of developing the mental powers as distinct from developing the understanding itself in breadth and depth. This introduces the idea that breadth of education can be seen in terms of the range of powers developed. Professor Elliott does not give us the comprehensive account of the powers that this approach would necessitate and such an undertaking would be formidable. From what I have said earlier however it will be appreciated that I consider this approach mistaken. If it is breadth of understanding that is the object of the whole enterprise then it is the full range of types of undertanding that matters and that is the basis on which disciplines should be chosen. Reference to any underlying powers there may be is then not relevant. And this brings me back to the need for us to know whether our understanding as a whole is or is not logically differentiated into several different forms. Maybe my own approach to distinguishing such forms by reference to the truth criteria for judgements is altogether too simplistic. Whether or not areas of understanding can be significantly distinguished by truth criteria is however not a simple issue, and the radical controversy as to whether there are truth criteria in such areas as morals or religion only complicates things, though Professor Elliott is mistaken in thinking I do not regard truth as necessarily an important concern in all areas of understanding. Nevertheless I remain of the opinion that an approach along these lines is not impossible, and I believe a clear grasp of the types of knowledge and understanding man has developed to be far more significant for education than a clear grasp of the structure of any mental powers that might lie behind these.

III

And now to my very brief final section. In the last part of his paper Professor Elliott comments on the question of justifying education in general, saying rather surprisingly, that this is a comparatively easy matter. The heart of the justification he gives seems to be that, in so far as education is the development of understanding, this is justified because the pursuit of understanding is, amongst other things, constitutive of the life of the mind which is an essential aspect of the life of a human being; and the life more abundant, rich and unlimited is to be preferred. To this statement he adds I think only certain appeals to kindness, children's birthright and their needs, all of which notions presuppose some other form of justification. Like Mr Langford, I am attracted by this kind of justification. But I am not convinved the search for justification can simply rest here. Does Professor Elliott have any reply to the question as to why the life more abundant is to be valued so much that it can over-ride young-people's wants? And is there nothing in a form of argument that if it is the pursuit of understanding one is seeking to justify, that justification can itself only come from understanding? In so far as his argument is, in the end, that one ought to develop what is an essential aspect of being human, then all Mr Langford's questions and difficulties have to be faced. What account of being human is being used? Are we being given simply a definition and an assertion of value? What of other necessary features of being human, ought these to be developed too? Perhaps Professor Elliott could comment on these well known criticisms of the kind of view he seems to hold. Mr Langford makes a most interesting suggestion that maybe this whole approach to justification runs into difficulties as it is essentially instrumental. Might we not instead consider education simply as one among many aspects of social life? Just what he has in mind I am not sure, for even as just one aspect of social life education would still need justifying. What is more, I suspect this move may tempt us to redefine education so that we in fact then search for a justification for some quite different activity. If indeed a new approach to the justification of education along these lines can be suggested, I hope Mr Langford will develop the point, for as against Professor Elliott any satisfactory justification seems to me very difficult indeed to formulate. We may all be for education because we are all for human being, but neither what that is, nor why exactly we value it, seems to me clear.

Postscript

R. K. ELLIOTT

I cannot hope to answer all the questions asked or comment upon all the points made by Professor Hirst and Mr Langford, but will confine my remarks to a few major issues in the hope of advancing the discussion further.

(1) In the second section of his Comments Hirst maintains, as he did in 'Liberal Education and the Nature of Knowledge', that his Forms of Knowledge are not to be identified with disciplines actually practised in universities and schools, yet he says that certain disciplines, including the sciences and literary criticism, are expressions or developments at sophisticated levels of particular Forms of Knowledge. I take his view to be that these disciplines, practised in universities and elsewhere, are expressions and developments of Forms of Knowledge if and only if they are being 'carefully and critically used' (p. 94). I did not deny that Hirst regards truth as necessarily an important concern in all areas of understanding; my objections were rather that in his view what truth and understanding are is determined separately by each of the radically different Forms, and that he assumes that the standards of truth and understanding of the sophisticated disciplines are necessarily superior to the standards of truth and understanding operative at less sophisticated levels. By distributing understanding and truth among entirely separate domains, and by making the public criteria of truth and understanding in each separate domain the ultimate basis of his accounts of understanding and mind, he leaves himself without any standpoint outside the disciplines from which he could criticise what they are doing or the directions they are taking. He can criticise them for not

being careful and critical in the application of their standards, according to conceptions of care and critical concern which are recognised by them, but he cannot on any account criticise the standards themselves. He cannot, for example, criticise a discipline because its standards of understanding are inferior to those of another discipline belonging to another Form of Knowledge. Whatever standards Philosophy may establish for itself, they are the standards of a particular Form of Knowledge, and cannot be used to criticise the standards of other, radically different, Forms of Knowledge. Nor can Hirst have any general conception of understanding by reference to which what counts as understanding in any 'paradigmatic' discipline can be criticised. Hence he cannot conceive how there could possibly be any justifiable objection to explanations provided by the physical sciences on the ground that although they enable us to control events they do not provide understanding of the world. What careful and critical physicists regard as understanding is for Hirst the paradigm of understanding of the world. Hirst starts from an affirmation of the present standards of certain advanced disciplines, (mathematics, physics, literary criticism, contemporary analytical philosophy). Thereafter he cannot legitimately criticise these standards even by reference to the less sophisticated standards from which they have developed, for to do that he would need a conception of what understanding within a particular paradigmatic discipline ought to be, or an independent conception of what understanding in general is. He thinks that the standards of each Form of Knowledge may have come into being accidentally, and is content if that is so. In his opinion the standards of the disciplines are what they happen to be, and the disciplines are in the process of evolving as they accidentally will. We, and the people we educate, must go along with the disciplines wherever they are taking us, and cannot conceivably have any cause for complaint so long as the disciplines are being carefully and critically used. Hirst's acknowledgement, in his comments, that the disciplines can go astray, is either strictly limited in scope or inconsistent with the basis of his doctrine.

It is essential, if education is to be based upon the Forms of Knowledge, that these Forms should be adequately characterised. Otherwise teachers will not know whether they are developing their pupils' minds or not. But Hirst has done little more than name the Forms, and that not altogether felicitously since his nomenclature makes it seem as if there is no such thing as empirical knowledge of persons. He does say that the Forms are to be distinguished by reference to the different ways in which judgements are validated, but not what the differences are. Consequently it is difficult to assess whether every true judgement can reasonably be classified as belonging to one or other of the seven or more Forms. It may be possible, on a 'family resemblance' basis, and with a good deal of pushing and shoving, to classify any judgement as either 'scientific', 'aesthetic', or 'moral', etc., but this would not in the least help to validate Hirst's doctrine, which is that every correct judgement belongs to one and only one of so many Forms each sharply distinguished according to precise logical criteria. At present nobody knows whether Hirst's contention that all correct judgements belong to one or other of the Forms is plausible or not, because nobody knows what the names of his Forms refer to. His readers are almost entirely justified if they try to understand the Forms by starting from the advanced disciplines which Hirst takes as paradigms and if they assume that these paradigmatic disciplines are the same as the disciplines which have the same names and are actually practised in universities and elsewhere. In Hirst's earlier writings it looked as if he was attempting to justify both education and breadth of education by identifying education with initiation into the Forms of Knowledge, and by representing mastery of the several Forms of Knowledge as necessary for the development of mind. In his comments, however, he says that no justification of education or breadth of education has yet been discovered. He refers us to philosophical controversy about whether there are Forms of Knowledge or not, and about what the Forms are if they exist, and expresses his faith in their existence and their educational relevance. This leaves the favoured disciplines somewhat exposed, and is less than an adequate basis for Hirst's powerful recommendations concerning mathematics in the secondary school.

I do not deny that there are forms of knowledge — a very

small number of them if one wishes to collect and unify, a very large number if one wishes to go on distinguishing and separating. My objections are not against the notion of forms of knowledge but against the manner in which Hirst has interpreted it, especially his view of the relation of forms of knowledge to mind and the educational conclusions he has derived from it.

(2) Hirst's account of education demands of the persons educated complete conformity to systems which, if they consider his account thoughtfully, they must regard as alien to them. Such a view of education makes 'opting out' seem imperative if a sense of human dignity is to be preserved. This is true also of Langford's account of education as the transmission of society's values. It was in reaction against this dispiriting aspect of contemporary philosophy of education that I tried in my paper to reassert the significance of the mental powers as constitutive of human being and originative of forms of knowledge. I did not maintain that the mental powers alone determined the character of the forms of knowledge, but that they did so in an intersubjective context and in relation to objects towards which they were directed. My concern was for a better understanding of how the mental powers are related to standards and conventions, and of the appropriateness and inappropriateness of kinds of such relation.

Hirst and Langford both argue, perhaps correctly, that no sense can be made of the notion of mental powers without reference to public standards. Langford writes 'It is surely unnecessary to argue that seeing involves a reference to public or as I would prefer to call them, social or inter-personal standards', and goes on to assert that people only see the same thing if they 'share the same criteria of application for the same concepts.' But both 'involve a reference to' and 'share' are ambiguous. 'Seeing involves a reference to public standards' might be taken to mean that we could not talk of anyone's seeing anything unless we had interpersonal criteria of seeing; or it might be interpreted, as Langford interprets it, as meaning that whoever sees anything applies standards which he has been taught. On the first interpretation the remark is true, but not inconsistent with anything I said in my paper. On the second interpretation it is false, since cats and infants see (and hear and make inductive inferences) without making any reference to any standards they have been taught. If cats and infants can see only if they 'share' public or social standards, then it must be possible for a being to share our public or social standards without its having been initiated into any public form of knowledge and without its belonging to any social group. But two beings can be said to share something (e.g. a taste, desire, attitude, house, the sunlight, etc.) simply because they both have use, or enjoy it, and they do not have to be in any social relation with each other in order to share in this sense. Langford may have been misled by this ambiguity. There is a sense in which animals and infants share certain of our concepts yet, clearly, they do not share them with us in the sense that they have received them from us and participate in our discourse.

All that Langford can properly claim is, first, that talking about seeing involves a reference to public standards; and, secondly, that if animals and infants see things *exactly* as we do they must have *exactly* the same concepts as we have, and therefore must have been taught our conventions. But though they do not have exactly the same concepts as we have, nobody who is not a philosopher, and not every philosopher, denies that animals and infants see; or that they see some of the same things that we do, under aspects which we find perfectly intelligible and under which we see some of the things ourselves. Cats see meat as food, mice and birds as objects of prey, ping-pong balls and pipe-cleaners as objects for play, items of furniture as obstacles to be avoided or surmounted in getting from place to place.

Langford points out that in our society we do not allow that people are seeing when they are hallucinating, and there are, of course, conventions concerning normal conditions which are relevant in the attribution of colour predicates. Nevertheless, our concept of seeing is very firmly based on what people, infants and animals do naturally, or which comes naturally to them: having visual sensations, for example, directing visual attention, responding to invitations to do so from the visual environment, picking out a figure from a ground, grasping or receiving the figure as a whole, and exploring with other senses what is encountered visually. These operations are not generally dependent on social tradition and do not have to be taught, but as soon as they occur with a sufficient degreee of co-ordination relative to something in the environment, seeing is taking place. Then whoever or whatever is seeing can be said to be satisfying our public standards for seeing, but it is equally and no less importantly true to say that he (or it) is satisfying *natural* standards or, rather, achieving a natural end. Langford maintains that there can be no effective use of the mental powers which does not involve a reference to public standards, but a cat or an infant is making effective use of its mental powers when it uses them to achieve a natural end, and it can do this without making any reference to public standards. Nor does its making this effective use of its mental powers in the least depend on anyone else's making, or being able to make, reference to public standards.

A child is not in the same way achieving a natural end when he learns to apply colour words in accordance with an idea of normal conditions. Yet this convention enhances his power of discrimination, facilitates communication, preserves clarity of mind, and need not impose any limitation on his sensibility. It is an appropriate convention for beings with natural powers such as he possesses, which during his infancy had a powerful tendency to make sense of his environment and which, so far as the distinction can be drawn, he had a powerful tendency to use to that end. Our present public notion of 'seeing the same thing' came into being through the supplementation of the naturally shared powers by a system of appropriate socially shared conventions, the learning of which also requires the exercise of pre-existing powers. The mind could not have been powerless before it had the conventions, nor, now that it does have them, are its achievements and operations entirely different from what they were before.

Since Hirst defines the Forms of Knowledge by reference to the mode of validation of their 'characteristic expressions' which he describes as 'true propositions' he, like Langford, presupposes that there can be no understanding prior to the acquisition of language, and both philosophers believe that prior to language there can be no definite mental powers. But if these presuppositions were correct language could never have begun, for no being who did not already possess language would have been able to grasp any proposition as a whole, connect one moment of its experience with the next, or make a unity of anything whatever. If prior to the invention of language what-is had been totally indefinite to the sensible mind, it could only have remained so thereafter. Prior to language an environment must already have been formed, and there must already have been a mind having definite powers by which an understanding of that environment had already been achieved, for these are preconditions of language, and so of public standards and public forms of knowledge. The idea that the minds of the originators of our language were far less highly developed than those of present-day cats and three-months-old babies is merely fantastical.

Our concept of understanding, though it makes reference to or incorporates socially shared standards, is not exclusively a concept *of* the application of socially shared standards, but covers understanding which does not depend on language as well as understanding which does. Hirst and Langford are not being asked to extend the concept to cover understanding which does not presuppose language, but not to restrict the concept arbitrarily to the artificially developed mode of understanding which they identify with understanding in general. Understanding which depends on language is not something altogether removed from pre-linguistic understanding, any more than post-linguistic seeing is something quite different from pre-linguistic seeing, but is centrally the same thing, namely the connection of phenomena on the basis of significances presented in them; and while certain extremely important types of understanding would be impossible without language, the only logically necessary connection between understanding and language is that we could not call anything 'understanding' unless we had a language in which to do so.

(3) At the level of a traveller's ordinary practical concern, understanding a region (e.g. Dartmoor) is being able to find

one's way around in it. To achieve an adequate understanding of this type, it is necessary to synthesise experiences of different parts of the area, and of the same parts from different points of view. Features have to be recognised as 'the same' when approached from different directions, but as having different parts of the region lying beyond them. Understanding the region involves being able to make the general synthesis afresh, and correctly, relative to wherever one is. A person who has an adequate understanding of the region is able, in principle, to assess and criticise existing routes across it — as circuitous, arduous, exposed, etc. —, to discover routes which are more satisfactory than existing ones, and to create new routes between places not yet connected by paths. Thus even at this comparatively primitive level, an adequate understanding is characterised as correct, clear, comprehensive, synoptic, creative, critical, appreciative, etc., and even as profound, since the person concerned will be able to judge correctly what is practicable and what is not, in a great variety of situations and conditions, and will seem to know the spirit and temper of the region.

In my paper I maintained that understanding has ends or norms by reference to which the disciplines as forms of enquiry may be criticised, and assumed that these norms could be discovered if we asked what are regarded as virtues of Understanding, or criteria of adequate understanding, in each and every discipline. A preliminary list of these was obtained by considering a sophisticated example of understanding (viz. understanding Wittgenstein's philosophy). Subsequently I suggested that one might criticise a discipline (physical science) on the ground that it was no longer providing understanding at all; or because it hindered the attainment of comprehensive understanding (aesthetic criticism); or because if taken as superseding other less systematic forms of knowledge it would lead to a decline in the sensitivity of our understanding (psychology). These disciplines have indeed been criticised for these reasons, and it is easy to imagine a discipline's being criticised for lacking profundity, clarity, creativeness, critical spirit or synoptic vision.

On this view of the nature of understanding, the disciplines do not determine what understanding is, but exist for the sake of understanding, and we do not have to go wherever they happen to be leading us.

(4) Hirst asks for a fuller account of the criteria for the sameness of the various mental powers. He seems to be concerned chiefly about the attribution of different instances of a power's operation to one and the same power, even though the objects upon which the power is operative are very different. He asks 'What then of Mr Elliott's mental powers?' a frightening question, but the mental powers are no invention of mine and criteria for their sameness and difference are available in ordinary language, which attaches importance to phenomenological considerations. We ordinarily speak of 'seeing' whether it is men we see, or trees, or stones, or triangles. That the concepts applied in seeing have different relations and the relevant perceptual judgements perhaps belong to different forms of knowledge is immaterial. There is no justification for supposing that because the objects on which a power is operative are different, or even very different, the power must be a different one in each case. Certainly, there are 'logical' criteria by which mental powers are discriminated, but by presupposing that these criteria are subordinate to those by which forms of knowledge are discriminated, Hirst begs the question of the relation of mind to forms of knowledge.

To the extent that mental powers are specified by reference to particular conventions, or to conventions in general, this dependence need not obscure the centrality of the natural element in them, any more than the conventions connected with seeing need obscure its impressively natural character. Nature does not disappear at the touch of a public standard. If reflection on the existence and importance of forms of knowledge causes us to misunderstand the nature of the logical connections between forms and powers, and to conceive and discriminate the powers in the manner Hirst does, this can only destroy our understanding of the independent reality of the mind, of the vitality it expresses through the forms, of the ends it transmits to them, and of the demands it legitimately makes upon them.

The distinctions we ordinarily make between mental powers may not be sufficient for all our purposes as philosophers of education, but we can, if necessary, draw on a very considerable philosophical and psychological literature in which many powers have been distinguished and their various combinations for the purpose of understanding described.

(5) Langford attributes my use of the expression 'mental powers' to a liking for drama, and prefers to talk instead of 'things which people can do'. Here again, phenomenological considerations, and with them our ordinary use of words, are ignored. Our mental life is dependent on passivities and spontaneities whose operations are not experienced as 'things that we do', but are recognised as things on which the 'things that we do' intimately and utterly depend. I cannot think effectively if ideas do not 'come to me', if memory 'fails me', if analogical connections do not 'occur to me', and perhaps if illuminating shifts of perspective do not 'happen to me'. Successful thinking depends on our ability to 'manage' the mental powers, and sometimes in our willingness to let them manage us. There are some things which normally we can 'do' fairly easily, at will, in order that other more important things may have a better chance of 'happening'. This is a matter of the first importance for education, and which Langford obscures by making 'doing' cover so wide a variety of 'things'. In talking of 'mental powers' I tried to avoid this too dramatic notion of the mind as sheer agency.

Talk about mental powers is neither dramatic nor romantic but derives from reflection on the life of the mind as a human being actually experiences it. One would have thought that a sensitive understanding of the phenomenology of enquiry would be of value to a teacher who wants to help a child to think effectively, and that philosophers of education would recognise this. Instead, on the basis of erroneous views of the mind and understanding, they lay overwhelming emphasis on public standards and rules, objective criteria, public structures of knowledge, and skills defined strictly and described exhaustively in terms of these. The life of the mind, as the individual experiences it, is either not thought worthy of consideration at all, or is not given the kind of consideration which lets it appear as it is.

(6) By 'the powers of Understanding' I mean powers used or operative in accomplishing understanding to whatever degree of scope, depth, clarity, etc. By 'the power of Understanding' I mean (i) the mental powers as capable of entering into combinations by which understanding is accomplishable to whatever degree; and (ii) the degree of understanding accomplishable. By 'development of the mental powers' I mean their improvement and strengthening by use in the pursuit of understanding, including increase of their capacity for entering into combination to that end. By 'development of the power of Understanding' I mean increase in the degree of understanding accomplishable by the power of Understanding (i). Development of the mental powers is development of the power of Understanding, but development of the power of Understanding may come about also through the invention and learning of conventions.

The question of the development of the power of Understanding is complicated by the fact that a particular discipline may increase the power of achieving depth for example, at the expense of scope or some other end or virtue of Understanding, and by the fact that a discipline may increase the power of understanding relative to matters other than those we want it to illuminate for us, while neglecting the things which we believe to be its proper concern. Nevertheless, since conventions and procedures which constitute forms of knowledge require constant correction by reference to the ends of Understanding, and since if conventions come into being accidentally they await ratification by Understanding and when so ratified lose their accidental character and become the work of the mind, I take development of the power of Understanding, rather than the mere acquisition and mastery of existing socially determined conventions and procedures, to be development of Understanding (i.e. of the cognitive mind) in the *full* sense of the term. And since conventions and procedures are in large measure created by the mental powers and the mental powers are necessary for the effective use of these conventions and procedures, I take development of the mental powers, rather than the mere acquisition of socially determined conventions and procedures, to be development of mind in the most *fundamental* sense.

Langford assumes that development can only be of the type exemplified in natural teleologies at the pre-conscious level, such as the development from acorn into oak, and believes that since this development is inevitable, talk about development in educational contexts makes talk about education pointless. But development of the power of Understanding is possible through appropriate use of the mental powers and through the invention and acquisition of conventions and practices which are truly instrumental to the ends of Understanding. Such development is by no means inevitable, yet it is justly called 'development', since what already existed — namely, the power of Understanding — increases and yet remains recognisably the same thing. Insisting on calling this development 'learning' effectively removes any suggestion of creativity, or of the criticism of any form of knowledge as such whether as a whole or in part. Though Langford would scarcely have intended this consequence, it is welcomed by Hirst. It is possible for an education to confine individual creativity and criticism to the repetition of what has already been achieved, and the desire to do so is comprehensible if education is conceived as the imposition of fixed or accidentally evolving forms or structures upon the minds of each new generation. It is not so readily comprehensible if education is conceived as handing over a continuing intellectual enterprise whose vitality and achievements have deeply depended on individual creativity and criticism and which will continue to do so in the future.

PART THREE:
QUALITY AND EQUALITY IN EDUCATION

7 Quality and Equality in Education

DAVID E. COOPER

(1) I have rather little to say about either quality or equality, and rather more about the relation between the two. It is not obvious what a philosopher has to say about this since, on a prevalent view, the relation is purely empirical. Whether education can embody both high standards and equality — once it is settled what these are — seems a matter for sociologists and planners. Writing of what he calls 'democracy' and 'humanism', which come close to the ideals of equality and quality, Raymond Aron says:

> (they) are not necessarily incompatible, nor are they automatically in accord ... humanism and democracy are ... only temporarily, not finally, contradictory.[1]

It is clear, though, that when equality and quality are understood in *certain* ways, the relation is no longer empirical, and the possibility or otherwise of reconciling demands for them becomes *a priori*. A utilitarian might assess quality in terms of education's 'social expediency'. Suppose this is combined with Mill's claim that

> all persons are deemed to have a right to equality of treatment except when some recognized social expediency requires the reverse.[2]

---

[1] 'Sociological comments on concepts of quality and quantity in education', in *Qualitative Aspects of Educational Planning*, ed. C. E. Beeby (Unesco, 1969) p. 136.
[2] Quoted in *Society, Law, and Morality*, ed. F. Olafson (Prentice—Hall, 1961) p. 398.

It follows that a system in which there is unjustified inequality cannot be one of the highest quality. For unjustified inequality is not socially expedient, and hence damaging to quality as defined. For a utilitarian of this type, the highest quality system cannot, logically, be one in which there is unjustified inequality. I suspect, too, that definitions of equality in terms of treating people only according to 'relevant' criteria, when coupled with definitions of 'relevance' in terms of what contributes to high quality, will also result in the conclusion that a high quality system must, logically, be one of equality. For if differential treatment according to certain criteria results in high quality, then the criteria are 'relevant' ones; if so, no inequality is involved in the differential treatment which accords with them.

So, one of the things I shall argue is that equality and quality are logically related; that, in fact, the relation is one of *in*compatibility.[3] I shall also want to spell out the exact nature of the dispute between egalitarians and 'qualitarians'; for this is not always appreciated. Then I shall argue — or at any rate *urge* — that the dispute be settled in favour of the qualitarian. If something has to give — and something does — let it be the demand for equality.

(2) First, though, I must say a few things about quality and equality taken separately.

(A) I limit severely but reasonably, I hope, what falls under the heading of 'quality'. Writers on this topic typically urge two distinctions. First, we must distinguish *extrinsic* from *intrinsic* criteria. Peters, for example, says that a course in Egyptology can be of high intrinsic quality, but of low quality when judged by a criterion like economic benefit.[4] Second, they say, we must distinguish an education's quality judged in terms of its *products* (i.e. the students emerging from it) from its quality judged in terms of its *processes*.

I shall only be concerned with intrinsic criteria, and with quality judged in terms of processes. These restrictions are

---

[3] More precisely, they are related as *contraries* in the logicians's sense; since while a system may embody neither quality nor equality, it cannot, so I shall argue, satisfy demands for both.
[4] 'The meaning of quality in education', in *Qualitative Aspects of Educational Planning*, op. cit., p. 160.

not arbitrary, since I doubt that there are extrinsic criteria for quality, and that quality is ever judged in terms of products. Peters, it seems to me, is wrong in supposing a critic could condemn the *quality* of a course in Egyptology on economic grounds. He could condemn its *value* on such grounds, since things have extrinsic value in a way that they do not have extrinsic quality. The economist should not think himself capable of judging the quality of the course, in any sense of 'quality'.

Nor is the quality of an education ever measured solely by reference to its products. It is not necessary that high-grade products emerge from a high quality education. A remedial school may be a very good one despite the fact that its products are well below the population's average. Nor is it sufficient for high quality that the students leaving the school are well-educated. They might have been well-educated before they went there. In other words, I doubt that the claim 'This is a high quality school' would ever be made purely on the basis of the quality of its products. (This is not to deny, of course, that the processes are themselves assessed, ultimately, by reference to the products they are likely to create).

This talk of 'processes' is too vague for our purposes. Let me introduce the expression 'educational transformation'. This refers to the change in a person's level of educatedness resulting from a certain education. One person may be more educationally transformed by a certain education than a second is, even though the second emerges better educated; this will be the case where the second person entered this stage of education at a considerably higher level of educatedness than the first. Now I shall say that one education is higher quality than another if the former, through its processes, produces greater educational transformation than the latter. The more an education of a certain duration increases the level of educatedness, whatever the initial level, the higher quality it is.

What I have said would have to be qualified in various ways for it to be realistic. For example, ages of students would have to be taken into account. A mediocre primary school probably brings about a greater increase in learning than even the best university, since young children have much more to learn than their teenage brothers; but we would not rate the primary school, therefore, as the better institution. Further, naturally, one would not expect each student receiving a particular education to be transformed at the same rate; so some averaging out, possibly of a very complicated sort, would be required before we could judge the quality of the education. But, granted the need for qualifications of this sort, I hope the idea is clear enough.

Criteria for what it is to be educated, I take it, provide us with the terms in which to judge the quality of education. The more the education increases educatedness, identified by these criteria, the better it is. I am not going to discuss what these criteria might be. First, I see no reason to think I could improve upon those suggested by others — such as Peters' 'wholeness', 'knowledge', and 'commitment' criteria, or Mary Warnock's 'imaginativeness'.[5] Second, it does not matter much as far as analysing the relation between quality and equality. If you prefer a list of criteria for educatedness markedly different from Peters' or Warnock's — if, in other words, you would measure rates of educational transformation differently — this will not affect the rest of what I have to say.

(B) Turning to equality, I again defend, rather breezily, a limitation put on the scope of my concern. I shall only be concerned with those inequalities which, in a good sense, are genuine educational ones, and not with various *social* inequalities which happen to manifest themselves in educational systems, as they also do in wage systems, housing allocation, and elsewhere. There would be genuine educational inequality in a grading method which failed people who should pass and passed people who should fail. It is not any similar educational inequality that most people who do well in a certain exam are from the middle-class. In the first case, there are relevant educational grounds for objecting to the grading. In the second, for all that has been said, there is no reason to think the exam is objectionable on any educational grounds. Educators, of course, can complain about those

[5] R. S. Peters, op. cit. pp. 152–6:; M. Warnock, 'Quality in education', to be published in *Philosophy of Education*, ed. R. S. Peters (O.U.P.).

social inequalities which result, *inter alia*, in certain people doing better at exams than others; but they do so not *as* educators, nor on educational grounds. Analogously, a person who complains that most musicians in symphony orchestras are from the middle-class is not, *per se*, objecting on any musical grounds to the staffing of orchestras.

The sort of point I am making often meets with the following ill-tempered reply:

> You're saying that we have educational equality when people are not excluded *on the grounds that* they are poor (black, female, etc.). But that is sham equality. It is like saying there is equality before the law when each man has the right to protection, even though only the rich can afford it.

Well, I am certainly not saying that equality is achieved provided, only, that the criteria for educational treatment do not formally exclude the poor, the blacks, or whoever; and the reply is based on confusion. The case of sham equality before the law is quite different from the one where a small proportion of the poor pass an exam, and as a result go to a certain school. In the legal case, each person has met with certain criteria for receiving certain treatment — each, that is, has the right to this treatment — but some are unable to exercise this right, to receive the treatment they are entitled to, through lack of money. The educational analogue to this situation is not a situation where the poor *fail* exams, but where they *pass* the exams and are then unable, for financial reasons, to take advantage of their success. (They cannot afford the uniform for, or the travel to, the school whose entrance exam they have passed). Were this the situation, it would be one of genuine educational inequality, of 'sham' equality; for persons are entitled on educational grounds to receive certain treatment, and it will be a genuine educational complaint that they cannot receive it.[6] So I am not saying we

---

[6] Bernard Williams, it seems to me, is guilty of confusing the legal case, with its sham equality, with a case like mine in which the poor tend to fail an exam. His case is one where the poor tend to fail the tests for becoming warriors in some country. But a relevant analogue to the legal case would be the situation where the poor *pass* the tests, but cannot afford their weapons or uniforms. See 'The idea of equality', in *Philosophy, Politics, and Society,* ed. P. Laslett and W. G. Runciman. (Blackwell's, 1964) 2nd series. p. 126.

have equality when, solely, the formal provisions for selection are impeccable; in addition, steps must be taken to ensure that those who are selected are able to take advantage of their selection. But once we move to complaining about the exams purely on the grounds that the poor do badly at them, we are moving to a quite different kind of problem — one of general social inequality. That poor people do badly on the exam is not, *per se*, any more of an educational criticism than the fact that people with short fingers do badly on it.

Of course, what might be true is that exams on which the poor do badly are *also* criticisable on educational grounds. If the exam tests for *achievement* by age 11, rather than for *potential*, then not only might it favour middle-class children but, according to some, it will also be testing for what is not educationally relevant. All I insist is that the two kinds of criticism be distinguished. The one has to do with educational fairness, the other has not. I, at any rate, shall only be concerned with genuine educational inequality, not with those social inequalities which may or may not be correlated with it.

My remarks so far might suggest, but wrongly, that I am going to understand equality, as it is fashionable among philosophers to do, in terms of treating people upon relevant grounds only; to understand it, for example, as the principle that likes be treated alike, and unalikes unalike.[7] I have no time to argue why I find this an unfruitful way of interpreting the egalitarian's demands. I shall remark only that if this is all that is understood by the principle of equality then it is difficult to see how we sort out the egalitarians among us from the rest; for I should think that, in this sense, we are *all* egalitarians, since we all think that relevant grounds for treatment should be preferred to irrelevant ones. But just as the fact that we are *not* all socialists now shows something wrong with George V's understanding of socialism, so the fact that we are *not* all egalitarians now shows there is something wrong with understanding equality solely in terms of relevant grounds.

[7] For such an account, see for example R. S. Peters, *Ethics and Education* (Allen & Unwin, 1966) p. 118 ff.

I am going to mean something more substantial by the principle of equality; something fairly meaty, with definite empirical implications. I defend my formulation of the principle on the following grounds: it captures the essence of what at least some notable egalitarians have urged; it is not patently mad, and has, indeed, been defended in terms of justice and fairness — by Rawls, for example;[8] and, finally, interesting questions can be asked about the relation between this principle and quality. If you don't like calling this principle 'the principle of equality', if you prefer, say, the 'relevant grounds' analysis, so be it. But I should hope you would agree — and this is the main thing — that the principle is an important one, dear to the hearts of some, and whose connection with quality in education bears examination.

The principle is this: only those inequalities are permissible from which everyone, in particular the worst off, benefits more than he would in their absence. For example, only those income differentials are justified which result in even the poorest doing better than they would without such differentials. Since we are concerned with educational equality, and with intrinsic educational benefits, the formula would read: only those inequalities in an educational system are justified which result in even the worst off getting a better education than they would otherwise. Put in terms of educational transformation: only those inequalities in rates of educational transformation are justified which result in even the least transformed being more transformed than in the absence of the inequalities. The defense of the principle is meant to be clear: only in conditions governed by it would no one be gaining at the expense of others, and only these conditions are just or fair.

(3) Now to the relation between quality and egalitarianism. Let us consider a highly simplified situation. A country contains just two schools, North and South. The relevant things to know about this educational system, the North-South (N-S) system, are the following:

(i)   The Northerners receive a better education than the Southerners; they are more transformed — and they also end up better educated.

[8] J. Rawls, *A Theory of Justice* (O.U.P., 1973) Ch. 2.

(ii)   Had any Southerner gone to North school, he would
       have been better educated, though he would not be as
       transformed as the actual Northerners are. Similarly,
       any Northerner, had he gone to South, would have done
       worse than he actually did, though not as badly as the
       actual Southerners do. In other words, the selection
       criteria are rational; those who can benefit most by
       going to North actually go there.
(iii) Educational resources cannot be increased; they can
       only be redistributed as between North and South
       schools.

Clearly there is inequality in the N–S system. Is it
unjustified inequality, and if so, can the egalitarian's demands
be compatible with qualitarian demands? Well, let's look at
the possible alternatives to the N–S system.

Obviously the inequality would be removed if either of the
following were done: raise the standard of South to that of
North, or lower that of North to that of South. To do the
first would clearly be to raise the quality of the system; to do
the second would be to lower it. Since either would achieve
equality, it seems to follow that equality might or might not
co-exist with quality. It seems to follow, that is, that there is
no *a priori* impossibility in satisfying the egalitarian and the
qualitarian.

I want to insist, though, that egalitarian demands, *when
appropriate*, cannot be satisfied together with demands for
quality. It seems to me that, were the only alternatives to the
N–S system those described, egalitarian demands in their
favour could not be appropriate. Hence the question as to
whether such demands, when appropriate, are compatible
with qualitarian demands, cannot arise. I say this for two
reasons. First, it is only appropriate to employ the principle
of equality in criticism if those who are doing less well are
doing so *because* others are doing better. If I am healthier
than you because I breathe in lots of fresh air, then my
health does not flourish at the expense of yours; and it would
be absurd to object to your sickliness on grounds of equality,
as opposed to health. Now if it was possible simply to raise
the quality of South school without affecting North, then it

will not have been the case that Northerners were benefiting at the expense of the Southerners. So a condition for appealing against the N—S system on grounds of equality would be missing.

Waiving this point, there is a second reason why egalitarian demands could not be appropriate in favour of the envisaged alternatives. A reason is only appropriate if it is neither morally grotesque, nor frivolous, to cite it. If someone were to cite equality as a reason for simply lowering the quality of North, with no improvement in South, this would indeed be grotesque. An egalitarian is someone who employs the principle of equality in certain ways; and he could not be taken seriously if he used it to justify the totally unjustifiable step of gratuitously, or out of pique, reducing the quality of some down to the level of others. If, to take the other alternative, someone were to cite the principle as the reason for raising the level of South up to that of North, this would be frivolous. The *least* complaint to level at a school which does not educate its students as well as it could — which would have been the case with South if it could be improved with no effect upon North — is that the students do not do as well *as others*. If a life-saver on Bondi beach saved a woman from drowning in the morning, but left another to be eaten by a shark in the afternoon because he didn't want to get his ice-cream wet, then the complaint that he had treated the two women unequally could only be a piece of black humour.

So, were the only alternatives to the N—S system those mentioned, then egalitarian demands for them could not be appropriate. The *likely* alternative, of course, would be quite different: that of achieving equality by raising the quality of South through lowering that of North. For if the Northerners have been benefiting at the expense of the Southerners, then it is only by shifting resources from the one to the other that equality could be attained. Suppose, in fact, equality is attained through replacing North and South schools by two new ones, East and West. The new schools provide the same quality education as each other, which is better than the old South's but worse than the old North's. I am going to assume that no meaningful measure of an *overall* rise or fall in the system's quality is applicable. It might be, of course, that parity was achieved by drastically reducing the quality of the better education to effect a marginal improvement in the poorer, in which case one could talk of an overall fall in quality. But were this the case, egalitarian considerations would, as before, be inappropriate. I want to take circumstances in which these considerations are at least appropriate.

The egalitarian, faced by the choice between the N–S and E–W systems, must opt for the latter; since the principle of equality cannot justify the inequalities of the N–S system. Not everyone benefited from them; on the contrary, the Southerners would do better in the E–W system.

The qualitarian, on the other hand, I am going to provisionally define as the person who would opt for the N–S system. For, he insists, the move to E–W would involve a sacrifice in quality – that found at North school – which ought not to be made.

It follows immediately, and trivially, that egalitarian and qualitarian demands cannot both be satisfied; for one prefers the very system the other rejects. The point is this: it is only under certain conditions, and faced with certain alternatives, that both equalitarian and egalitarian demands are appropriate. Where these conditions hold, the respective demands can only be understood as contrasting with one another. Cases where the two seem compatible are illusory; they are cases, like those described, where the nature of the alternatives makes egalitarian demands inappropriate. These demands become appropriate where quality for some flourishes at the expense of lower quality for others; and this situation, which is necessarily intolerable to the egalitarian, is precisely what is tolerable to his opponent. In short, egalitarian demands are appropriate only where they conflict with quality.[9]

(4) We cannot, however, rest content with the present characterisation of the opponents' positions. For there is a problem with my qualitarian's position which his opponent

[9] The distinction between a principle and the demands based upon it is of general importance. A legal system may be compatible with both the principle of utility and the principles of justice. But I doubt that utilitarian *demands* are ever compatible with those of justice; since either they are not appropriate, or they are put forward in opposition to the demands of justice.

will be quick to seize upon. What, he will ask, can the qualitarian mean by saying that the N—S system is preferable to the E—W on grounds of *quality*? He cannot mean that the overall quality of the system is higher since, *ex hypothesi*, no measurement of such an overall change is applicable. Perhaps he means, simply, that the quality of the Northerners' education would fall in the E—W system. But, if that is all that is meant, the egalitarian can quickly show that a shift from E—W to N—S would *also* mark a fall in quality; for then the Southerners would do worse than they might. So the qualitarian's complaint about the change from N—S to E—W can be matched by a complaint about the reverse change — since both changes mean that the quality of some people's education falls. If so, what right does the qualitarian have to his title? It is not, so the charge goes, that he is, and his opponent is not, concerned with quality. Rather he concerns himself with quality for some, the Northerners, while his opponent concerns himself with quality for others, the Southerners.

The challenge to the qualitarian is fairly clear. He must provide a sense of 'rise in quality' in which only the change from E—W to N—S would mark a rise in quality; a sense in which the reverse change, despite the improvement in the Southerners' lot, does not. I think he can provide such a sense, and to see what this is is to begin to see the essence of his position.

If a Harrods' representative says 'The quality of our sausages has risen', he might mean one or both of two quite different things. He might mean that more of the sausages are now of the quality that the better ones have always been. Or he might mean that the better ones are now higher quality than any had been before. We might distinguish between *distributional* and *ontological* changes in quality. The distribution changes when some things come to have a quality *they* did not have before. Qualities change ontologically when things come to have qualities which no things had before; if, that is, one creates *new* qualities. An ontological change entails a distributional change, but not vice-versa. If 4th division football clubs are brought up to the standard of 3rd division ones, there has been a distributional rise in quality only; whereas if 1st division clubs start playing better than ever before, there has been an ontological rise as well.

A change from the N—S system to the E—W one will involve a distributional rise in quality; for the Southerners will now be doing better than before. Equally, a change from E—W to N—S will involve a distributional rise, since the Northerners will do better than they did before. But — and this is the important point — the change from E—W to N—S will involve an ontological rise in quality which is not involved in the reverse change. For, not only will the Northerners be doing better than they did before, they will be doing better than anyone did before. A quality of education, so to speak, higher than any present before, will have emerged.

So the qualitarian can meet the charge of incoherence, and can defend his claim to his title; for he can point to a sense of 'rise in quality' in which only the move to the N—S system involves a rise in quality. His opponent can point to no similar rise, an ontological rise, in the move from N—S to E—W.

(5) But the qualitarian's problems are not over. For the egalitarian can point out that while it is only the change to the N—S system that involves an ontological rise in quality, it is only that change which also involves an ontological *fall* in quality. For some persons, the Southerners, would not only be doing worse than they had done before, but worse than anyone had done before. He will accuse the qualitarian of an arbitrary concern with ontological rises in quality, to the exclusion of ontological falls.

The heart of the qualitarian's position emerges with the way he handles this charge. He might begin by stressing that when we assess the quality of a system, practice, or institution, it is typically the heights, not the depths, upon which we focus. Quattrocento art is judged by the achievements of its geniuses, and it would be absurd to criticise the art of that age by pointing out that some amateur, backstreet Florentines were very poor painters indeed. When it is said that the quality of football in a country is risen, it is not meant that the poorest teams have improved, but that the best teams are better than ever before.

The qualitarian will use such cases to exemplify a fundamental human concern: the concern, in whatever field, with excellence, with satisfaction of the highest aspirations; a concern quite distinct from, and typically outweighing, concern with how many shall do well, or with ensuring that none fall below a certain level. What is essential is that the highest quality be attained by those who can. The pursuit of excellence and ideals must, no doubt, be tempered by the demands for universal participation in basic human goods; but, once the latter is assured, special energies and special resources should be devoted to that pursuit. It is this fundamental concern that you will find, turning to philosophers, expressed drunk in Nietzsche, and sober in G. E. Moore.[10] To the field of learning this concern is applied by Hesse's 'magister ludi' in these words:

> We train them (the students of the glass-bead game) to an ever higher standard of perfection. You all know that in ours as in every art there is no end to development, that each of us . . . will work away all his life at the further development, refinement, and deepening of himself and our art . . . The existence of our elite has sometimes been denounced as a luxury . . . (but) only here is our Game played properly, and correctly, to its hilt, and with full commitment.[11]

To point out to a man with this sort of concern that 'perfection', 'refinement', or 'full commitment' have their price is not to present him with something he can regard as relevant, or at least as overriding. It is not that he places no value on improving the lot of all men; rather, he insists, this is not to be done by obliterating the chances that some have to attain the heights, to discover new channels of human excellence.

(6) Like most ideals, the qualitarian's is not one which admits much in the way of positive argument in its favour. (You'll have noticed, already, that I have switched from argument to rhetoric.) But this is not to condemn the ideal. And the qualitarian might at least defend himself against

[10] See Nietzsche, *Untimely Meditations*, and G. E. Moore, *Principia Ethica*, Ch. 6.
[11] Hermann Hesse, *Magister Ludi* (Bantam books, 1970) pp. 213 ff.

misguided objections, and perhaps move to counterattack.
Let us see, briefly, how he might do this.

The egalitarian might object, first, to the qualitarian's
claim to be the one concerned with ideals and aspirations.
For cannot equality be an ideal and aspiration? There is a
sense, certainly, in which the pursuit of equality is the
pursuit of an ideal. Like the qualitarian, the egalitarian
does not base his case upon satisfaction of wants, so that
both principles are, to use Barry's expression, 'ideal-
-regarding'.[12] But, in a sense too, the principle of equality is
necessarily opposed to a concern with ideals. This comes out
clearly in Rawl's defense and discussion of the principle. For,
first, he argues the principle is one which would be adopted
by those following the more fundamental, prudential
principle of 'maximin'. This principle tells us that

> we are to adopt the alternative the worst outcome of
> which is superior to the worst outcome of the others.[13]

It is significant that, in order to make this sound a principle
each of us would adopt, Rawls has to suppose that, in the
position of original choice, men do not have ideals, or have
no 'knowledge of their particular conception of the good'.[14]
If they did have these then, as Nagel asks, why should they
'be prepared to commit themselves to principles that may
frustrate or contravene their deepest convictions?'[15] The
point is that egalitarianism necessarily outlaws any inequalities that do not benefit all, and it is surely hard to
think of many ideals that could be realised without such
inequalities. The highest attainments, typically, require specifically favoured conditions. Rawls, indeed, makes explicit the
conflict between equality and the concern with ideals and
aspirations, when he says that his principles are inconsistent
with the policy that 'a certain minimum of social resources
must be kept aside to advance the ends of perfection'.[16]

[12] See Brian Barry, *Political Argument* (Routledge & Kegan Paul, 1965) pp. 39 f.
[13] J. Rawls, op. cit., p. 153.
[14] Quoted in T. Nagel, 'Rawls on justice', *Philosophical Review*, LXXXII,
220—34, p. 226.
[15] Ibid., pp. 228—9.
[16] Op. cit., p. 326.

It is worth insisting that the qualitarian's concern with ideals is special; for his ideal is not one among others, but is, if you like, a higher-order one. It is the ideal that men should have (first-order) ideals and aspirations, and should be provided with the conditions under which these, or some of them, can be attained. The egalitarian, by opposing those aspirations which cannot be attained except at the expense of some men — which, one feels, will encompass most aspirations — is thereby opposed to that higher-order ideal. So the qualitarian can insist that he is the one with a special concern for ideals and aspirations.

A second egalitarian objection might run as follows:

> Men do not agree either on what the highest qualities are, or on which should be given the greatest weight. To gear institutions to the production of the highest qualities will, therefore, entail *imposing* the standards and weightings of some men upon others. And this is to interfere with men's equal liberty. Such institutions will be doubly unjust. Not only do some gain at the expense of others, but some will have their qualitative preferences overridden. [17]

The question, I think, is whether the problem of equal liberty need be a particularly serious one in education. Certainly in some areas, it is impossible that the ideals of some be pursued at the same time as those of others. A government cannot satisfy both the nationalist's and the internationalist's aspirations. But there is no obvious reason why, granted different conceptions of educational quality, these cannot all find a place in the educational system. Schools can differ from one another; and within a school, different kinds of education, representing different valuations of quality, need not be impossible. Experimentation and novelty, expressive of different qualitative preferences, should indeed be encouraged. If anything, it is the egalitarian's system which is likely to conflict with equal liberty. The egalitarian is not *committed* to advocating a system in which all schools provide a similar kind of education; but,

[17] This provides the gist of Rawls' main objection to adopting the 'principle of perfection' as a policy. *Op. cit.*, pp. 327 ff.

administratively, such a system provides us with the easiest way of ensuring equality of educational transformation. It is no accident that comprehensive schools find their staunchest supporters among egalitarians; and it is precisely this one-school system which, rightly or wrongly, is criticised on grounds of equal liberty to educate and be educated according to one's preferences. If all of this is so, the 'equal liberty' objection is one that the qualitarian is able to turn against the egalitarian who forwarded it.

(7) The qualitarian, finally, may go onto the offensive, with a challenge to the coherence of his opponent's position. The egalitarian does not simply demand equality; he must add that the benefits each enjoys should be as high as are compatible with every other person enjoying like benefits. In education, he must demand that each should receive the highest quality education compatible with every other person receiving a like education. He then insists that achieving this state of affairs overrides the attainment of excellence by some at the expense of others.

But the question arises, how is the egalitarian to identify the level of quality which all are to be brought to enjoy? How does he know what is the highest quality education that each might receive? Typically we identify what it is feasible to strive towards by first seeing certain persons reach it. Unless certain scientists *had* achieved certain results, we would have no reason to suppose these provide feasible aims for others to be set. It is the successes of yesterday which set the goals that all may be urged to pursue today. Now unless some, initially, enjoy privileged conditions, it is just not likely that such successes will be had; hence we should not be in the position of identifying feasible goals.

There is something peculiarly self-defeating, it seems to me, in coupling egalitarian demands with the claim that all children should enjoy the sort of education advocated and practised by daring and experimental educators. For that these men have been able to practise what they advocate, and to *test* what they advocate, has been due, typically, to the very inequalities that the egalitarian proscribes. A. S. Neill, for example, is the first to admit that the successes of his methods would not have been possible except under specially favoured conditions; a small number of pupils, very high teacher-pupil ratios, and so on.

I am not making the utilitarian point that the inequalities of today may eventually rebound to the benefit of all. This, too, presupposes a prior identification of what is beneficial. My point is the more fundamental one that in a system of equality, where the favoured conditions in which it became possible to progress to new levels of attainment are forbidden, there cannot be the most obvious and vital means for even identifying what the methods of high quality education could be. The egalitarian wants us all pulled up to higher levels which, however, he makes it difficult, if not impossible, to identify.

8 Quality and Equality in Education: A Critique of David Cooper

TIMOTHY O'HAGAN

Rather than make a direct attack on Mr Cooper's position, I shall attempt to isolate it, to show the limits of its applicability and to reject the author's illicit overstepping of these limits.

I AGAINST THE SPECIOUS *A PRIORI*

Mr Cooper promises to show that egalitarianism and qualitarianism are logically incompatible (p. 113). I take him to mean that it makes sense to talk of egalitarian demands only in a context where (a) goods are relatively unequally distributed and (b) egalitarians demand redistribution of these goods at the expense of those who have the greater share (p. 122f); and conversely that it makes sense to talk of qualitarian demands only in a context where (a) goods are relatively equally distributed and (b) qualitarians demand redistribution of these goods on a more unequal basis in order to promote a higher level of absolute quality. Both terms are relative in that egalitarianism is a movement for greater equality at the expense of quality, while qualitarianism is a movement for greater quality at the expense of equality.[1] Thus in a particular context the egalitarian may simply be opposing new inegalitarian distributions rather than proposing his own egalitarian ones. In a sense this is

[1] cf. Felix E. Oppenheim, 'egalitarianism as a Descriptive Concept', *American Philosophical Quarterly*, 7.2 (Apr 1970).

obvious, but it is only obvious once it is recognised that the problem of demands for quality or equality in education is a problem of political philosophy:[2] in particular that the demand for educational goods, which in turn is a sub-species of the broadest category of political equality, equality of access to a limited quantity of goods.[3]

So far then I agree with Cooper's thesis: egalitarianism and qualitarianism are programmes of political demands which are necessarily incompatible because the goals of the one are attainable only at the expense of the goals of the other. But in what sense is this an *a priori* truth? (pp. 113ff.) Consider a standard text-book definition of *a priori* in its post seventeenth century usage[4]:

> *A priori*: universal, necessary and wholly independent of experience... An *a priori* proposition is one which (it is claimed) is independent of experience... Thus we know *a priori* that a whole is equal to the sum of its parts; for once we understand the terms involved, we see that it is universally and necessarily true and that no experience could refute it.

Is it possible to demonstrate that the proposition 'Quality and equality in education are incompatible goals' is true *a priori* according to the text-book definition? One conventional method of doing so would be to analyse the key terms ('quality' and 'equality'); to demonstrate that they are (*a priori*) incompatible; and to infer from this that under any application (including education) they would be incompatible. (To use the most tired example, if 'being red all over' and 'being green all over' are incompatible, then if *anything* is red all over it is not green all over.)

This approach looks promising in what may be called *the philosophy of the grocery store*. In the grocery store we buy one litre of orangeade (dilutable in an unlimited quantity of

---

[2] Martin Hollis has pointed out that the obviousness of this fact should not be taken for granted. See his article, 'The Pen and the Purse', *Proceedings of the Philosophy of Education Society of Great Britain*, Supplementary Vol. 5, no. 2 (July 1971).

[3] Cf. Brian Barry, *Political Argument* (Routledge & Kegan Paul, 1965) p. 120.

[4] The Concise Encyclopaedia of Western Philosophy and Philosophers, ed. J. O. Urmson (Hutchinson, 1960) p. 23.

water), to be divided among ten people. Assume that the quality of the orangeade increases in direct proportion to its strength, i.e. in proportion to the quantity of orngeade per unit of water.[5] Then on an equal distribution, each person will receive ten centilitres of orangeade: each will receive the same quantity of the same quality of orangeade. Any other distribution will leave some people with either more of the same quality orangeade or the same quantity of higher quality orangeade than the rest (depending on how they choose to dilute it). This blindingly obvious fact can be expressed as $n/n' > n/(n' + 1)$. Given the identity 'stronger' = 'higher quality', it is true (true *a priori* if you like) that quality and equality are incompatible goals in the distribution of a finite quantity of orangeade. Before we go on to consider whether they are incompatible goals in the distribution of other goods (including educational goods), let us consider the conditions under which they are incompatible in the grocery store example:

(i) The quality of the goods is in direct proportion to their intensive magnitude and it is (or is thought to be) to the benefit of each party to gain a maximum quality goods.

(ii) The goods are limited in quantity.

(iii) The quality of the goods at any moment of time is not affected by the way in which they are distributed.

(iv) The model is static: neither quantity nor quality of the goods are affected for the future by the way in which they are distributed at present.

It is necessary to assume (i), otherwise it is incomprehensible why these demands should exist at all.

It is necessary to assume (ii), otherwise the two demands would not necessarily be at the expense of one another and so talk of 'egalitarianism' and 'qualitarianism' would be inappropriate. As Cooper says, it does not under normal circumstances make sense to talk of 'egalitarian demands for equal access to the air'. He makes the scarcity assumption explicit in his 'model' (pp. 119 121), in which 'educational

---

[5] The strength of the orangeade is an 'intensive magnitude', i.e. a point on a continuum between pure water and neat orangeade.

resources cannot be increased, they can only be redistributed'.

It is necessary to assume (iii), otherwise the qualitarian will be open to the 'utilitarian' criticism mentioned by Cooper on p. 113: the 'utilitarian' will claim that quality pursued at the (gratuitous) expense of equality is not real quality, or as R. S. Peters puts it:[6] 'the nature of education can be seriously influenced by its manner of distribution.'

One can think of analogies in the field of welfare: hygiene, for instance, must be distributed pretty well evenly or not at all, since the highest standards of hygiene for some cannot coexist with substandard conditions for others within one system. But the qualitarian will reject the analogy on the following grounds: the upper limit on hygiene is more or less fixed, so the existence of unequal standards of hygiene will mean the existence of *sub*standard conditions. Whereas in education the situation is different: he (the qualitarian) is not accepting the existence of substandard education in the system; all are entitled to a recognised standard of education, but some are entitled to something *above* this standard. I am not sure how satisfactory this reply is: I simply note that (iii) is a necessary premiss for asserting the incompatibility of egalitarianism and qualitarianism.

It is the last assumption (iv) which is the crucial one, for the nerve of Cooper's thesis is that only qualitarianism and egalitarianism but also quality and equality are ultimately and eternally incompatible. If this is to be true, it must be the case that egalitarian demands at time t cannot lead to an overall rise in quality at t'. He must reject the possibility that the lowering of standards of some group at t may be a necessary condition for raising standards for all at t'. In order even to consider such a possibility, we have to introduce the notions of (a) the development of an educational system over time and (b) the existence of different social groups or classes within the system. For evidently (by definition) those individuals affected by egalitarian reforms, whose educational standards have been lowered at t will not be *the same individuals* who make up the body of people whose standards

[6] R. S. Peters, *Ethics and Education* (Allen & Unwin, 1966) p. 136.

are raised at t'. What will have happened can be represented by this table:

	t_0	t	t'
	Time immediately before egalitarian reform	Time immediately after egalitarian reform	Time after development of reformed system
Class I	50	75	150
Class II	100	75	150

The figures represent 'units of educational quality' accruing to the two groups. It should be emphasised that this is a purely abstract model, deployed to illustrate the logical point that the incompatibility of qualitarianism as political programmes does not amount to an incompatibility of quality and equality as ultimate states. In real life, the idea that purely 'educational reforms', not combined with fundamental politico-social reforms, are capable of altering the unequal access of different social groups to educational goods is a major illusion of certain educationalists. In fact any educational reform (including – or perhaps especially) comprehensivisation can be *used* by the dominant classes to reinforce and increase the inequality of access to educational goods. Therefore the *type* of reform bringing about the changes envisaged in the table is left entirely open.

In summary, Cooper's contention that qualitarianism and egalitarianism are incompatible political programmes is absolutely correct. But once we have spelt out the conditions for this incompatibility, the intimidating universality of the *a priori* proposition begins to shrink. It shrinks in fact to the following proposition: since egalitarianism is the demand for equality at the expense of quality and since qualitarianism is the demand for quality at the expense of equality, egalitarianism and qualitarianism are incompatible demands. But from this quasi-tautology we cannot derive the conclusion that a higher level of both quality and equality cannot ultimately be achieved together. In order to derive that conclusion we must make assumption (iv) above, but the possibility envisaged in the table shows that that assumption may be false; alternatively we can adopt a very different notion of quality (to be considered at IV below), but neither Cooper nor I will be willing to adopt it, since it entirely *relativises* the notion of educational quality.

Cooper's argument is important in that it demonstrates the common philosophical trick of reducing broad *a priori* propositions to quasi-tautologies of extremely limited application (in this case a proposition about incompatible political programmes) and then reapplying these restricted terms in the abstract realm of the traditional *a priori* (quality and equality). The political consequences of this move are evident: without denying the validity of his own trade, a teacher can hardly advocate a policy which must lower educational standards, so, it would seem, a teacher cannot consistently be an egalitarian.

II A NOTE ON THE APPLICABILITY OF COOPER'S THESIS

The extent to which Cooper's thesis is applicable is well illustrated by the work of a writer on education in developing countries. C. E. Beeby[7] describes a situation of extreme scarcity of educational resources, in which it may be necessary to deprive some people even of primary education in order to concentrate resources on producing university and technical college graduates, thereby ensuring that there will be enough teachers to raise the next generation to a higher educational level overall. Here the merits of 'quality' and 'equality' are assessed and 'quality' is preferred. But such a decision has nothing to do with Cooper's positive theses concerning educational 'excellence'. Having a few university graduates and many illiterates is not *intrinsically better* than having no university graduates and fewer illiterates. On the contrary, both options are assessed relative to a further goal, that of ultimately raising both quality and equality of education.

[7] C. E. Beeby, *The Quality of Education in Developing Countries* (Cambridge, Mass: Harvard U.P., 1966) pp. 9–10.

III A NOTE ON 'HOLLOW EQUALITY'[8]

Cooper distinguishes firmly between 'genuine educational inequality' and 'general social inequality' (pp. 117—119). It is his contention that the latter topic, though important in itself, has no bearing on the question and equality *in education*. In his terminology, to criticise an educational system on the grounds that in it certain classes consistently fail to succeed (or even gain access to its goods) is not 'an educational criticism' (p. 118). A situation which is open to 'educational criticism' is one in which 'persons are entitled on educational grounds to receive certain treatment . . . it will be a genuine educational complaint that they cannot receive it'. The restriction of discussion to 'genuine educational inequality' thus defined is to be rejected for the following reasons:

(i) It does not in fact distinguish 'educational inequality' as a type of inequality *sui generis*. For cases of 'educational inequality', we are told, are cases where members of a social class complete the educational requirements for access to certain educational goods, but are prevented by extraneous factors (poverty etc.) from taking advantage of the goods to which they are entitled (p. 117). However these are not peculiar 'educational inequalities', but social, legal, political, moral inequalities or unfairness *in the field of education:* they are therefore subject to criticism and reform by social, legal, political and moral measures.

(ii) As a stipulative definition, it simply excludes by fiat the possibility of comparing the extent to which two educational systems tend to promote or restrict the access to education of the greatest number of persons; or rather it allows us to make such comparisons, providing we do not call them 'educational' comparisons.

(iii) It trivialises the question of quality and equality in education by refusing to consider the relation between the

---

[8] For a classic (almost tongue-in-cheek?) statement of 'hollow egalitarianism', see Edmund Burke, *Reflections on the Revolution in France* (Penguin Books, 1969) p. 132: 'We know that the British House of Commons, without shutting its doors to any merit in any class, is, by the sure operation of adequate causes, filled with every thing illustrious in rank, in descent, in hereditary and in acquired opulence . . .'

'purely educational' *content* of an educational system and socio-political features (including inequalities) of the overall system of which the educational system forms a part. For instance in the classical Chinese examinations system, which provided the most important method of recruiting the imperial bureaucratic elite, we are told that:[9]

> (whereas) all males were able, in principle, to compete for the highest occupational goals, not all males had the same access to the requirements of mobility . . . peasants' sons competed at a decided disadvantage with officials' sons. The culturally sanctioned goal was open to all comers, while the actual opportunities for success . . . depended to some extent at least on one's family background.

The 'educational content' of the examination system was

> long years of memorization and mastery of the ancient classics, the dynastic histories, commentaries, poetry and a highly rigid form of essay competition . . .

Now it is quite clear that the link between (a) this kind of 'educational content' and (b) the 'hollow equality' described above is not merely contingent. (a) is a powerful instrument in maintaining (b).

IV NEGATIVE INEGALITARIANISM AND POSITIVE INEGALITARIANISM

We can now distinguish two importantly different ways in which quality and equality can be said to be incompatible goals. These can be labelled *negative* and *positive* inegalitarianism.

Negative inegalitarianism corresponds to the kind of programme noted in section II above. It is the thesis that, given limited resources, quality may have to be pursued at the expense of equality in order to attain a situation in which both quality and equality can be promoted together. This is a sane thesis. It is consistent with the Rawlsian stipulation that

[9] Robert M. Marsh, *The Mandarins. The Circulation of Elites in China, 1600–1900* (New York: Free Press of Glencoe, 1961) pp. 5–6.

> only those inequalities are permissible from which every-
> one, in particular the worst off, benefits more than he
> would in their absence (p. 119)

provided that the contracting parties are seen to be social
groups taken over a period of time (see above section I).

Positive inegalitarianism claims that inequality in education (unequal access to and distribution of educational
goods) is a value to be pursued for its own sake. Cooper
would rebut the claim that he is a positive inegalitarian in this
sense. But his positive qualitarianism, coupled with an
eternalisation of the thesis that any *worthwhile* system must
embody one of the incompatible goals of quality or equality
(cf. p. 114, n. 3) amounts to a thesis of positive inegalitarianism.
Other philosophers have been less bashful than Cooper in
adopting such a stand. By the way of illustration, I shall list
three versions of positive inegalitarianism and show reasons
why we should be suspicious of them, either because they
turn out to be merely versions of negative inegalitarianism or
because they embody dubious metaphysical or pseudo-
scientific assumptions about the nature of man. These
versions are

(A) Eternalised scarcity (which turns out to be a version of
      negative inegalitarianism).
(B) Inegalitarianism corresponding to inegalitarian models
      of man.
(C) Market inegalitarianism (which turns out to be relati-
      vism).

In presenting the presuppositions of certain qualitarian
theories, I challenge him and other qualitarians to produce
the presuppositions (empirical/metaphysical) of their own
theories.

(A) ETERNALISED SCARCITY

According to this thesis, scarcity of educational and other
resources is an eternal and inevitable feature of human
society. Since this is so ('fact'), quality should be pursued at
the expense of equality (normative claim). Some such notion
of 'eternal scarcity' has been an implicit premiss of elitist

arguments from Plato to Hastings Rashdall[10] but that is no reason to accept that it is correct. In a famous passage of the *Anti-Dühring* Engels comments:[11]

> It is clear that so long as human labour was still so little productive that it provided but a small surplus over and above the necessary means of subsistence, any increase of the productive forces, extension of trade, development of the state and of law, or foundation of art and science was possible only by means of a greater division of labour. And the necessary basis of this was the great division of labour between the masses discharging simple manual labour and the few privileged persons directing labour, conducting trade and public affairs, and, at a later stage, occupying themselves with art and science.

Engels claims that historically the attainment of a high level of division of labour, both technical and social, involving unequal access to educational and cultural goods has been the only way of advancing out of a state of scarcity and low productivity. But both he and Marx believed that under the rationalised system of production inaugurated by socialism, scarcity would be overcome and such inequalities would no longer be a necessary condition of progress. In an exuberent passage of *The German Ideology* Marx and Engels had expressed this as a vision of the suppression of *all* specialisation:[12]

> society regulates the general production and this makes it possible for me to do one thing today and another to-morrow, to hunt in the morning, rear cattle in the evening,

---

[10] Hastings Rashdall's chilling views should be studied by all who are tempted by the extremes of 'qualitarianism'. Cf. *The Theory of Good and Evil*, I (Oxford, 1907) p. 238: 'Sooner or later the lower well being — it may be ultimately the very existence — of countless Chinese or negroes must be sacrificed that a higher life may be possible for a much smaller number of white men. It is impossible to defend the morality of such a policy upon the principle of equal consideration . . . If we do defend it, we distinctly adopt the principle that a higher life is intrinsically, in and for itself, more valuable than lower life, though it may only be attainable by fewer persons and may not contribute to the greater good or those who do not share it.'

[11] F. Engels, *Anti-Dühring* (Moscow, 1962) p. 250.

[12] K. Marx and F. Engels, *The German Ideology* (Moscow, 1964) p. 44.

criticize after dinner, without ever becoming hunter, fisherman, shepherd or critic.

The utopianism of this picture should not blind us to the correct underlying thought that massive *social* division of labour is necessary only under conditions of scarcity. The 'eternalisation' of the division between hand and brain is both the instrument and also one of the major effects of a particular and transitory socio-political system.

It may be objected here that an illicit play is being made on the notion of scarcity; that in fact all that need be assumed for the universal (*a priori*) applicability of Cooper's thesis is that resources are *finite;* that the orangeade model (see I above) is therefore always applicable, since resources (including educational resources) are always finite and since a greater intensive magnitude always produces higher quality. But this last qualitarian assumption is (at least with regard to education) false: for it is simply not the case that e.g. the continued improvement of the student/staff ratio (an intensive magnitude) will continue to improve educational quality *as infinitum.*[13] The point at which it will no longer do so is a matter for (non-philosophical) research.

(B) INEGALITARIAN MODELS OF MAN

According to many traditional theorists, inequality of education is justified by the essential inequality of men. I shall consider briefly just two inegalitarian models of man, labelled 'political' and 'aesthetic'.

(i) Political: according to this version, the goal of political and social planning should be the unequal distribution of goods (educational goods included) since this corresponds to and satisfies certain 'natural' inequalities in men. In the classic accounts of Plato and Aristotle, satisfaction involves administering justice through 'proportional' rather than mere 'arithmetical' equality, i.e. distributing more to the greater and less to the lesser. The function of education, on this view, is to promote the peaceful co-existence of naturally

---

[13] Cf. The adoption of the public school system in preference to private tuition by the British ruling classes.

unequal groups. Dahrendorf has rightly called this view 'pre-sociological',[14] since it gives no account of the extent to which these very inequalities are themselves socially determined. Modern advocates of 'natural inequalities' proceed from alleged genetic determination of educational aptitude. While espousing the widely accepted thesis of 'interactionism' (intelligence = product of both nature and nurture),[15] they place themselves firmly in the line of Plato and Aristotle in holding that the environmental component is definitely subordinate to the genetic. This thesis yields an inegalitarian political and social programme for education: it claims that *manipulation* of (a) the genetic component is not practicable, whereas manipulation of (b) the environmental component through political-social-economic intervention is practicable; that (b) is fundamentally ineffective; therefore the aim of a fundamental alteration of educational inequality is at best a waste of time and money and at worst dangerous utopianism.[16] The statistical and experimental inadequacies of this thesis have already been fully documented[17] and I do not intend to add to that polemic. In brief, these inadequacies are so glaring that the onus is on the inegalitarian to demonstrate the egalitarian is wasting his time in aiming for a measure of *real* equality of opportunity in education.

(ii) Aesthetic: it is hard to give a clear picture of this more bizarre version of positive inegalitarianism. There are hints of it in some of Cooper's remarks on 'excellence' and in his allusions to Nietzsche. But a more striking account is to be found in Nietzsche's own writings:[18]

---

[14] Ralf Dahrendorf, 'On the Origin of Social Inequality', *Philosophy, Politics and Society*, 2nd Series, ed. Laslett and Runciman (Oxford: Blackwell, 1964).
[15] See e.g. H. J. Eysenck, *Race, Intelligence and Education* (London, 1971).
[16] 'Is there any likelihood of ever being able to boost IQ by . . . changes of environment? . . . Environmental manipulation, even if it should prove successful, cannot be the answer; the cost is staggering . . . Furthermore, it does not go to the root of the negro-white differential . . . it seems likely that white children would benefit equally, thus maintaining their superiority.' ibid pp. 132, 134.
[17] For a good polemical selection, see *Race, Culture and Intelligence*, ed. Richardson and Spears (Penguin, 1972).
[18] F. Nietzsche, *Unzeitgemässe Betrachtungen*, III (*Schopenhauer als Erzieher*) section 6.

Mankind must work continually to produce individual great human beings ... (and live) to the advantage of the rarest and most worthy exemplar and not to the advantage of the majority who, taken individually, are the most worthless exemplars ...

And how is this production of 'outstanding exemplars' to be assured? Like Plato (but less confident than he of success) Nietzsche advocates 'genetic engineering':[19]

How one would like to apply to society and its goals a doctrine derivable from the observation of all animal and vegetable species: namely that the only thing that matters there is the highest individual exemplar, the rarest, the strongest, the most complex, the most fertile ...

An examination of aesthetic inegalitarianism in Plato (whose *Republic* contains elements of both the political and the aesthetic versions of the doctrine) should remove one common misapprehension. Several commentators have claimed that it is social egalitarianism (the movement to equalise opportunities for children in all domains amenable to social control), which will, if taken to its extreme, lead to 'genetic engineering', to an attempt by policy-makers to produce identical genetic structure in children.[20] Yet its two most important advocates in the history of philosophy (Plato and Nietzsche) have had as their goal the reinforcement of *un*equal distribution of excellence. In fact 'genetic engineering' may form part of the equipment of *any* advocate of wholesale 'social engineering',[21] for whom society is an object to be moulded and manipulated at will. It is important to emphasise this point, otherwise 'genetic engineering' becomes a kind of science-fiction bogey of egalitarianism. In fact the sane egalitarian must weigh egalitarian values against other political values (respect for privacy, for the autonomy of the personality etc.) and moderate one against the other.

[19] Ibid. For Plato on 'genetic engineering', see *Republic* V, 457 ff.
[20] See B. Williams, 'The Idea of Equality', Laslett and Runciman, op. cit., p. 128; R. S. Peters, op. cit., p. 129. Cf. J. Rawls, *A Theory of Justice* (Oxford: Clarendon Press, 1972) p.108.
[21] The term coined by Popper in *The Open Society and its Enemies*, 4th ed. (London: Routledge & Kegan Paul, 1962).

But aesthetic inegalitarianism has more fundamental defect for Cooper's purposes, its tendency to break down into one or other of two unacceptable theses. It may break down into a version of 'eternalised scarcity', the thesis that a few highest exemplars should be pursued because it is impossible to attain many. Alternatively it may break down into a version of 'market inegalitarianism' (see below), that is a high evaluation of rarity simply for the sake of rarity. This latter is a genuine version of positive inegalitarianism, but one which abandons the notion of an absolute standard of value.

(C) MARKET INEGALITARIANISM

This is perhaps the purest, but also the most trivial, form of positive inegalitarianism. According to it, the value of a commodity is directly proportional to its scarcity: thus a tendency towards equalising access to a commodity must lower its value. As noted above, there are hints of this approach in aesthetic inegalitarianism (the 'rarity value' of a work of art). But apart from being absurd economics, this approach is useless for Cooper, since it relativises the concept of value, making it impossible to grade the absolute ('onto-logical') rise or fall of the value of an object.[22]

In short, the versions of positive inegalitarianism considered above appear to be either versions of negative inegalitarianism or to be based on dubious premisses (whether frankly metaphysical or pseudo-empirical) or to be trivial and relativistic.

[22] The classic exposition of politics as a 'zero-sum game' of this market type is Hobbes' *Leviathan:* see C. B. Macpherson, *The Political Theory of Possessive Individualism* (Oxford: Clarendon Press, 1962) and T. A. Spragens, *The Politics of Motion* (Croom Helm, 1973) pp. 191, 200–1.

9 Chairman's Remarks

R. F. ATKINSON

Mr Cooper seeks to show that quality and equality in education are incompatible, but not by taking the easy course of arguing that they are definitionally inconsistent, or the still easier one of treating them as stand-ins for the opposed policies of egalitarianism (preferring equality to quality) or 'qualitarianism' (preferring quality to equality). Instead he tries to find a middle position in which it can be argued that, when demands for quality and equality are both 'appropriate' they are incompatible in the sense that neither can be satisfied without detriment to the other. The question, obviously, is whether such an intermediate position is tenable. Mr O'Hagan thinks not, arguing that Cooper's incompatibility thesis is virtually tautological under the conditions on which alone it is true, and, consequently, that it does not rule out the substantial possibility of equality and quality being sometimes simultaneously promotable in the real world. My own educational and social preferences are closer to Cooper's than O'Hagan's, but I have to concede to the latter the better of the argument on the main question ostensibly at issue. On the other hand it seemed to me, both when I first read the papers and more strongly since, that the authors somehow fail to get properly to grips. O'Hagan may have something of this in mind when, towards the end of his paper, he forsees the objection that he has 'merely spelt out areas of agreement'. The *fundamental* conflict between them is, I suspect, about individualism and collectivism, but this does not come to the fore in the papers, presumably because Cooper takes an individualist standpoint for granted, whilst O'Hagan, as becomes a second symposiast, deals with the topic largely in Cooper's terms.

The main stages in the dispute seem to be these: Cooper (section 2) gives his accounts of quality and equality and proceeds (section 3) to set out the relations between them. In sections 4, 5 and 6 he attempts to deal with egalitarian objections, and in section 7 to demonstrate the incoherence of egalitarianism. O'Hagan begins (*his* section 1) by pointing out the artificiality, as it seems to him, of the conditions under which quality and equality are genuinely incompatible, and next (section 3) insists that it is impossible to accept Cooper's sharp distinction between specifically educational and general social inequalities. He devotes about the last third of his paper to an attempt to demonstrate the incoherence of inegalitarianism.

The symposiasts are too free with charges of incoherence. Any educational principle it is worth arguing about must have a coherent alternative, even if its opponents have as yet failed to formulate it. A principle could not be the foundation of educational *policy* unless it admitted an alternative. On can neither carry out, nor disregard, a tautology.

I will look at the main stages of the argument in turn.

COOPER ON QUALITY (section 2A)

O'Hagan seems not to object to Cooper's theses here, nor in the main do I, though I have some reservations about the detail of his arguments to the effect that educational quality has to be judged *intrinsically* and in terms of *processes* not products.

On the former point he contends that quality is never judged extrinsically; that, *pace* Peters, we could not condemn the *quality*, though we might the *value* of, say, an Egyptology course on economic grounds. But I am doubtful whether the words 'quality' and 'value' are really differentiated in this way; and, moreover, think it at least difficult altogether to exclude means/end considerations when *courses* are being assessed. It would seem perfectly natural to hold an Egyptology course to be high quality on the grounds that it is useful for would-be keepers at the British Museum.

The other argument, about educational quality being assessed in terms of processes, also seems defective as stated.

It is true, no doubt, that high quality people (if this sort of shorthand is acceptable) emerge from low quality education and *vice versa,* much depending on the initial quality of entrants to the systems. But all this shows is that the quality of people emerging may not be altogether the result of the system. It does not show that the quality of a system is not to be assessed in the light of the quality it genuinely produces. Puzzlingly, Cooper himself allows that processes are ultimately to be assessed by the products the are likely to yield. Maybe my difficulties with this and the previous argument derive largely from Cooper attempting to hurry through the preliminaries, though it is also true that the intrinsic/extrinsic and process/product distinctions are quite slippery and can confuse as well as clarify.

Cooper next argues that quality in eduation has to do with the capacity of a system to effect 'educational trans-formation'. Again O'Hagan has no objections, though some are possible. It seems, for instance a little strange to contemplate judging all schools — primary, secondary, tech-nical, etc. — on the same scale, by reference to their power to bring about educational transformation, and apparently *without* reference to their different functions as institutions. Furthermore, whilst one can understand Cooper's wish not to be drawn into discussion of what it is to be educated, it is impossible to believe that the adoption of criteria markedly different from those culled from Peters and Mrs Warnock could fail to affect the rest of his paper. Another thing that struck me at this point was the way in which Cooper thinks of quality in relation to an educational system as a whole. Simplified models apart, it is surely more natural to think of it in relation to institutions within a system. This affects the relevance of the incompatibility thesis, for the people against whom it is directed may well intend no more than to hold that it is a contingent matter how far the quality of particular elements, or the proportion of high quality elements, can be improved in an increasingly egalitarian system.

COOPER ON EQUALITY (section 2B)
Here Cooper seeks to help on the incompatibilty thesis by firmly distinguishing educational from general social equality/

inequality and by considering a very tough principle of equality. He thus narrows his own claim whilst enlarging that of the egalitarians. O'Hagan takes exception to both moves.

In the course of the former Cooper illustrates his position by distinguishing between the educational inequality of an examination which places people in the 'wrong' order, perhaps because the examiners pay more attention to the social class of the candidates than their scripts, and the social inquality that would be manifested if most of the people doing well in a educationally unexceptionable examination came from the middle class. He is not, of course, claiming that any actual examination is equal on either count. His point is only that there are two distinct sorts of complaint that can be made. So far, for my money, so good. And I can still follow him when he contends that a selection examination is not made *educationally* unequal by the fact that working class candidates tend to fail, although there would be educational inequality if such working class candidates as passed could not afford to take advantage of doing so. But he goes too far when he holds, as he appears to do, quite generally that all that educational equality requires, in addition to educationally impeccable selection procedures, is that those selected should be able to take advantage of their selection. It would seem very strange to hold that an examination was inoffensive from the point of view of educational equality if the poor were excluded by a stiff entrance fee or main force. O'Hagan very effectively makes this point in his account of the civil service selection procedure in the former Chinese Empire. He does not, however, convince me that no distinction can ever be made between educational and social inequality.

A full discussion would require more consideration of the notion of education than either symposiast had time for, but on a superficial view I see no reason to doubt that there is a range of cases over which it is reasonable to make an educational/social equality distinction. But it can as reasonably be conceded that in conditions of extreme social inequality it betrays a want of proportion to commend elements of the educational system for their educational equality in the narrow sense. One might well fail to be impressed by the, so far as I know, perfectly true claim that there is no racial bias in the *examining* in South African Universities.

On one point, however, O'Hagan seems clearly right — that is, in his contention that it is the social inequalities expressed in the educational system, not simply educational inequalities in the narrrow sense, about which egalitarians typically object. Cooper's anti-egalitarianism is too narrowly conceived fully to match up with the sort of egalitarianism that is actually encountered in the real world.

Turning next to the principle of equality, one can only applaud Cooper's determination to avoid a vacuous formulation. He is quite right that we are not all egalitarians now. But it so much suits his book to consider a principle strong enough to rule out concern for quality, that one must ask whether it is not stronger than most egalitarians would accept. Even O'Hagan, who presumably regards himself as an egalitarian, does not accept it without qualification. He insists that other values have to be balanced against, and sometimes preferred to, equality. Indeed, it seems that most self-styled egalitarians really object only to flagrant cases of unnecessary discrimination on irrelevant grounds. They are usually happy enough to discriminate where 'necessary' (say, as a step towards the classless society) or on 'relevant' grounds (say, against the poor, or the rich, or women).

These considerations are, however, by themselves insufficient to bring to light the root difference between the egalitarianism contemplated by Cooper and that actually embraced by O'Hagan. This is that, whereas the former thinks in terms of equality between individuals, the latter is concerned with equality between social groups taken over a (possibly quite long) period of time. O'Hagan writes as if he thinks this a minor difference, or simply a move in the direction of greater social realism, but in fact it is plainly an absolutely fundamental difference of moral and political standpoint. The difference is so great that any concentration of scarce resources on a minority, which Cooper would have to see as inconsistent with equality, need not be so viewed by O'Hagan — provided only that he can believe that there will be future advantage for the presently disadvantaged group, even if only in the long run in which all its present members are dead. With egalitarianism of this sort around it is more than ever important to be in the right minority.

THE RELATION BEWEEN QUALITY AND EQUALITY

Cooper argues, referring to his N—S/E—W schools example, that, where demands for equality and quality can both be approporiately made, they are incompatible. What brings them into competition is, of course, scarcity of resources — if there is no scarcity demands for equality are inappropriate. One can see the point, which recalls Hume's observation that in conditions of abundance justice would be superfluous, though I think that the notion of inappropriateness could have stood a little more examination. Doubtless the idea is not that in the absence of scarcity demands for equality do not make sense, but rather that they are in some other way out of place. Anyway the relevance of scarcity is recognised by both symposiasts, Cooper with his schools and O'Hagan with his orangeade distribution example. The difference is that, whereas the former takes it for granted that educational resources are scarce in relation to demand, the latter, very strangely to my mind, appears to doubt it.

There may be some cross purposes between them over the notion of scarcity, which is at least *quasi*-technical. It does not imply that resources cannot be expanded, nor that there is a fixed upper limit on them, but only that their expansion for any purpose takes time and will be at the expense of other uses to which they may be put. For scarcity not to be a problem, as O'Hagan thinks it need not, resources would have either to be infinitely expansible or demands on them, in all fields not just education, to be finite. There is a hint, in O'Hagan's section 5, that he thinks educational demands at least might be fully satisfied, but this would not eliminate scarcity so long as there remain insatiable demands of other sorts. It is possible too that he thinks the insatiability of demand to be less a feature of the human condition than of capitalist society, though he does not say so in his paper. The fact that the doctrine of eternal scarcity has appeared in élitist argument from Plato to Hastings Rashdall does not entail its falsity. I could not help feeling that O'Hagan was inclined to move fallaciously from the truth that educational resources are not fixed at any particular level to the falsehood that they are not fixed at all.

But even though Cooper is right on the matter of scarcity all that follows is that equality and quality will come into conflict in the long run. It does not follow that there cannot be actual situations in which it is possible to make concessions to them both. Obviously this could not be done forever. But a great deal of what can be done in the here and now could not be done forever. There is much justice in O'Hagan's observation that what is true of simplified models need not be true of the real world.

I will pass very quickly over Cooper's sections 4–6, though they contain interesting material, and would have been important in a debate with a less radical antagonist. One thing that is worth noting is that is section 5 he is prepared to temper qualitarianism with the requirement that there be universal participation in basic human goods. Unless a very narrow view is taken of basic goods this represents a considerable concession to egalitarianism. Finally, in section 7, he tries to show that egalitarianism is incoherent. The argument is that, to the extent it is effective, it tends to rule out the sort of situation, one of privilege, in which alone it is possible to achieve, and hence to identify, the goods that the egalitarian wants to see equally distributed. I do not, as I said above, much like charges of incoherence, but I agree that equality, as a *distributional* principle, cannot very well be anybody's sole practical principle. There has to be a *content* to distribute.

O'HAGAN'S CRITICISM OF INEGALITARIANISM (section 4)

A distinction is drawn between negative and positive inegalitarianism. The former is the thesis that, because of limited resources, quality may have to be pursued at the expense of equality: the latter that inequality is in some way valuable in itself. ('Instrumental' and 'intrinsic' or 'essential' might be better terms.) Negative inegalitarianism is allowed to be 'sane' though, of course, vitiated by being based on the 'false' premise of eternal scarcity. The positive variety, however, is claimed either to reduce to the negative or to be incoherent.

This is a large claim, that so plainly requires more explanation and supporting argument than it could receive in context, that it is perhaps unfair to criticise it severely. All the same it does seem to me that a rather short way was taken with the varieties of positive inegalitarianism.

Is it enough, for instance, to dismiss 'political inegalitarianism', the view that distribution should reflect the inequalities of people, as 'pre-sociological'? Its being pre-sociological surely does not entail its falsity, but at worst that it was not, and perhaps is not, known whether its social presuppositions are true or false. It can hardly be maintained that sociology (*whose* sociology?) has established that all human differences are socially determined. And if the idea is rather that sociology presupposes this — but why should it when there is small reason to think it true? — one could still ask why one should be obliged to consider all practical questions in a sociological perspective. In any event, even if all human differences were social in origin, they would remain real, and it would not be self-evidently absurd to hold that account should be taken of them in framing social policies.

With regard to 'aesthetic inegalitarianism' I have to confess that I have been unable to form a perfectly clear idea of it, though it seems to include the thought that human inequality is not merely to be accepted but maintained or increased. In this connexion O'Hagan considers the possibility of value being conveived as proportional to scarcity, from which it might follow that goods of high quality would always be in too short supply for wide equal distribution. 'Market inegalitarianism' he calls this view. He rightly observes that Cooper does not adopt it, and himself dismisses it on the ground that it makes value wholly relative. (Gone apparently are the days when absolutism needed to be argued for.) It seemed to me, though, that this was too simple. Evaluating is typically a matter of discriminating between items on the basis of their having or lacking, or having in a higher or lower degree, some feature or complex of features. Where all items of a kind regularly achieve the desired quality, as in the case of a sheet of postage stamps, one does not usually say that they are all of high value, but rather that it is impossible to make value discriminations among them. This does not mean that a particular stamp is the worse for being no better than any of the rest — and this perhaps is the notion that O'Hagan objects to in market inegalitarianism — but it does mean that the idea of high value lacks application in such circumstances. I am not trying to defend market inegalitarianism, but simply suggesting that it builds upon features of evaluation that cannot be dismissed out of hand.

In making my comments and criticisms I am very conscious of ignoring a great deal that both authors must have considered important. My excuse is that between them they cover an extraordinarily wide range. This is the other side of their failure squarely to confront each other, which results, I believe, partly from their attempting to discuss what are at bottom matters of educational policy in excessively abstract terms, and partly from the wide, but insufficiently explicit, ideological divergence between them.

Postscript

DAVID COOPER

I have comments to make on three topics, arising out of the reply and discussion. First, let me try to clarify the nature of the incompatibility between quality and equality for which I argued. It is not, in any straightforward way, an incompatibility between states of affairs. The state of affairs in which something of the highest quality is enjoyed is compatible, sometimes at least, with the state of affairs in which everyone equally enjoys it. Mr O'Hagan is right to stress that I couldn't have meant to deny this, and intended to focus upon the incompatibility of the *demands* for quality and equality. Mr O'Hagan does not deny this sort of incompatibility, but he does make it sound rather more obvious and trivial than I think it is by saying, for example, that it follows as a 'quasi-tautology' from my definitions of the principles of equality and quality. He seems to think I defined them in terms of their mutual opposition, in which case, to be sure, the ensuing incompatibility between demands would follow trivially enough. But that is not what I did. I didn't define the principle of quality at all, and my definition of the principle of equality was Rawls' one — to the effect that only those inequalities were permissible which were to the benefit of everyone. I then *argued* that the only conditions under which this principle could be appropriately, non-frivolously, and non-grotesquely cited in favour of some policy would necessarily be ones under which a qualitarian would have to advocate an opposed policy. If it were possible to bring the rest of the population up to a level so far enjoyed only by some, without in any way affecting the latter, then since they would not have been benefiting at the expense of the rest, any appeal to the principle of equality in favour of improving matters would be out of place and frivolous.

Second, the distinction I drew between what I called 'genuine educational inequalities' and 'social inequalities which happen to manifest themselves in educational systems' did not go down too well either with Mr O'Hagan or some of the participants. Part of the objection, I think, was simply to the labels. Well, I'm not particularly concerned with the labels, though as I shall argue in a moment I don't think they are inappropriate, but with the distinctions they were intended to highlight. It seems to me that the three following criticisms of a school's selection system must be distinguished:

(a) Stupid people pass the examination and intelligent ones fail it.
(b) The people who pass the examination are often unable to take up their places because of financial hardship, despite being thoroughly suited for the places.
(c) Poor people tend to do badly on the examination.

If the objection to my distinction is that (c) should not be separately treated from both (a) and (b) then it is misguided. I don't see anything odd in describing the inequalities or injustices criticised by (a) and (b) as 'genuine educational ones' in a way that what is criticised by (c) are not. The first is a criticism of the educational criteria being employed by the school. The second is a criticism of the failure of the school to be run in accordance with rational educational criteria. The third criticism, on the other hand, has nothing to do with educational criteria or the implementation of policies governed by such criteria. Only a person with some expertise on the questions 'What persons are suitable for such-and-such an education?' or 'What are the criteria for a good education?' is in a position to offer the first two criticisms. Anyone at all can make the third. None of this is to suggest that educators should not concern themselves with the third type of criticism. Equally, to hark back to an anlogy I used in the paper, musicians should no doubt be concerned with the predominately middle-class composition of orchestras — but to complain about this is not to complain on musical grounds, as it would be if they were to complain that half the players can't play their instruments properly.

Finally, a word on the type of 'qualitarian' or 'inegalitarian' that I am — for I don't recognise myself in any of the parts Mr O'Hagan offers me in the last section of his reply. Certainly I am more than his 'negative' inegalitarian, who tolerates inequalities in the short run only if they can be expected to lead to equality in the long run. I should want to defend inequalities which have very little likelihood of resulting in equality. On the other hand, I don't see myself as adopting any of his versions of 'positive' inegalitarianism, for I don't find any value in inequality 'for its own sake'. My position is, simply, that first I see no good reason for always sacrificing excellence in the name of equality (and it's only where some sacrifice would be involved that an appeal to equality could be appropriate), and second that unless some persons are placed in specially favoured circumstances there are general reasons for supposing that the highest standards will not even be identified, let alone attained. Naturally, I am in favour of as many persons enjoying high standards as is compatible with their attainment by some.

PART FOUR:
THE NEUTRAL TEACHER

cf. p. 41 on neutrality

10 The Neutral Teacher

MARY WARNOCK

I must begin with a brief apology. My paper will be extremely simple-minded. It may seem that the questions raised in it are almost all of them empirical and practical rather than philosophical. If anything philosophical is discussed it is because the issue arises by the way. I find that this is the regular order when one is supposed to be discussing the philosophy of education, but I can only hope that in the course of the later discussions I shall learn different.

Those who advocate neutrality in teachers do so, in my experience, with great passion. There appear to be two major grounds for their advocacy, which are not, however, totally distinct from each other. The first ground is the desire to avoid turning teaching into indoctrination. The second is the desire that pupils may learn whatever they do learn by discovering through experiment, trial and error and genuine argument; that they may have the pleasure of coming independently to their own conclusions, with the teacher simply as chairman of their meetings.

I want briefly to consider the indoctrination argument first, but this will not take long, since it will be clear already how this argument shades off into the second. It is worth considering the *word* 'indoctrination', however, since it is rather a vogue word just at the moment. Indoctrination means the imposing upon a captive child the body of doctrines held by the teacher (or supposed to be held by him. It would obviously be possible for a freethinking teacher to impose Christian doctrine on a child, but we need not consider this case.) The essence of the situation is that what the teacher says is true is to be accepted by the child uncritically. The bad feature of indoctrination therefore (and

159

the word is obviously pejorative) lies precisely in the docile and uncritical state of mind which it produces in the pupil. The concept of indoctrination certainly has some use; but there are great difficulties in marking off its limits exactly. For instance, if the teacher is a charismatic person it may well be that his pupils are disinclined to doubt what he says, even in areas where doubt is perfectly reasonable. If he is the opposite, whatever he says may seem dubious or at least unmemorable to his pupils. Again, it is not clear whether the word 'indoctrinate' means 'to induce uncritical belief deliberately' or not. If I am an absolutely convinced believer in the single authorship of the Iliad and the Odyssey, such that I have never even raised the question whether Homer was one author or several, then I may teach my class that the Iliad and the Odyssey were written by one Greek whose name was Homer, and they may go through the rest of their lives believing this, especially if they do not develop any particular interest in Greek poetry. It may become simply part of the seldom-examined furniture of their minds. Have they then been indoctrinated? I certainly did not *mean* to indoctrinate them. I simply meant to tell them what I took to be the truth. I did not even know that it was controversial. But, it may be asked, does anyone ever set out deliberately to indoctrinate another? Do we not always attempt simply to teach them the truth? Perhaps sometimes, in cases where there is a received body of dogma which hangs together, and belief in which is thought to be particularly desirable in its effects, a teacher may say, like the Jesuits, I will catch him young, and ensure that he accepts it all, lock stock and barrel. But when you come to think of it this is a pretty rare phenomenon. For most teachers the question whether or not to indoctrinate in this narrow sense, hardly ever arises, Apart, then, from 'indoctrination' in the narow sense, the word seems mostly to be used of other people, when we ourselves disapprove either of the content of their teaching, or of the methods. As such it is perhaps not a very useful word to analyse further.

Let us move on, therefore, to consider the second ground for holding that a teacher should be neutral. This is the desire that pupils should learn by discovering things for themselves rather than by being told; and this course of discovery will include among other items the discovery that it is possible to hold different views about a vast number of subjects, between which views he will have to choose. Thus, the neutral teacher will present to his pupil the different views that exist, will put him in the way of evidence or other considerations which might favour the different views, and will then sit back and allow him to make up his own mind. Now it will be obvious at once that this kind of description of the teacher's role applies only to certain kinds of material, if at all. There are some sorts of teaching situations in which the question of the pupil's deciding something for himself does not really arise, and this even where the material is , in a sense, controversial. Let us suppose, for example, that I am trying to teach someone to do something. In the very simple kind of cases, such as where I may try to teach you to ride a bicycle, there will be very little theoretical content to my teaching; I will merely guide your efforts with advice and physical support. If I am trying to teach you, on the other hand, to drive a car or play the French horn, there may be a good deal of theory involved. But nonetheless my aim in teaching is to get you to be able to do something. And when you can do it reasonably efficiently, then you can perfect your technique by practice, rejecting some of my teaching if you find it better to do so, that is if you find it more efficient. The question of neutrality can hardly be made to bear on such cases at all. A great deal of what one teaches at school is in fact of this kind, disagreeable though it may be for some theorists to accept this. Reading and writing are indeed often spoken of as 'skills' and it is acknowledged that in teaching them we are teaching children how to do something. But a great deal of mathematics must also be learned as a matter of skill or technique; and in the case of languages, the aim is also to teach people how to talk, write, or translate. Of course a teacher may get things wrong. He may simply teach his pupils to write bad French, or give them a cumbersome or confusing method for solving equations. But this again has virtually nothing to do with whether he is neutral or not. It is a matter of whether he is intelligent and understands his subject matter. I mention these cases only to show that there is a vast area of very important teaching, (though somewhat neglected in the writings of educationalists) which is the teaching of techniques or skills, and where it does not enter our heads to demand the neutrality of the teacher. The question of whether he is neutral or not, again, does not arise.

But obviously, embedded in these technique-subjects there generally lies a core of fact and of theory. I teach someone to read Latin, and teach him in doing so *that* Cicero uses the subjunctive in relative clauses to convey this or that nuance. This is taught as a fact, which can be verified by appeal to the texts. And behind this fact lies a theory, or at least a system, which enables me to split up written words (in this case) into sentences, and sentences into clauses, to distinguish nouns from verbs, and to distinguish, within the class of verbs, those which are indicative from those which are subjunctive in mood. And so on. At last we may begin to see some of the difficulties. How are we to distinguish, in what lies behind the taught technique, between fact and theory? Are we to teach the theory as well as the fact? Must we preface all our teaching of Latin syntax (to stick to this example) with the words 'This is a subjunctive verb according to our present classification; but of course there could be other classifications'? How much do such provisos actually add to a pupil's understanding? Do we want him to be thinking all the time about alternative geometries, or do we first want him to learn a bit about Euclidean geometry, and then contemplate alternatives? One thing is certain. In teaching such subjects as Latin syntax, a teacher cannot simply act as a chairman. His duty is to provide positive information, which he must make intelligible by as many examples as he can. No child can be expected to discover Latin syntax unaided from the ancient texts. In such a case the teacher must actually teach, that is pass on information and understanding which he has and his pupil, so far, has not. Whether or not he wishes to preface all his teaching with remarks of the form 'things being as they are' or 'using the syntactical classification we do', he must at some stage actually assert what is the case. I think that, empirically speaking, it would create endless confusion if he always put in the covering clause; and no sensible teacher who actually wanted to get his pupils to learn something would think of doing so.

We have come upon a case, then (and there are very many such) where although it is logically possible to regard the matter in a wholly different light, yet the teacher is justified in teaching certain facts as facts, as an aid to teaching certain skills. He need not continually point out that someone else might deny that what he had taught was a fact. If he wishes he may suggest that there could be a different frame of reference within which things would look different, but to point this out is most of the time irrelevant to his purpose. A teacher who never pointed this out, who either did not believe it, or had never thought about it one way or another, need not be described as doctrinaire, nor need his teaching be described as indoctrinating. A man who accepts some facts as such, and passes on his knowledge of them is not failing to be neutral.

However, up till now, we have been dealing with the easy cases. We have looked only at cases where the pupil has little scope either for discovering facts for himself or making up his own mind between conflicting accounts. But we have only to think of a few more lessons in the school day to come upon subjects where the distinction between what is a fact and what is not is much harder to draw. In the discussion of history and geography (as they used to be called), indeed of the social sciences generally, it is frequently claimed that it is absolutely impossible to distinguish between facts and non-facts, that the notion of a fact is dangerously misleading, and that teachers must not deceive or bully their pupils by telling them things on the assumption that this distinction can be made. I want now to examine this claim a little further.

In the first place, it will be agreed that in the teaching of, for example, history, there has to be considerable selection of material, even if a teacher himself does not do it, but relies on a text book or syllabus-maker to do it for him. Selection, notoriously, may be biased or onesided. The good teacher will do his best to supplement material which he feels is inadequate in this sort of respect; but he would find it very hard radically to change the assumptions of our whole culture about what is worth discussing and what is not. The main historical issues to be examined will remain the same, changing only gradually, for many generations. The teacher cannot aspire to a god-like status as far as selecting material goes. If he chooses, he may preface all his remarks with the warning that he is looking at the thing from the standpoint of a twentieth-century historian. But this warning, like the general warnings we looked at before, turns out to be empty, because he cannot specify at all exactly what alternatives there may one day be. He *is* after all a twentieth-century historian. That he will be teaching from largely preselected material, then, is necessarily true, and need not be taken to impair his neutrality, nor need it be taken to undermine the whole concept of the fact. But this is not the whole story. In most branches of the social sciences, the main purpose of the teacher is not only to impart information but to give to his pupils a sense of evidence, of what does and what does not count as an argument, so that they may if they wish go on with the subject by themselves. It is in this area that the demand for neutrality is likely to become insistent. A teacher must present evidence fairly; he must not conceal evidence, nor exaggerate that which is favourable to one side or the other. His pupils must weigh the evidence, and decide on the truth. Is the teacher thus put, whether he likes it or not, into the chair? Is chairmanship enough? Let us take a concrete example. Suppose a class to be discussing the history of Mary Queen of Scots. They have arrived at the stage of the murder of Darnley. The question arises, was Mary or was she not implicated in this murder? Now one thing is certain. Pupils in an ordinary school class cannot examine any fresh evidence on this point. They cannot even read the secondary sources in detail, still less can they go back to contemporary sources. They must use evidence which is merely described to them, rather than presented in detail. The teacher must tell them what the sources are, and must tell them, for example, that Buchanan's history was specifically designed to incriminate Mary, that it contains inconsistencies, and cannot be taken as true or unbiased. The teacher must help his pupils to reconstruct the probable course of events, relying on his own knowledge of the period, and his own common sense and experience of how people in general behave. But in helping his pupils, is he not to tell them what he thinks is the most likely account? Of course in a case like this no one cares very much one way or the other, and no one is likely to attack the teacher for non-neutrality even if he does say what he thinks. But there is a point in choosing such an example since the principles governing the teacher's behaviour in this case are general, and apply equally to cases in which the passions are likely to be involved. I would argue that unless the teacher comes out into the open, and says in what direction he believes that the evidence points he will have failed in his duty as a teacher. For what his pupils have to learn is not only, in an abstract way, what counts as evidence, but how people draw conclusions from evidence. The whole notion of evidence independent of any probable conclusion is meaningless. Of course there may be cases where the teacher thinks the evidence is genuinely inconclusive, and in this case he must say that there is really no ground for coming down on one side or the other. But such cases are rare. If all evidence were inconclusive, then the concept of evidence itself would be, if not empty, at least radically different. Thus the teacher must if he is to teach his pupils to assess evidence fairly, give them actual examples of how he does this himself. His pupils may disagree with him. The more adult they become, and the better their earlier experience of arguments, the more capable they will be of weighing the probabilities differently. But unless they see before them the spectacle of a rational man drawing conclusions rationally, they will never learn what rational probabilities are. Obviously all kinds of factors personal to the teacher come in here. If he is dynamic and likeable his views may tend to be uncritically accepted. If he is despised, they may be uncritically opposed. But all the same to see that the teacher is committed to a view which he thinks rationally follows from the evidence is of tremendous value in itself, whether his pupils follow him or not. The teacher must be a *leader* in argument if he is to teach argument. And a leader cannot sit on the fence for ever.

So far I have been treating only of facts, albeit selected and dubious facts. In this area I hope I have suggested that uncommitted neutrality in the teacher, in so far as it is possible, is not desirable. I want now to consider whether this conclusion has any bearing on the real question, the problem that all the fuss is about, namely the question whether or not a teacher should be neutral when the subject of the class is a matter of values. I do not wish to embark here on the problem of distinguishing facts from values. It is sometimes argued that as there is no such thing as a pure fact, no proper distinction can be drawn between fact and value. If so, then perhaps we could take a short way with the subject and say that what has been said about facts ought to be said about values since they cannot be distinguished. But this would not be convincing. I would rather assume that we can all of us give examples of what, in non-philosophical moments, we should be prepared to call statements of fact. An example would be that Mary Queen of Scots knew that Darnley was to be murdered on February 9th 1567, or that she did not know. (The fact that many people would be inclined to condemn her for conniving at the murder of her husband, however unsatisfactory, is neither here nor there. The factual question is, did she know about it or did she not?) We can, I shall assume, also all of us produce instances of obviously evaluative statements, such as that the publication of pornography ought to be severely restricted by law. It is to the second kind of statements, and the arguments which may take place in class about them that I want now to turn.

Now it is a truism that matters of fact may be relevant to the drawing of evaluative conclusions, though they may not entail these conclusions. That being so (and especially since relevance is one of the main lessons he has to teach), it follows that all the duties a teacher may have with respect to evidence in the historical examples already considered will be equally incumbent upon him in the evaluative case. And of course many of the historical cases may also be evaluative. But the collection and presentation of evidence is likely to be fraught with difficulties in the evaluative cases. Notoriously, for example, it is hard to discover what the effect of pornography is upon its willing consumers, even if an agreed starting definition of pornography can be arrived at. It is perhaps still harder to discover its effects upon those who have to consume it whether they like it or not. All evidence of the form 'people in general do or suffer x' is extraordinarily hard to collect or present fairly. Still worse is evidence of the form 'people suffer harm if x is done to them'. For it is not only the scope of the generalisation which causes difficulties, but the conceptual content as well. What is to count as harm? Such difficulties as these must be faced by the teacher who is trying to present the material on which his pupils are to base their judgement of whether or not pornography ought to be radically further restricted by law. But he must be neither daunted nor deflected by this. He must plough his way on as best he can, making it absolutely clear what he is doing, where he is assuming something that he cannot prove, and what he is preparing them to do. He must use the material, as far as he is able to collect it, as *grounds* upon which to found a judgement. But now what happens? Does he jib at forming a judgement himself, and simply demand that his pupils make one? Or does he state, as I have maintained that he should in the relatively 'pure' historical case, his own view? Once again, I have no doubt whatever that he should state his own view, and thus demonstrate to his pupils the whole process of basing a judgement on an interpretation of the facts. Insofar as the argument we are supposing is just an argument, the very same considerations apply to it as applied to the argument about Mary Queen of Scots. A pupil cannot understand the relevance of factual considerations to conclusions, without experience of the conclusion's being actually drawn. But in the evaluative case there are other and more important considerations as well.

First, as will be obvious from a consideration of the foregoing example, the facts cannot be absolutely determined. Interpretation is going to enter into the presentation of the grounds right from the start. It is therefore virtually impossible to separate a conclusion from its grounds. The conclusion, as it were enters into the presentation of the grounds. But even if such separation were possible in practice, other objections would remain. There is a psychological objection to the spectacle of some one's remaining neutral in a highly charged dispute about a subject which is supposed to affect everyone and therefore be everyone's concern. The neutral man cannot but seem uninterested, and however much he claims to be *putting aside* his own beliefs, in order to act the part of neutral chairman, this does not prevent his seeming either alarmingly remote, or positively scornful or patronising, if he will not join in the dispute. There is a kind of nightmare in which one is in danger or pain or in some state of emotional tension of a painful kind and all the time on the sidelines, there is a perfectly impassive observer, taking no steps to help or comfort, or even to acknowledge the existence of a crisis. It is the nightmare of the knitters at the guillotine, or of the absolutely rational parent observing a child's tantrum and letting him simply go on screaming. Something of this nightmarish sense is conveyed to pupils whose teacher will not take part in a debate, or state his own moral view.

It may be argued that this is a neurotic, or at any rate an exaggerated, reaction. Any such disagreeable effects are far outweighed by the desirability of getting pupils to see both sides of any question so as to ensure that they judge, when they do, rationally and without prejudice. Since a teacher has, it is argued, no right to impose his own prejudices on his pupils, he had better not voice them. He cannot expect his pupils to eliminate prejudice from their minds if he is seen to be guilty of prejudice himself. So runs the argument for neutrality. The weakness of the argument lies, self-evidently, in the word 'prejudice'. I wish to distinguish between a prejudice and a moral belief, and thus to conclude that if a teacher states clearly his own moral belief, he is not displaying prejudice. He has not *pre*judged anything. In the case supposed, he has examined and assessed the signifcance of what facts he has been able to assemble, and then made his moral judgement of what ought to occur.

Very well, it may be said, let him express his moral belief, provided that he both shows how he has arrived at it, and is careful to say that it is simply *his opinion*. Let him by no means seek to impose this opinion on his pupils If he cannot keep his mouth shut, or if he feels that he must state his own conclusion in order to demonstrate the drawing of a conclusion, let him at least clearly show that he realises that other opinions are just as good (or, as people prefer to say, as valid).

But alas, this is impossible in the nature of the case. And here we have come upon the real nature of evaluative judgements. It is strictly impossible at one and the same time to say 'this is wrong' and 'but you need not think so'. Although we all know perfectly well that values are relative to our society and our culture (or even to our little bit of society or culture) yet it is impossible to assert this truth *and* in the same breath seriously to assert a value judgement. We are inevitably and for ever divided in our minds. Either we make no value judgements, and are content to stand outside the making of them, or, if we do make them, we must for the time being put on one side our anthropological spectacles through which we survey the conflicting opinions of the human race. Moreover, if we have come to our moral judgement by the route of serious thought and a considera- tion of the evidence as fair as we can make it, then we cannot think that an opposite judgement follows equally 'validly' from this same evidence. If we have concluded that some- thing is wrong, we *must* think that everyone ought to hold it wrong, even though we know that they do not, and that we must put up with this, Now this feature of evaluative judgements is something that at some time or other pupils must learn to recognise, and, if possible, understand; and they can start to understand it from the expression of genuine moral convictions by their teacher. They will learn that someone who sincerely holds a moral conviction does not and cannot feel that any other conviction is *just as good*. That is the nature of the case. Moral relativism may be a fact; but it is not a fact that we feel while we are forming moral judgements. If we really believed that any moral view was as good and worthy to be adopted as any other, then we would of course make no moral judgements at all. And the same is true of all other, non-moral, evaluations. We cannot evaluate, and accept another evaluation at the same time as equally sound. Moral views, then, are not prejudices; but they are also totally distinct from matters of opinion.

One may, of course, raise the question what is the point of getting people at school to discuss such topics as whether or not the legislation about pornography should be changed. Part of the point, as has been suggested already, is to teach them to judge fairly on the evidence, and to understand the arguments both for and against the proposition. But part of the point is also actually to get them to think about right and wrong, good and evil, to think, that is to say, about morals. If this is accepted as part of their education, then they must not be deprived of the spectacle of a teacher who holds, and clearly expresses, moral views. There is nothing but benefit in the contemplation of a man of principle. A man without moral views is after all a monster, and it is hard for pupils, especially if they are quite young, to realise that the neutral teacher is only play-acting. Moreover, if they do realise this, they resent it. Practically speaking, one of the things one learns from teaching children is that play-acting is despicable. The first rule of teaching is sincerity, even if one's sincerity is dotty or eccentric. A man ought to have and to express moral beliefs, and this entails that as a teacher he cannot remain neutral. For holding a moral belief is in some respects like having a vision. It is in a sense, an imaginative vision of how things ought to be though they are not. Expressing a moral belief is thus attempting to share a vision or way of looking, and this cannot be done without in some sense attempting to get your interlocutor to see things as you do, if only for the time. A pupil may discover, in the course of discussion, what he himself thinks, what moral views he holds. But he cannot do this without exercising his imagination to see *in* the material under discussion a moral issue. He must see it as a starting point from which he may envisage a world in which such things do not happen, or do happen freely. The teacher must help him to exercise his imagination; it is indeed his only serious function; and thus he must help him to see the material as morally significant. This he can do only by demonstrating that it appears so to him. If a teacher, by the attractiveness of his personality, causes his pupils for the most part to share his vision, aesthetic or moral or of whatever other sort, the passage of time will remedy this, if remedy is needed. To have been conscious at some stage of one's life how someone else, a grown up, actually saw the world is far from harmful, even if later the viewpoint is totally abandoned. I conclude therefore that in the sphere of the evaluative, as of the factual, the teacher has a positive obligation, if he is to teach well, to be non-neutral; and that this is necessary because of the nature of moral, and other evaluative judgement.

It will be noted that in the foregoing argument I have seemed to assume that the teacher is older than the pupil, more knowledgeable and more rational, and also possessed of more experience, common sense and imagination. I make this assumption knowingly. I realise that there are .teachers who are in all these respects (except generally that of age) the inferior of their pupils. Nevertheless the teacher's essential role is to be in all these respects his pupil's superior, and this is the role he must try to fill, necessarily. It is the role which creates the teaching situation, with all its intrinsic authority, and it is this *role*, not any particular occupier of it, which has been the subject of discussion. In such a role, I have maintained, the teacher will fail if he attempts to remain neutral.

11 The Neutral Teacher? [1]

RICHARD NORMAN

Mrs Warnock concludes that the teacher will fail in his role if he attempts to remain neutral. I agree. I shall not, however, simply leave the matter there, not only because it would make for a rather boring symposium, but also because I suspect that there remain important aspects of this subject on which Mrs Warnock and I would disagree. I hope that the disagreement will emerge. At any rate, what I shall do is to take Mrs Warnock's conclusion and push it further — further, I think, than she would be prepared to take it.

INDOCTRINATION

Before turning to the main theme I should like to say something briefly about the notion of 'indoctrination'. Mrs Warnock speedily dismisses it, concluding at the end of a paragraph that it is 'perhaps not a very useful word to analyse further' (p. 160). But can it really be so easily dispensed with? One would perhaps like to think so, but unfortunately the phenomenon to which it refers remains depressingly familiar. The only reason which Mrs Warnock offers for abandoning the term is that, although teachers may in fact 'induce uncritical belief', they rarely do so deliberately; most teachers simply aim to impart the truth, and if they fail to present other points of view, this will be because they do not regard what they are teaching as controversial. This is probably true. It shows only that the teacher's intentions are neither here nor there, and that the process we are talking about may have to be described by saying that, although the teacher indoctrinates, he does not do so deliberately.

[1] I would like to thank Lesley Norman and Sean Sayers for their comments and assistance.

172

What *is* it, then, that people refer to as 'indoctrination'? The phenomenon is marvellously captured in a passage from Laurie Lee's *Cider with Rosie* which, though it refers to the writer's own childhood, can be all too easily updated:

> Through the dead hours of the morning, through the long afternoons, we chanted away at our tables. Passers-by could hear our rising voices in our bottled-up room on the bank; 'Twelve-inches-one-foot. Three-feet-make-a-yard. Fourteen-pounds-make-a-stone. Eight-stone-a-hundred-weight.' We absorbed these figures as primal truths declared by some ultimate power. Unhearing, unquestioning, we rocked to our chanting, hammering the gold nails home. 'Twice-two-are-four. One-God-is-Love. One-Lord-is-King. One-King-is-George. One-George-is-Fifth . . .' So it was always; had been, would be for ever; we asked no questions; we didn't hear what we said; yet neither did we ever forget it. (Op. cit., Penguin edition, p. 53 ff.)

Here we have, delightfully conveyed, the continuity between traditional ways of teaching mathematics, for example, and the implanting of the 'received truths' of religion and politics. If the latter seem more to warrant the label 'indoctrination', this is only because the subject-matter is more controversial; the procedure is the same — 'Twice-two-are-four, One-God-is-Love, One-King-is-George'. The essential contrast is between learning which is based on sheer repetition, and learning which proceeds from understanding. Now of course there is no absolute dichotomy here; all human learning, even the mechanical memorising of multiplication tables, involves some degree of comprehension. It is never just the parrotting of mere sounds. For this reason, the term 'indoctrination' *may* be misleading. It suggests some special, refined technique, totally distinct from the normal processes of teaching, whereas what one is really concerned with is a matter of degree — a failure to produce sufficient understanding, a failure to teach well enough or to effect more than the retention of ritual formulae.

It is of course the desire to produce genuine understanding that lies behind the recent progressive developments in education — child-centred education, the New Maths, the whole stress on the learner's own activity and experience. As Mrs Warnock rightly observes, the argument about indoctrination shades off into the argument about learning through discovery. I do not need to emphasise this theme. I am sure that many of the participants in this conference will know far more about it than I do (the universities have yet to catch up with the primary schools in this field).

But it does seem to me that Mrs Warnock obscures the matter. She presents an unreal either/or; the teacher is either the conveyor of truths, or the near-silent chairman of meetings, leaving the pupils to discover everything for themselves. This second alternative is of course untenable. The teacher is an active participant in the process. But so are, or should be, the pupils. What Mrs Warnock's either/or rules out is the possibility of education as *dialogue*, as a *co-operative* activity. The pupils, as much as the teacher, have something to bring to the educational process. They have their own experience to draw on, and unless they are helped and enabled to articulate that experience, what they are 'taught' will remain external and mechanical. This sounds like a bland truism. In practice, I think it raises great difficuties. I know from the teaching I do (and I am sure this is general) that one can all too easily miss the point of what a student is saying. In order to appreciate its relevance and importance, one may have to set aside one's own preconceptions, and the difficulty is that these preconceptions may well have become one's own implicit definition of 'the subject', so that whatever cannot be assimilated to them is seen as irrelevant. I am sure that what goes for the teaching of university students goes equally for the teaching of five-year-olds. How much of children's painting, for example, is dismissed as inadequate or incompetent because the teacher's own unconscious preconceptions make it impossible to recognise what the child is doing?

The general point I am making is that the term 'indoctrination' is regularly used to contrast with learning which proceeds from genuine understanding, achieved by the active participation of the learner in the educational process. The term may not be ideal, but in this sense indoctrination is a reality, and needs still to be attacked.

Nevertheless, I would *not* attack it in the name of any ideal of 'neutrality' — and this now brings us to the central topic under discussion. According to Mrs Warnock, 'the desire to avoid turning teaching into indoctrination' is one of the major grounds for the advocacy of neutrality in teachers. It might consequently be expected that, since I have been emphasising the need to attack indoctrination, I should go on to defend neutrality. But that is not what I intend. I do not want to set up 'neutrality' as the desirable alternative. Such an ideal presupposes as its conceptual background an extreme and untenable liberal individualism. It assumes that education consists essentially in the child's (or the learner's) being left alone, left to grow and develop under his own impetus; the task of the teacher is to make experiences available to the learner for him to draw upon, but not to influence him positively in any preconceived direction, since this would be to impose one's own values on another. The picture at work here is the classical liberal one of an area fenced around, within which the individual lives his own life, immune from the influence of others. I would reject this picture. I regard the activity of education, like all characteristically human activities, as one of social interaction and mutual influence. And I would aim to avoid indoctrination not because I want to avoid imparting my values to others but, on the contrary, because I am committed to certain values and want to promote them. I want those whom I teach to become free human beings, sceptical of authority, capable of seeing through and rejecting the ideological props of existing social institutions, capable of directing their own lives and their own society. To talk of 'imposing' these values is self-contradictory; but I would certainly want others to acquire them, and I would certainly teach with that end in view.

POLITICAL VALUES AND THE TEACHING OF 'FACTS'

We have arrived, then, at what Mrs Warnock calls 'the problem that all the fuss is about' — the question of neutrality in relation to values. But notice — and this will be my theme for the remainder of the paper — that Mrs Warnock understands this question in a very restricted sense. She glosses it as 'the question whether or not a teacher should be neutral when *the subject of the class* is a matter of values' (p. 166; my emphasis). In other words, she is concerned solely with what one ought to do when one is explicitly teaching *about* values, and it is within this context that she suggests that the teacher ought not to be neutral. Her only example is the following: if the class is discussing the censorship of pornography, the teacher should state his own view. Insofar as one can generalise from this, one supposes that Mrs Warnock has in mind something like a sixth-form 'General Studies' or 'Current Affairs' lesson, or perhaps a trendy version of Religious Instruction. But is this really 'what all the fuss is about'? Well, some of it perhaps. Certainly, the practical dilemma is one which teachers do genuinely face. And if one resolves it as Mrs Warnock recommends, this may well give rise to a certain amount of controversy, especially if the moral beliefs which one presents to a class are unorthodox ('TEACHER IN SEX LESSON ROW' — *Daily X*). Nevertheless, where questions of neutrality are concerned, the following example seems to me to be much more typically controversial. Just over a year ago, a lecturer in English at the University of Lancaster was threatened with dismissal on the grounds of 'political bias'. He had previously been removed from a list of examiners on the grounds that 'a candidate writing answers for a known socialist would be under invidious pressure'; and it was subsequently suggested by one of the examiners that the scripts showed 'clear evidence of an undue orientation in the teaching towards political rather than literary themes'.

Notice how this example differs importantly from Mrs Warnock's example. In moving to the discussion of questions of value, she says:

> I do not wish to embark here on the problem of distinguishing facts from values . . . I would rather assume that we can all of us give examples of what, in non-philosophical moments, we should be prepared to call statements of fact . . . We can, I shall assume, all of us produce instances of obviously evaluative statements, such as that the publication of pornography ought to be severely restricted by law. (p. 166)

Mrs Warnock's assumptions are quite legitimate. Some such distinction can undoubtedly be made; there certainly are statements which are undeniably statements of fact, and others which are undeniably evaluative statements. But Mrs Warnock actually assumes much more than this. She assumes not only that there are clear instances of factual statements and clear instances of evaluative statements, but also that one can talk quite separately about the teaching of facts and the teaching of values. However, as my example shows, the important questions about neutrality arise precisely because the two kinds of teaching may coalesce. The problem is whether the teacher should be evaluatively neutral, not just 'when the subject of the class is a matter of values', but when the subject of the class is history, or literature, or philosophy. For, at the level of logical and linguistic distinctions, though facts and values can in some way be distinguished, the philosophical problems stem from those cases where statements of fact seem to be at the same time evaluative, that is, where values seem to be built into the facts. Correspondingly, at the practical level, one may teach facts, and one may teach values, but one may also teach facts in a way which is clearly value-laden. One may then be accused of importing one's own values into an area where they do not belong; and it is at this point that the ideal of 'neutrality' may be invoked or questioned.

Notice also a further feature of our example. The 'fuss' here is not so much about 'values' in a general and rather woolly sense, but, characteristically, about *political* values. When teachers are accused of failing to be neutral, what is regularly meant is that they are *politically* committed, and that this commitment is apparent in their teaching of history, or literature, or sociology, or philosophy, or whatever.

Therefore the crucial question which we ought to consider is this. Can one exclude values, and in particular political values, from one's teaching, either by eliminating them entirely or by reserving them for a specific occasion — perhaps some special slot on the timetable, of the sort that Mrs Warnock refers to, in which the class is specifically required to 'discuss values'? In attempting to answer this, there are obvious distinctions to be made. Some kind of teaching are more obviously value-free than others. For example, the teaching of the natural sciences, in contrast to the human sciences, undoubtedly can be, and normally will be, politically neutral. Even here, however, there are problems, of the sort which emerge from current debates about social responsibility in science; thus the intellectual abstraction of scientific knowledge from the social uses to which it is put could well be seen not as 'scientific neutrality' but as 'political irresponsibility'. In other words, the decision whether to exclude from one's teaching any political judgement about the applications of scientific knowledge is, even if it is made by default, necessarily a political decision, and one which the science teacher as such cannot escape.

Again, there is the area which Mrs Warnock identifies, for other purposes, as the teaching of skills and techniques. Here too it seems plausible to suggest that one's teaching can quite feasibly be politically neutral. The teaching of reading, for example, might seem to have its own purely internal and purely technical criteria of success. Yet one has only to invoke the notorious 'Janet and John', or their equivalents, to be reminded of how political values enter in even here. The normative status which is implicitly attributed to the respectable middle-class home, the nuclear family, masculine superiority, in reading material of this kind, is familiar and easily mocked. It is a fit subject for ridicule, but the point is a serious one. Reading is not a pure technique. What the child learns to read has a content, and in particular it is likely to have a moral and social content of one sort or another. Moreover, the content that is chosen will reflect a particular conception of the social use which the technique of reading is intended to serve. Reading may be taught either as the passive initiation of the child into an alien universe in which language is a scarcely-comprehended mystery and hence an instrument of domination, or as a process of making language available to the child as an instrument appropriate to his needs, an instrument for understanding and assessing his own world and reflecting critically on it. The choice is a political one.

The most interesting cases to consider, however, are

obviously the teaching of the humanities and the human sciences. To the question of the possibility of political neutrality in these areas, certain standard arguments about the logic of the human sciences are clearly relevant — arguments about whether history, philosophy, sociology, etc., can be *written* in a way which is politically neutral. There is, for example, an argument familiar from the philosophy of history and the philosophy of the social sciences, about the necessity of *selection*. The reality which is the potential subject-matter of any of the human sciences is an infinite multiplicity. To provide an exhaustive account of it would be impossible. One has to select — and one necessarily does so on the basis of values, in accordance with what one takes to be important in human life, practically or morally or politically. Now, this is sometimes taken to be no more than a pragmatic point: one has to choose how to apportion one's time, one cannot study everything, nor can one teach everything, one has to choose what to concentrate on. It is then supposed that this still leaves open the possibility that, having made one's choice, one can go on to study or to teach whatever one has opted for, in a purely neutral, purely factual way. Values may enter into one's choice of what to focus on the subject, but they can be excluded, it is assumed, from what one then says about it.

This assumption is questionable, and so is the distinction on which it is based. To the extent that values enter into one's selection of what to study or teach, they also enter into one's conception of the subject-matter. Take the case (not an imaginary one) of a student who, having read Kafka, wishes to study further the question of the meaninglessness of life, its depersonalised and alienated character, in modern bureaucratic society. He is told by the teachers of literary criticism: 'We can discuss with you questions about Kafka's literary technique — the means he employs to convey such ideas, his use of symbol and allegory. We can perhaps discuss also questions of interpretation — whether, for example, Kafka's presentation of the predicament of the individual in an absurd and incomprehensible world is to be read primarily as a religious or as a political statement. What we cannot discuss is whether Kafka was right; that is a philosophical question, and for that you must go to the philosophers.' By the latter, however, he will no doubt be told: 'We can help you to analyse the concepts that are employed here. We can discuss with you whether such statements are intelligible, and how, if at all, they are to be verified. But we cannot enter into the substantive questions; if you want to talk about the alienated character of life in modern society, you should read novels or plays, rather than turn to philosophy.' If the student is not by now completely disillusioned, he may think of turning to the sociologists or the psychologists. But from them he will receive the answer: 'These large-scale metaphysical and political questions cannot be dealt with by an empirical, value-free science such as ours. There are no hard data to be gathered here; there is nothing to be measured. You had better return to the philosophers.'

The upshot is, of course, that the student can find no academic subject in which he can engage in what interests him — an overall moral and political understanding and assessment of his own society. The self-justification of his teachers will be: 'Such questions no doubt have their place. But we simply do not choose to concern ourselves with them. They belong elsewhere.' But the fact of selection actually carries a wider significance. It carries with it some such implication as the following: 'Questions of that sort do not warrant serious intellectual enquiry; they can properly be relegated to the realm of irrational reactions; they are no more than the product of adolescent emotion.' And the crucial point is then that the dismissal, the exclusion of certain kinds of political discourse as unimportant or improper or irrational, is itself a political stance. In short, to exclude is as political a step as to include.

So the necessity for selection is not just a matter of personal convenience. It inevitably imports certain moral and political evaluations into one's conception of the subject-matter. And this point can be taken a stage further; the necessity for selection is not just a practical necessity, it is an *epistemological* necessity. The argument will again be familiar from the philosophy of history, so let us take history as an example. It is not just that the historian has to direct his interest in one direction rather than another. Given the infinite multiplicity of the potential data of history, the historical facts are not even *describable* except insofar as they are formed into a pattern, viewed from a perspective within which some things come into prominence as foreground and others merge into a background. This selection of one pattern rather than another will again have evaluative implications, and this will again be apparent in the teaching of the subject. The conception of history which I was first introduced to at primary school was the history of the British monarchy and the growth of the British empire. This was replaced by what was still, I suppose, a conception of history as the history of nations, but with the emphasis now on the development of mankind towards the liberal-democratic nation-state. If I am now more inclined towards a conception of history as class-struggle, I do not regard this as differing from the others in being more political, but only in being more valid. I would not criticise the two former versions for being political; but I would criticise them for being ideological — for being based on political preconceptions rather than on reality, for being an uncritical reflection of the political status-quo. Each of these historical perspectives, however, is equally a political perspective — and so would be any other alternative.

The argument in terms of 'selection' here merges into another argument familiar from the philosophy of history. The relevant claim, with which I would agree, is that the historian (and likewise the teacher of history) is inevitably committed to one political point of view or another by *vocabulary* which he employs. Consider the following passage taken at random from a standard work, avowedly written for sober educational purposes, not for those of political partisanship:

> The most important fact about all three single-party states (Nazi Germany, Fascist Italy, and Stalinist Russia) was not economic but political: the fact that they were governed by men who wielded, more completely than any other rulers in history, absolute power of life and death over all their subjects. The unique feature of modern dictatorship is that it tends to be totalitarian; that is, it contrives to concentrate in the hands of the ruling group a degree of

power which enables them to control all aspects of the national life . . . Ballyhoo and brutality were made the foundations of the state. Behind the party, engaged in monopolizing and running all the important organizations of society and state, stood in each country the terrible power of the secret police . . . Each dictator found that he could muster, from modern society, a large enough number of utterly unscrupulous, devoted, and brutal henchmen to gain him this power of terror . . . The story of tortures and cruelties, of total degradation of the human personality and of vicious sadism, was by the mid-twentieth century familiar enough. There is little mystery left about how a single-party dictatorship works. The more difficult question is how such absolute power could be generated and accumulated in apparently civilized cultured European communities of modern times. One explanation is the appeal made to fanaticism — the astounding force of ideologies whether Marxist, nationalist, or racialist . . .

> (David Thomson: *Europe Since Napoleon*,
> Penguin edition, pp. 728–9)

In this passage the political attitudes of the writer are blatantly apparent. The very fact that he classifies Nazism, Fascism and Stalinism under the single term 'totalitarian' immediately commits him to a specific political stance — to the claim that the similarities between these regimes are more important than their differences. The use of the term implies that what is significant about Stalinism is the concentration of power rather than the direction in which it is aimed; therefore Stalinism can be lumped together with Nazism and Fascism. The defender of Stalinism[2] would of course use a different vocabulary. He would not use the term 'totalitarian'. Still less would he describe Stalin's actions in terms of 'brutality' and 'cruelty'. And he would certainly not characterise the driving force of Marxism as an appeal to 'fanaticism'. Instead, he would describe Stalin's policies as the harsh

---

[2] In view of misunderstandings which have arisen on occasions when I have read this paper, I should make it clear that I would not myself accept the defence of Stalinism which follows.

measures necessary to safeguard the fruits of the revolution, and without which the whole movement towards socialism, and therefore the hopes of humanity, might have been shattered for ever.

The question then is whether, as historian or as teacher of history, one could abjure both political vocabularies and give a purely neutral description of the history of Stalinism. Certainly one could say that each of these two descriptions is over-simplified, and that the reality of Stalinism was much more complex. One might have to use elements of both vocabularies, and say that though the original impetus behind Stalin's policies was an authentically revolutionary one, it led to the creation of a ruling group set only on perpetuating its own power. Numerous variations are possible here; but each of them would constitute another *political* perspective. Less plausibly, a desperately liberal historian intent on doing justice to both sides might oscillate between one vocabulary and another; but this would simply produce a bizarre history, not politically neutral but politically incoherent. Could one, however, abjure all politically-loaded vocabulary and employ nothing except purely neutral descriptions? Well, in a sense one could do so. One could confine oneself to stating that from the year 1924 onwards, Stalin uttered certain commands and signed certain documents, which resulted in the deaths of such-and-such persons and the creation of such-and-such institutions. This would be neutrality of a sort. But it would not be history. It would reduce Stalin's actions to unintelligibility, and turn them into dehumanised motions of an automaton, a set of meaningless physical movements. As soon as one even begins to ascribe to Stalin one motivation or another, one is embarked on the enterprise of political justification and political criticism.

It may be objected that my argument is fallacious insofar as it runs together the activity of the *writer* of history with that of the *teacher*. For, it might be said, though the historian cannot escape being committed to a political perspective, it is the task of the teacher to acquaint his students with the competing viewpoints of different historians. With the latter suggestion I would agree. But I do not think that it requires political neutrality on the part of the teacher. It is at this point that I would invoke Mrs Warnock's discussion. The good teacher will make his students aware of the strength of competing arguments; but he cannot do this properly, he cannot help his students to develop a sense of the difference between a good argument and a bad argument, unless he commits himself, unless he 'states his own view and thus demonstrates to his pupils the whole process of basing a judgement on the interpretation of the facts' (p. 167).

I have, I am afraid, concentrated overmuch on the example of history (though what I have said is applicable to other disciplines). In doing so I have raised issues in the philosophy of history which demand a discussion to themselves, and which I have had to treat rather cryptically. Let me therefore end this section by reiterating the basic claim which I hope at least to have substantiated. In leaving open the question of the relation of facts and values, Mrs Warnock obscures a crucial aspect of the question of neutrality. If, as I think, the logical separation of facts and values is untenable, if our factual knowledge is essentially value-laden, then correspondingly, we have to recognise the inevitable intrusion of values, and in particular political values, into the teaching and learning of facts.

Insofar as I talk here of a *necessary* intrusion, I am going beyond Mrs Warnock's conclusion in a further respect. She concludes that the teacher *ought not* to be neutral. I would say that the teacher *cannot* be neutral.

THE POLITICAL CHARACTER OF TEACHING METHODS

I want now to propose a second way in which Mrs Warnock's discussion of the problem needs to be extended. In considering whether or not the teacher is neutral, we need to look not just at the *content* of his teaching, but at the *manner* of his teaching. At the end of my earlier discussion of indoctrination, I suggested that my own wish to avoid indoctrinating was to be explained as stemming not from an ideology of neutrality but, on the contrary, from a specific political commitment. Here, the impossibility of neutrality applies not to *what* one teaches, but to *how* one teaches. Or rather, the two cannot be separated. The teaching of values is not limited to 'moral education' classes of the kind that Mrs Warnock seems to have in mind. One puts across certain values not just through what one explicitly says, but through the way in which one organises the learning situation. Here again, this is something which one cannot help doing. For example, every teacher, especially in a primary school, faces a choice between organising the classroom on a basis of competition or on a basis of cooperation. The children may be perpetually encouraged to aim at doing better than one another, and made constantly aware of their relative 'superiority' and 'inferiority' by the usual paraphernalia of marks and stars, and the ordering of the class in terms of 'top' and 'bottom'. Alternatively they may learn to work together, to pool their abilities, to adapt their work to that of others in joint activities; they may be taught that, where one can do easily what another child finds difficult, the appropriate response is to help him, not to feel superior. The point is, once more, that the choice, even if it is made by default, is one which the teacher cannot help making. And thus he cannot help inculcating certain values.

What may seem more controversial is the suggestion that the values in question are *political* values. This can be made more obvious if, in our example, we remember the kinds of justification likely to be offered on either side; on the one hand, that the child should be prepared for the competitive society in which he will have to live, or, on the contrary, that teaching can be a form of political action directed at changing the kinds of social relations which constitute our present society. At the very least, then, competition and co-operation in education are *causally* related to wider social relations which are undeniably political. But we can go further. If the choice between different social relationships, when these characterise a whole society, is a political choice, then it is surely equally political when made on a smaller scale. To take another example: if the conflict between authoritarian and libertarian tendencies is a political conflict when it occurs in the wider society, why should it cease to be political when it occurs within education? What is really needed here is a proper examination of the concept 'political'.[3] At the very least, we need to get away from the

---

[3] Such an examination can be found in Tony Skillen's article 'The Statist Conception of Politics,' *Radical Philosophy 2*.

idea that the sphere of 'the political' is delimited by the phenomena of governments, elections, electoral parties, etc.

THE POLITICAL CHARACTER OF INSTITUTIONS

I turn now to my third and final extension of Mrs Warnock's discussion. Mrs Warnock seems to assume that a teacher's neutrality or non-neutrality is determined simply by his own individual choices and actions. I think that it is fair to see this kind of individualism in her discussion, even if she would not explicitly avow it. In contrast to this, it is important to recognise that human actions can have a meaning which goes beyond the conscious intentions of the agent — a meaning which is given to them by the social context and the social institutions within which they are performed. As a teacher one is, whether one likes it or not, working within institutions which have a specific political character and political functions. I take the facts here to be obvious (though no doubt they would be contested). Through its processes of streaming, selecting, examining and grading, our educational system services and perpetuates a complex hierarchical society, separating social class from social class and preparing some for privilege and others for drudgery. By the very fact of being compulsory, and through more specific disciplinary procedures, it establishes patterns of obedience and acquiescence towards authority. And insofar as teachers work within such institutions, their activity is, through no choice of their own, correspondingly political. This is an unpleasant fact to have to face. One would like to be able to deny it. For my own part, as a university teacher I have to recognise that, insofar as I mark examinations and give assessments and compel students to study prescribed courses instead of exploring their own intellectual interest, I am helping to maintain a political system which I loathe.

This is not to deny that teachers can consciously attempt to counter these tendencies, or to change the institutions. One can attempt, for example, to work as a libertarian teacher within an authoritarian structure. One's activity will then combine contradictory political characteristics; and although this may be rather a shattering experience, it need not necessarily be futile. Nor should one suppose that 'the system' is something totally monolithic. So the political character that is given to one's teaching by the institutional structure does not prevent it from having other political characteristics as well; but it does mean that it cannot be politically neutral.

CONCLUSION

One often hears it said that education suffers from being made a matter for political dispute. This tends to be accompanied by the proposal that we should 'take education out of politics'. Such a proposal is usually itself a transparently political manoeuvre — 'Lets take education out of politics' means 'Let's keep things as they are'. No philosophical knowledge is needed to see this. More important, perhaps, is the fact that one finds philosophers of education talking as though questions about the desirable aims and methods of education were questions about which, at least in principle, all rational men could agree, whatever their disagreements elsewhere. One finds this manifested, for example, in the apparent assumption that such questions can be settled simply by examining 'the' concept of education. I would say, on the contrary, that questions about what to teach and how to teach it can be answered only in the context of some political perspective or other. And since those of us who are involved in education obviously disagree politically, this means that we are also bound to disagree about education. I therefore conclude that, within the foreseeable future, education will be an arena of political conflict.

12 Chairman's Remarks

ALAN MONTEFIORE

'I want those whom I teach to become free human beings, sceptical of authority, capable of seeing through and rejecting the ideological props of existing social institutions, capable of directing their own lives and their own society. To talk of "imposing" these values is self-contradictory; but I would certainly want others to acquire them, and I would certainly teach with that end in view.'[1]

So runs Richard Norman's declaration of faith; apart perhaps from its use of the word 'ideological', it has, surely, a 'liberal' ring about it. There are many important differences of mingled substance and expression between such evident liberals as T. H. Green, R. M. Hare, H. L. A. Hart and J. S. Mill — to take a few distinguished names at near random. But would one not take this declaration to come from one of the same family of thinkers? Only a few sentences earlier Norman speaks of 'the classical liberal [picture] of an area fenced around, within which the individual lives his own life, immune from the influence of others', adding, 'I would reject this picture'.[2] Yet leave out the reference to 'classical liberalism' and the rejection could come straight from T. H. Green. When one reflects that even Bentham and Mill would almost certainly have spoken of immunity from interference rather than of immunity from influence by others, one might think that Norman's real complaint against Mrs Warnock should be that her generation and is predecessors have not succeeded in being liberal enough. Of course, it is well known as a 'liberal establishment' move to seek to absorb would-be

[1] p. 175.
[2] p. 175.

188

opponents by representing them as 'really one of us all the time'. Nevertheless, there is positive as well as negative (negating) substance to the claim that the values of much radical intellectual protest are those of liberalism taken further than the founding fathers were able to take them; and that in their origins at least they are thus very different from those of working class revolutionary socialism.

With this last remark Norman would most probably disagree; the evidence of his book, *Reasons for Actions*,[3] at any rate is that he sees 'socialist' ethics as a development of 'liberal' ethics. Yet on the general face of it, his reaction to Mrs Warnock's paper seems to be a mixture of 'this is too good to be true' and 'It's merely that she doesn't go far enough'. (Or perhaps it should be the other way round: 'She doesn't go far enough — but anyhow it's too good to be true.') Both of them certainly come out against the idea of the neutral teacher; such a stance is said to be undesirable or even impossible — with varying degrees of emphasis on the one thesis or the other. But if they appear so close to agreement with each other on this central issue, what then are these arguments about the possibility, desirability or impossibility of neutrality in the class, lecture or seminar room really about? Tiresome though it may seem as a routine philosophical reflex, something has to be said about some of the key terms of debate.

First, the word 'neutral' itself. It has sometimes been suggested that much of the controversy generated by the original Humanities Curriculum Project might have been avoided if its chosen key phrase had been rather 'the impartial teacher'.[4] Unsurprisingly, ordinary language furnishes us with no hard and fast rules of speech in this area of few hard and fast distinctions. Yet concepts going under the labels of neutrality, impartiality, objectivity, open-mindedness, disinterestedness, detachment, indifference, independence, etc. may all be distinguished from and

---

[3] Oxford: (Basil Blackwell, 1971).
[4] Lawrence Stenhouse himself toyed with this suggestion at one time, but would now reject it. As he has put it in a comment to me: 'Impartiality can be seen as a virtue in itself: neutrality cannot. It is quite clear that the teacher is not neutral, he is only fulfilling a neutral function. Impartiality seems to blur this.'

sometimes even opposed to each other. *Any* firm way of taking any of these terms is going to involve a certain degree of stipulation. Still, it is a reasonable first stipulation to say that neutrality is always to be conceived of as being in or towards some actual or potential conflict and that, this being so, there can be no such thing as a position of absolute neutrality in the sense of a neutrality towards all actual or possible conflicts at once; a would-be neutral in conflict A must by definition be open to involvement in any conflict B over whether neutrality in A is either possible or desirable. Impartiality may, in certain conflicts, be exceedingly un-neutral; nor is there any general reason why attitudes of neutrality should be any more (or less) likely to be disinterested than attitudes that are openly partisan. These points are merely by way of example; there are many other similar distinctions and contrasts to be made. [Not all is contrast, however; in certain specific contexts, and given certain specific assumptions, neutrality and impartiality may come to the same thing; as in others again impartiality and objectivity.]

So of course there can be no such thing as the un-restrictedly neutral teacher[5] — just as of course there may always be certain limited conflicts in or towards which teachers may, if they choose, preserve or pretend to preserve an attitude of neutrality. If the terms are defined precisely enough, neither Mrs Warnock nor Richard Norman (nor certainly the Humanities Project team) need or indeed would seem likely to disagree on this *general* point. But it by no means follows that they must agree on what is to be counted as neutral behaviour in each particular situation or even on which situations do or do not present neutrality as a possible option — let alone as one which may be desirable. And indeed this essential contestability of what is to be recognised as neutrality is written deep into the foundations of the concept.

[5] No one would think to argue that those who demand that Britain should remain neutral in any conflict between the U.S.A. and the U.S.S.R., do so from a position of absolute or overall political neutrality; nor that the teaching of a so-called neutral teacher could be neutral with respect to conflicts between the 'values' that he may be seeking to inculcate and those from which he is explicitly seeking to get away.

One reason for this may be indicated as follows. Whether neutrality be interpreted in terms of non-alignment with any of the parties to a conflict or, more widely, in terms of total non-involvement (including such involvements as those of knocking all heads equally and impartially together), a necessary condition for the meaningful applicability of the concept is that the potential neutral should be in a position to choose whether to exercise some effective influence on the conflict or not. But if the causal possibility is effectively open to him of, say, helping A rather than B, then a refusal to do so may be seen as a partisan way of helping B rather than A. One quite powerful line of argument exploits considerations of this sort with the aim of showing that the concept of neutrality is ultimately empty because ultimately incoherent. This argument is not pointless. Nevertheless, people *are* sometimes faced with recognisable choices of whether to involve themselves in conflicts or not or, at the very least, of how far to go with such involvements; indeed, I should be prepared to argue that this is not a wholly contingent matter. In general they may be counted as having such choices where there appear to be commonly recognisable criteria for identifying a conflict as occurring or continuing within a framework of on-going normality independently of any reference to their own participation. But this will depend in particular cases on what is there taken for granted about the nature and structure of social situations and about the ways in which individuals, groups, classes and institutions may be and in fact are related to each other. Between those whose assumptions on such matters are different — and such discrepancies are particularly likely to occur in periods of fundamental social change — differences must naturally be expected in assessments of neutrality and non-neutrality. Nor in evident principle can there be any 'neutral' way of bringing these differences to definitive judgement.

It is not surprising, therefore, that Mrs Warnock and Richard Norman, while agreeing that absolute or overall neutrality is a senseless and inapplicable notion, may yet disagree over what more limited options of neutrality may in practice be available, over what forms of behaviour are to be counted as neutral in cases where the option exists and over when it might be desirable to take it. Nor, for that matter, is it surprising that they should see such disagreements as most likely to arise in what they identify as the area of values, Norman more specifically as that of political values. Unfortunately, both these apparently unavoidable terms, 'values' and 'political', carry their own full share of widely ramifying complexities.

Where is the borderline to be drawn between the political and the non-political? Norman claims that 'when teachers are accused of failing to be neutral, what is regularly meant is that they are politically committed . . .';[6] and later that 'the crucial point is then that the dismissal, the exclusion of certain kinds of political discourse . . . is itself a political stance. In short, to exclude is as political a step as to include.'[7] In many contemporary contexts both of these claims would seem to me to be generally justified. But part of their force is lost if one does not at the same time see why they need have no compelling universal validity. At one time major controversies turned around the question of whether teachers and the schools should or should not adopt attitudes of religious neutrality. Should one have said that a decision to exclude certain kinds of religious discourse was itself a decision to take a particular kind of religious stance? That would have depended, of course, on the religious perspective from which one spoke; indeed, the question of the status of such decisions might itself have belonged to the controversy over what decision should be made. The same may be said of the status of any decision to exclude certain kinds of political discourse — with the added complication that the question of whether the position of religion in schools is of political significance itself involves essentially contestable issues. Norman cannot, and presumably would not, claim that his denial of the possibility of political neutrality is itself politically neutral. This by no means constitutes any kind of *reductio ad absurdum* of his position. It does, however, shed light on the combative peculiarity of its status and of the way in which its own sense depends on the possibility of

[6] p. 177.
[7] p. 180.

giving some relative sense to the position to which it is opposed.

This, clearly, is not easy; for it is of the nature of a case like Norman's that opposing theses, setting limits to the range of the political, should be seen as essentially incoherent. One answer — in so far as there can be a determinate answer — will be that they too need fall into incoherence only when, forgetting the conditions upon which they depend, they claim universal validity for themselves. One of these necessary conditions is that the general structure of society, the framework within which all particular struggles take place, should be commonly taken for granted as beyond serious threat or question. Another presumably is that there should be some limit to any prevailing demand for conformity and control over all that is thought and done by members of society. Under stable conditions the line between what is of public political concern and what falls for one reason or another outside may be drawn in diverse ways and places; but in principle there need be no insuperable problem about discovering where it is in fact drawn in any particular case. Within the accepted framework people may normally choose whether or not to participate in such political struggles as take place. Unless these struggles themselves involve efforts to enrol teachers as combatants on one side or the other, or demands that they should at least remain silent on what is going on, there is no general reason of principle why they should not be able, if they see fit, to provide neutral presentations of the issues in conflict. But these conditions may not always be satisfied. In particular, when the very frameworks of society are called into question, the fiercest battles may take place precisely over the question of where the line between the political and the non-political is to be drawn; and the demand that certain areas be recognised as non-political may become one of the most politically significant of all. It hardly needs to be added that since it is in the education of coming generations that the future lines of social and political classification must be maintained or redrawn, the political or non-political status of education may itself become one of the most bitterly contested political issues; and that to seek to be a (procedurally) neutral teacher by reference to one framework of assumptions and expectations is bound to appear substantially unneutral to those whose principal aim is to bring these assumptions and expectations into question.

What about the term 'value'? In many ways I wish that one could get on for a while without having to use it or other members of its family, so confused and interwoven have debates on their proper meaning become. Is the question of value-neutrality, for example, the same as that of whether value-judgements can be derived from statements of fact? Has this latter question itself any one determinate sense? It is clear that many of the most famous proponents of the 'Wertfreiheit' of the social sciences intended principally to insist that from the hypotheses or statements of their analyses there followed in strict logic no value-judgements on the facts therein conjectured or reported; that is, that the acceptance of such statements left everyone entirely free as to the attitude, for or against, which they might adopt towards these facts. There is, certainly, much that is problematic in this doctrine; but the much used arguments in terms of selection and interpretation, however important in themselves, in themselves go no way to disprove it. There is very little real disagreement between the symposiasts on this point; and indeed Max Weber himself went out of his way to stress that research whose direction and selection of material was guided by no presiding 'values' would be likely to be of merely curiosity or exemplary interest — at best. So far as Weber was concerned, the crucial thing was not to pretend that one's choice of topic and material in no way reflected one's 'values', but on the contrary to lay them openly and explicitly on the table. Gunnar Myrdal prescribed the same line of conduct; and so, incidentally, did the authors of the Humanities Curriculum Project.

All this is really very well known; so why, when there is so much that needs arguing about, do people still go on as if they were arguing seriously about this? Partly, no doubt, because of the (mistaken) way in which different versions of the doctrines of Autonomy and of 'Wertfreiheit' have been presented as establishing the neutrality of the purely technical adviser; and partly again because of the individualist and pluralist assumptions that were undoubtedly built into them. It was not — it could not be — that individuals might do or say things in a manner that would carry none of the implications of having chosen to do or to say one thing rather than another. It was rather that it seemed that it must always be possible for autonomous individuals explicitly to dissociate themselves from any 'values' of which they might become or be made aware as otherwise implicit in their theoretical or factual work. So at the level of that which was consciously discoverable and identifiable the ultimate responsibility for a man's 'values', for his identification or alignment with one group or another, must lie with the individual himself — whether by clear-sighted, mature choice or by the default of bad faith. This was and is a doctrine with strong and striking implications for education. It is true that there can be nothing in it officially to rule out a commitment to fanatic intolerance; from purely theoretical considerations, no value-judgements, it asserts, can follow. But if moral and personal maturity is characterised in terms of self-conscious choice of one's own leading values and if — which is a natural, if logically gratuitous assumption — one regards such maturity as desirable, then education must have as one of its objects the inculcation of habits of autonomous individual choice in matters of ultimate value. So, understandably, some have looked to 'the neutral teacher' to put his pupils in positions of learning to choose for themselves what side to be on independently of any pressure from him or of the clues that they might pick up if they knew what his own choices were. In so doing, he opts for the values of individual autonomy and responsibility in matters of ultimate evaluation. But, as we have noted, *no one* could seriously need to argue that his neutrality could be absolute or that his own attitudes were not directed by and to certain 'second-order values' rather than others.

But is this not irresistibly reminiscent of Norman's own declaration of faith? Yes; so perhaps the real area of disagreement between him and Mrs Warnock touches less on how far free and independent self-awareness and determination are ideally desirable than on the questions of the conditions under which they may be generally attainable, and for and by whom. Both of them are sceptical of any real or pretended neutrality on the part of the teacher as an instrument for encouraging the growth of autonomy. Mrs Warnock — perhaps — is prepared to accept the going institutions of society, give or take a reform or two; Richard Norman — apparently — is not. Given his radical questioning of the framework conditions under which alone it may be possible to realise what may still be called liberal values, it is hardly surprising that Norman should insist on the political implications of adopting positions of apparently substantive neutrality in the classroom; nor that he should in effect maintain that the urgent present need to change that framework demands a committed non-neutrality on most if not all of the substantive issues by which we and our students or pupils are confronted at present. For myself I should certainly agree that at the present time any thoroughgoing philosophy of education must also be an explicitly political philosophy. Norman may well take a wider view of the nature of politics than does Mrs Warnock; but whatever the disagreement between them on this general theoretical point, it needs to be assessed in the light of such disagreements as they may have on the actual policies involved.

To return, however, to the work of Lawrence Stenhouse, John Elliott[8] and their colleagues on the Humanities Curriculum Project, work which lies at the heart of so much recent debate in educational circles on the role of the neutral teacher, but to which neither of the two symposiasts make direct reference. I have already noted that the authors of this project make no bones about their explicit commitment to recognisably liberal values or the evident fact that the neutral teacher could not be supposed to remain neutral on all issues at once. As I understand it, moreover, their idea was not that teachers should adopt a neutral, chairman's stance in the teaching of any or all of the standard subjects on the school curriculum, certainly not in mathematics, but not even in regular history or literature periods. It was rather that certain periods on the timetable should be set aside for the discussion of what were called 'human acts in social

---

[8] To both of them I am much indebted for comments on an earlier version of these remarks.

situations and the controversial value issues they raise'. These were essentially topics on which different members of the contemporary community, including notably the parents of different pupils, might be expected to disagree even violently: disputed topics in current affairs. The working assumption was that in the normal course of events by which the teacher would make known to the class his own views on such controversial matters, the effect of his intervention, carrying inevitably the authority of his role as teacher, would be to stifle any movement in attitudes and further to entrench existing prejudices without any increase in general understanding either of each his own point of view or of those of others or, indeed, of what was at stake. If, on the contrary, the teacher stuck to the job of refereeing the rationality of the argument without letting his own views be known on the matter of substantive dispute (the main 'factual' elements being supplied in the form of material embodying the 'evidence' adduced by the conflicting parties in support of their respective positions), then, it was claimed, there would be gains first in the growth of all round understanding and hence, secondly, in the development of autonomy and mutual respect. Moreover, greater respect would have been shown by the teacher, functioning as he does in a pluralist society, not only for his own students, but also for the rights of parents and the diversity of their sincerely held views.

There are evidently a number of problems with this thesis over and above, if interwoven with, those arising out of the terminology through which it has been expressed. It assumes that for all main operational purposes a clear enough distinction can be made between the 'factual' and 'evaluative' substance of a viewpoint and the validity of the arguments by which it is supported. More problematically, the conflict or controversy in which the teacher is to remain neutral is to some extent interpretatively identified in advance; that is, the teacher has to adjust his neutrality not simply to the conflict as he may or may not find it arising in the classroom, but as he understands, selects and interprets it (or as he receives it already interpreted for him and his class in the materials prepared for their use) on the basis of evidently contestable general assumptions. (Here are the views of Mr Enoch Powell: there are those of Mr Bonham Carter. But expressed over what period of time, in what terms, adapted to what purposes and audiences, etc. etc.?) There are special difficulties concerning the key concept of 'understanding' and the fact that its connections with other key concepts in the area are also perhaps essentially contestable. Is there a clear conceptual gap between insightful theoretical understanding and given patterns of practical action — or must a modification in the one find necessary continuation in the other? Is there really any necessary connection between understanding a viewpoint and gaining an increased human respect for those who hold it? How far are these measurable empirical questions and how far 'evaluative' and conceptual — and how are these different aspects linked (or not, as the case may be)? Is there not some tension, both theoretical and practical, between the anti-authoritarian aspects of the Project's re-definition of the teacher's role and the conservatism implicit in its explicit respect for the *existing* range of opinions and attitudes on the matters of real dispute with which it is directly concerned?

I want to end, however, by focussing attention on certain other, themselves rather problematic aspects, or possible aspects, of the concept of neutrality, which seem to relate surprisingly directly to some of the ways in which the recommendations of the Project have been received in the teaching world.

There is a striking passage in Mary Warnock's paper which runs as follows:

> There is a psychological objection to the spectacle of someone's remaining neutral in a highly charged dispute about a subject which is supposed to affect everyone. . . . The neutral man cannot but seem uninterested. . . . There is a kind of nightmare in which one is in danger or pain . . . and all the time on the sidelines, there is a perfectly impassive observer, taking no steps to help or comfort, or even to acknowledge the existence of a crisis. It is the nightmare of the knitters at the guillotine, or of the absolutely rational parent. . . . Something of this night-

marish sense is conveyed to pupils whose teacher will not take part in a debate, or state his own moral view.[9]

As she presents this as 'a psychological objection', the suggestion might seem to be that it rests on contingent and verifiable matters of fact. If so, the Project evidence is, so John Elliott tells me, that the relevant facts are not all that secure. Many pupils certainly, appear to start by feeling disorientated and insecure at the apparent withdrawal of the quasi-parental authority of the teacher and the thoroughgoing modification of his role that goes with it. But it seems that it is in the end the teachers, or at any rate some of them, who feel themselves the more threatened, for whom the situation may take on an almost 'nightmarish' quality, but who, perhaps, find it natural to attribute the nightmare (in suitable transposition) to their pupils. (I am also told that such worries more usually afflict teachers who have not themselves actually worked on the Project.)

'The neutral man cannot but seem uninterested.' Why this 'cannot'? The neutral teacher surely does not have to pretend that he has no view of his own; he has only to conceal what it is. But he does not at all have to conceal his interest in the subject of debate. Nor does he necessarily have to be thought of as not taking part in it, only as not participating as a partisan. As for the knitters at the guillotine or the absolutely rational parent, who appear in nightmares . . . what are they doing in a philosophy of conceptual analysis?

The answer to this latter question may be obscure; but there is no doubt that to many contemporary philosophers from the continent they would carry messages coded in some sort of psychoanalytic terms. I do not pretend to have any clear view at the moment as to what to make of this fact — except to make the obvious point that its interest here has nothing whatsoever to do with the personal histories of particular individuals. Nevertheless, I am struck by the

[9] p. 167 f. Mrs Warnock goes on to say: 'Since a teacher has, it is argued, no right to impose his own prejudices on his pupils, he had better not voice them. He cannot expect his pupils to eliminate prejudice from their minds if he is seen to be guilty of prejudice himself. So runs the argument for neutrality.' As I hope to have indicted, the Humanities Curriculum Project's central argument for neutrality does not run in this way.

apparent relevance to the experience of the Humanities Curriculum Project of many of the dominant themes to be found in a recent article by Louis Marin on 'Le neutre et le discours philosophique'.[10] Taken out of context, the French term 'neutre' may, of course, be translated as either 'neutral' or 'neuter'; and much of Marin's (extremely complex) discussion of the topic makes use of this apparent ambivalence. We find ourselves here in an area of few basic conceptual implications (or semi-implications) and many conceptual associations of a more shifting nature. In default of a unifying theoretical structure the relationships between the two are far from easy to spell out. But simply to list some of Marin's themes:

(i)   The association of the idea of 'le neutre' with someone (or something) who neutralises or neuterises, that is who renders impotent.

(ii)   The sense in which a would-be neutral arbiter of an intrinsically unequal contest may be led so to act as to contrive between the contestants a new balance of equally opposing forces, a situation in which he can then act as deciding judge.

(iii)   The way in which the notion of neutrality is linked with that of a ceaseless but in itself contentless questioning. The neutral/neuter position is that of the man who is neither-the-one-nor-the-other of the rival contestants; he is the man who has no substantive position of his own, but who brings all positions into question. But this means that he has constantly to bring into question his own 'non-position'[11] *qua* 'neutre'; which leads to the further themes of

(iv)   The 'neutre' as committed to a continual reflexivity, a constant turning back upon itself, and at the same time to

(v)   A perpetual movement from one 'position' to another. Indeed, for Marin 'le neutre' is to be found in the

---

[10] To be found in English translation (in every sense of the word) in *Neutrality and Impartiality: the University and political commitments* (C.U.P., 1975). There are also plans for a French version of this book.

[11] In this sense the neutral position is, as Marin would also point out, Utopian in the strict sense of the word.

movement between 'positions', which are only so much positions to the extent that they are neeed to supply a principle of movement. This continual movement and questioning can present itself in one light as open-mindedness and in another as evasiveness, in one light as lack of commitment and in another as ultimate self-awareness.

As I said, I am as yet quite uncertain as to how all these themes should best be handled in their complex relationships to each other; but there is clearly much that is suggestive in them both of the activities of the 'neutral teacher' and of the joint fascination and fear that may so clearly be inspired by the overall theme of 'le neutre'. John Elliott has said, for example, that one of the most common reactions of 'misunderstanding' to the Project proposals has been precisely this fear on the part of teachers (objectors rather than practitioners) of being rendered powerless or impotent;[1][2] they are, as it were, being asked to give up their 'standing', to bring their own position and status into question. For Marin, 'le neutre' is to be found, in so far as he is ever to be found, at the originating heart of Western philosophy — he is the pure Socratic questioner, the 'neutral teacher' of those who engage in discussion with him. It is perhaps deeply significant that the theme of the value or danger, necessity or impossibility of neutrality should have re-emerged in so many reiterated forms in so much modern thought and practice at a time when the whole of this tradition of philosophy has been so widely called into question. And not least significant that people should now be concerning themselves with the need for or impossibility of a neutral teacher, 'le neutre' in the classroom where society stands *in loco parentis* to itself as it faces itself in the mirror of its own changing self-awareness across the generations.

As to the question, 'What are these arguments about the possibility, desirability or impossibility of neutrality really about?', it would seem as well, therefore, to cast about more widely for possible answers than one might normally do

[1][2] 'The words often used were "less than hman", "emasculated", "a mechanical robot".'

within the bounds of traditional conceptual analysis of the meaning of the term 'neutral' alone — though that, in fact, is complicated enough. But this is not something to be done lightly or at random. It is better to start by following Richard Norman's suggestion and, adopting a position of temporary neutrality towards ourselves, seeking to define more clearly our own explicitly existing areas of actual and potential disagreement.

PART FIVE:
ACADEMIC FREEDOM

13 Academic Freedom

STUART BROWN

What is an issue of academic freedom? When is academic freedom at stake? These are questions which do not, to my mind, admit of a general answer. For the phrase 'academic freedom' tends in practice to be used when some restriction is threatened or imposed on any of a wide range of privileges, rights and discretions enjoyed by academics, both individually and collectively. It is a phrase which belongs in particular to the repertoire of the orator in university politics. But there is no one cause whose defence occasions its use. Vice-chancellors and other university representatives talk about academic freedom when defending the principle that universities should be run by academics and not by the Department of Education and Science.[1] The phrase is also used when the tenure of a university teacher is thought to have been denied on political grounds rather than grounds of academic competence. Again it is used when freedom of speech is denied on a university campus or when publication is in some other way denied to controversial views within an academic community.

I do not believe that there is any factor common to all such cases. In this paper I confine myself to a particular class of cases in which academic freedom has been supposed to be at stake — namely, in which the *rights* of certain persons have been involved. I shall be concerned with the question whether, and if so how, the rights of academic freedom are to be taken to belong to a special class of persons (loosely referred to in what follows as 'academics') or whether they belong to citizens generally. My contention will be that the

[1] See, for example, V. H. H. Green, *The Universities* (Pelican, 1969) pp. 343ff.

rights of academic freedom attach to the *role* of academic person, properly understood.

In what follows I shall use the word 'academic' of persons who occupy a certain role and not in the narrow but common way to refer simply to those holding a certain sort of paid position in a university. For reasons which will become apparent the role of academic cannot be fulfilled in isolation from other academics. It will therefore involve membership of what I term an 'academic community'. I should stress at the outset that, when I use the phrase 'academic community' I do not mean 'university or similar institution'. The phrase is a vague one but not the less useful for that. (It is perhaps worth noting that we can count 'academic communities' by counting disciplines as well as by counting institutions.) I shall use the word 'role' in a familiar way to refer to a socially recognised function to which responsibilities and rights attach. Familiar roles include those of parent, teacher, magistrate and employer. Other classes of person, under such descriptions as 'football fan', 'art lover', 'cousin' and 'women', do not occupy social roles. Football fans have the right to travel by public transport and the responsibility not to cause damage to the vehicles in which they are travelling. But that right and that responsibility do not attach to them *qua* football fans. Those who defend the rights of women are not attempting to defend a special role for women. On the contrary they reject such a role.

We may distinguish, at least in a preliminary way, between two sorts of right which have been mentioned in connection with academic freedom. In the first place there are rights which citizens have, academics or not, on or off the premises of academic institutions. These include the right of free speech and the right not to be denied employment on account of one's religious or political creed. In addition to these civil liberties, however, academics are often thought to have rights *qua* academics. For instance someone offering a criticism of a prevailing theory for publication in an academic journal has a right not to have his contribution refused on doctrinaire grounds. And this right is not obviously reducible to one recognised even in a liberal society as belonging to the public at large. Consider, by contrast, the rights which would-be contributors to the correspondence columns of newspapers have. If their contributions are accepted then they have a right to have their views represented in substance and not shortened in such a way as to be distorted. But a newspaper editor has a different role from that of an editor of an academic journal. A newspaper editor is not obliged to give views which would displease his readers a fair hearing and is quite entitled to reject contributions in a doctrinaire way. It would, by contrast, be an infringement of the rights of his correspondents were the editor of an academic journal to do this, for reasons which will be made clearer at the end of Section I.

I distinguish these two sorts of right in a preliminary way since some have found it tempting to deny that there are any special rights which, in the context of a liberal society, should be accorded to academic persons as such. John Searle, for instance (*The Campus War* (Pelican, 1972) Ch. 6), holds that in a society which values intellectual freedoms generally the rights of academic freedom cease to belong peculiarly to members of academic communities. On his account the rights which in a repressive and authoritarian society take the form of exemptions for academic persons become in more liberal societies civil liberties to be enjoyed by all. Searle thinks he is justified in taking the rights of academic freedom to be, in a more liberal society, rights of a civic sort exercised in an academic context.

Searle refers to as 'the Special Theory' of academic freedom that traditional rationale which has been provided for according special rights to members of academic communities *as academic persons* which they and other citizens cannot lay claim to *as citizens*. To this he opposes his own 'General Theory' in which the rights of academic freedom are derived as a corollary to claims about 'the general social values of free inquiry and free expression' (op. cit., p. 177). He claims that all the rights of academic freedom are derivable within the General Theory and that many such rights are not derivable within the Special Theory, hence that the General Theory is preferable. I wish to maintain, on the contrary, that there are rights derivable on the Special Theory which are not derivable on the General Theory and that the General Theory involves an unwarranted confusion of academic freedom with civil liberties, hence that the Special Theory is preferable.

In what follows, therefore, I shall present a version of the Special Theory. I am in agreement with Searle that the right way to develop a theory of academic freedom is in an axiomatic manner, beginning with a set of assumptions and deriving the rights in question from them. An advantage of such a procedure is that, provided of course that the derivations are correct, there is some prospect of deflecting objections to respecting academic freedom to those assumptions. When I have considered objections to the account of academic freedom I put forward I shall then consider difficulties with the assumptions from which the rights of academic freedom are derived.

I A 'SPECIAL THEORY' OF ACADEMIC FREEDOM

The theory of academic freedom I shall present is in substance not original, though my version of it differs somewhat from that given by Searle. Because the substance is not novel, I shall present it dogmatically. The assumptions are as follows:

(A) Some value attaches to the advancement and dissemination of public knowledge or, which failing, to determining and making known which of competing beliefs it is most reasonable to accept.

(B) There are objective standards for deciding whether a putative proof does or does not constitute a contribution to human knowledge and for deciding which of competing beliefs it is most reasonable to accept. In the case of more complex or otherwise difficult justifications, moreover, there are objective standards by reference to which it can be decided who is competent to assess them.

(C) For the advancement of knowledge to be promoted those qualified to engage in inquiry should be free to pursue those lines of research they consider profitable and to make known the results of their inquiries to one another.

We may now define an 'academic community' as 'a body of persons concerned with the advancement and dissemination of public knowledge (etc.), including those competent to engage in and assess the results of complex inquiries'. Given that assumption (A) extends to matters which call for complex inquiries and — what is latent in (C) — that a claim is more likely to be right if it has survived the scrutiny of those competent to assess it, it follows that it is desirable that there should be well-functioning academic communities. And from (C) again it follows that certain freedoms should be allowed individuals as members of such communities.

It is tempting to move directly to the thesis that any restriction on the free pursuit and publication of research is a restriction of 'academic freedom'. But if academic freedom is something certain people have a *right* to and not merely an ideal state they hope for, this would be a mistake. Given, for example that there is only a finite amount of money available for research it is inevitable that some people will be prevented by lack of funds from undertaking the projects that seem to them most worthwhile. Again there may be insufficient space in appropriate journals for publication of all articles which are up to standard. These restrictions are, perhaps, matters for regret. But they could hardly be represented as infringements of anyone's rights. For it seems clear that the rights which are commonly defended in the name of academic freedom are rights which it is possible to respect. And if that is so, a restriction on academic autonomy — even though it may delay or prevent some new discovery — which was made inevitable by limited resources could not in a reasonable man give rise to the kind of moral indignation associated with alleged violations of academic freedom.

It seems, then, that the rights of academic freedom cannot be derived from the assumptions I have stated alone. Indeed I think it is not possible to identify an issue of academic freedom as an issue about rights by means of a wholly unhistorical account. In this respect, as I think in several others, academic freedom is analogous to freedom of the press. In both cases the rights have come to be recognised as a result of a conflict between the interests of powerful parties and the purposes of growing institutions. But for the existence of powerful parties with an interest in censoring for their own ends what is published in newspapers, we should not have had the concept of the freedom of the press. Nor should we, but for newspapers establishing themselves as institutions with objectives which, but for such censorship, they would fulfil. On an unhistorical account Galileo's treatment at the hands of the Inquisition would seem a paradigm case of an infringement of academic freedom. But there seems something anachronistic about so representing that case. True, Galileo was a university teacher (first at Pisa, then at Padua). His credentials as a member of an academic community could hardly be questioned. I am inclined to conjecture that what was lacking in seventeenth-century Italy was any widespread recognition of the truth of assumption (C) or appreciation of the — to us — obvious distinction between the man who is doctrinaire and one whose approach ai open-minded. At any rate, that distinction seems now to be indispensable in defining the recognised role of academic persons.

What I am suggesting is that, while the role of academic person and the attaching rights can be derived within a theory of academic freedom, the rights can only intelligibly claimed in an historical context where such a role is recognised. Outside such a context such freedom could only appear as a privilege. But to the role of academic person obligations also attach, to represent opposing opinions fairly, take responsible criticism of one's own position seriously, and so on. These are as integral to a theory of academic freedom as any rights. In this respect a theory of academic freedom is like a theory which provides a rationale for freedom of the press. Both specify the purposes to be served by freedom being respected, both allude to roles which can be fulfilled with greater or lesser responsibility. Both freedoms may be misused.

I referred earlier to the rights enjoyed by those who submit articles for publication in academic journals. Characteristically such persons have special qualifications and special kinds of employment. But the role of academic person is not confined, as is that of magistrate, to those on whom it has been conferred. Some specialised knowledge must have been acquired by with even an *interest* in many specialised areas of inquiry. But, with that qualification, anyone who offers a *bona fide* contribution towards the advancement of learning may be regarded as *eo ipso* a member of an academic community. Someone who sends an article for the consideration of an editor of an academic journal assumes, in so doing, the role of academic person with its attendant rights and responsibilities if he did not already occupy such a role.

The rights of academic freedom do not, therefore, belong to an elite group of persons. At the same time the existence of a special role of academic person is connected with the need for some people to invest a good deal of their time if the cause of learning is to be advanced. There are religious denominations who accept the 'priesthood of all believers'. The distinctness of that role is not lost by its being widely undertaken by members of those denominations. Nor are they inconsistent if they engage full-time clergy to devote themselves to discharging the responsibilities attaching to the role of priest. Similarly the role of academic person would not lose its distinctness were the advancement of learning a national obsession.

The rights of academic freedom, I am suggesting, attach to academic persons *as such*. Unlike those rights which attach to persons in the community generally, their infringement gives no moral right of redress. For the harm done is not strictly to an individual person but to the academic community. The right of free speech, by contrast, attaches to individual persons and it is they, individually, who are harmed if this right is denied to them. And moral, if not legal, rights of redress would attach to them in that event. If an academic person is prevented from teaching, then it is likely that where his academic freedom has been infringed an injustice will have also been done to him. But those harmed by the infringement of his academic freedom will include those who were to have been taught by him. The injustice, on the other hand, will have been done to him alone and it is in respect of that alone that he would have a right of redress. It is not surprising that issues of academic freedom promote solidarity amongst academics much as threats to the freedom of the press do amongst journalists.

I have hinted that the rights of academic freedom are rights members of academic communities have over against those who are doctrinaire. In one way I think it is worth stressing this. For insofar as education is directed to enabling individuals to work out for themselves what it is reasonable to believe, those undergoing education have rights which are closely analogous to the rights of academic freedom. Corresponding to the right to be free from what doctrinaire persons would impose externally on members of the academic community, there is a right not to be indoctrinated. If the enemy of academic freedom is not also an indoctrinator it is, I suggest, because he is denied the opportunity. And if the indoctrinator is not an enemy of academic freedom it is, I suggest, because he lacks the power.

To say this, however, is at best to bring two problems together. Both the theory of academic freedom and this educational corollary stand in need of an account of what it is to be doctrinaire or to indoctrinate. I think that the most satisfactory account will be given in terms of the intentions[2] of the doctrinaire man in relation to those whom he seeks to influence. It seems too crude, however, to say that the doctrinaire man *intends* to prevent free discussion or open-minded assessment of some doctrine. He *may* have such intentions, perhaps. But commonly the doctrinaire man does not *intend* to insure that the truth of some matter is not discovered. At least that description of his intentions might be alien to him. For the possibility that the doctrines he upholds might be false or at any rate call for further assessment might not — and I think quite characteristically *will* not — have occurred to the doctrinaire man.

What we have to say of the doctrinaire man, I think, is that he attaches a certain importance to some belief being held which cannot be explained by reference to considerations which relate to whether it is reasonable to hold it. A parent will drum into his children the belief that roads are dangerous

---

[2] I agree with much of what J. P. White has to say on this score. See his contributions to *Concepts of Indoctrination*, ed. I. A. Snook (Routledge, 1972).

to cross or that smoking is bad for their health. It may be important to him that his children should believe such things firmly. But an essential part of an explanation of why it is important to him will refer to his reasons for thinking those beliefs are true. He has nothing to lose if the child is able at a later stage to assess those beliefs in a critical way. The doctrinaire man, on the other hand, has an interest in upholding beliefs which is in conflict with an impartial interest in whether or not they are true. His purposes *are* frustrated if rational assessment of those beliefs becomes possible.

Rather more needs to be said about the doctrinaire man. But I would expect refinements and corrections of the account I have sketched to affect how an issue of academic freedom is to be identified in terms of a 'Special Theory'. The rights of academic freedom are not rights to any provision as such but rights over against those with an interest in upholding beliefs whose truth might be put in jeopardy by free inquiry. They are rights not to be prevented from exploring a line of inquiry or publishing its results for doctrinaire reasons.

II SOME OBJECTIONS TO THE 'SPECIAL THEORY'

I would like to consider briefly certain criticisms which have been made of the 'Special Theory' of academic freedom and to which therefore my account may appear exposed. I shall concentrate primarily on the objections raised by Searle.

(A) I have remarked that by no means all those rights which are defended in the name of academic freedom are derivable within a 'Special Theory'. Bodies such as the Council for Academic Freedom and Democracy certainly do concern themselves with cases which I would regard as having to do with civil liberties in academic institutions. And I do not of course wish to quibble at their doing so. But I think it helps to be clear about whether, in any given case, one is defending someone's right of free speech and is therefore concerned with his *civil* rights or whether one is defending academic freedom in some such sense as I have defined it. There was a recent case in which an academic person was prevented from giving a lecture at a university. A prominent member of CAFD supported his not being allowed his say on the ground that it was irrelevant in this case that this person was an academic. He was quite consistent, he argued, in believing in academic freedom and supporting those who prevented the lecture. And, supposing him to accept some version of the Special Theory and to be right in his expectation that the lecture would have consisted essentially in the defence of a political policy, his position would appear to have been consistent. What puzzled me about his defence of his position is that he was anxious to stress that had the academic in question been threatened with the loss of his job on account of his political views, that would have been quite different. He evidently thought that, in that event, it *would* have been an issue of academic freedom. I do not see how it could be argued that academics have a *special* right not to be dismissed for their political views. The right not to be dismissed for one's political views is surely a right academics share with other employees in the community. These rights are not in any way lessened by not considering them as rights of academic freedom.

It may appear, from my remarks, that Searle's objection that there are rights of freedom on the campus which do not follow on the Special Theory comes down to a terminological preference for using 'academic freedom' more widely. But there is more behind his objection than this. His view is that the rights of academic freedom can be derived from a generalised version of the theory, extended to provide a rationale for the social values of free inquiry and free expression. He does not show, however, just how this can be done. His objective is to provide some underpropping for the rights of teachers and students alike to engage in political discussion on campuses without interference from university authorities.

This raises issues about free speech. And while it may be right to extend to the community generally the rights of free inquiry by means of an extension of a theory of academic freedom, I do not think that the right of free expression can be derived within a theory about the conditions under which truth is most likely to prevail. It is tempting to defend free speech by arguing, as Mill did in *On Liberty*, that one cannot be certain that those with whom one disagrees are wrong. And I think that Searle has some such defence in mind. But, in the first place, it is doubtful whether political and religious creeds can be represented as straightforwardly right or wrong and some would argue that such notions do not get much purchase in connection with such creeds. That aside, however, it would seem to me unfortunate to rest the right of free speech on the foundation of scepticism. The right of the man who believes that the earth is flat or that the moon is made of green cheese to say so would be rendered highly precarious if the only reason we should respect that right is that there is some chance that, after all, what he believes is true. I think that a man's rights of free expression do not depend at all on there being some risk that he is right and should be respected even though no risk of error is incurred by not taking the views he expresses seriously.

A less precarious foundation for the right to have one's say is as one aspect of the liberty of action. Just as people are said to have a right to do ludicrous things provided they do no harm to others, so with the same proviso they may be said to have a right to *say* ludicrous things. Respect for another person's freedom of speech is founded, I would have thought, on the value attached to tolerance generally. That does have a connection with what it is thought a good society should be like. But it does not seem to me even remotely to connect with anything recognisable as a theory of academic freedom.

It seems to me that only a theory which confused the basis of the right of free speech with the right to make known the results of one's inquiries would seem to provide the basis both for the right to be free of the impositions of the doctrinaire and the right to engage in political discussions on the campus. Tolerance does not free us from the doctrinaire altogether, though it may curtail his harsher actions. The right to be free from the doctrinaire as such does not follow from the right to be tolerated. The basis of the rights of academic freedom are quite different from those which may provide a rationale for civil liberties.

(B) Another objection to the Special Theory which is pressed by Searle is that it has nothing to say about the rights of students. There are, of course, a lot of rights which may be claimed for students, including the right not to wear a gown or live in residence, not to mention more serious civil rights often denied them by university authorities. And none of these is derivable either within the Special Theory of academic freedom nor any other, if what I have said in the previous paragraphs has been right. But the right of students not to be indoctrinated can be derived as a corollary to the theory, as I have already tried to show.

(C) Searle also thinks it makes a practical difference which theory of academic freedom one accepts. He writes

> . . . university administrations which are committed to the Special Theory but not to the General Theory will feel themselves justified in placing all sorts of arbitrary restrictions on the out-of-class behaviour of students and faculty members, even though those restrictions cannot be justified as part of any coherent educational theory. (*The Campus War*, p. 180)

Since Searle thinks the Special Theory itself is to blame for these undesirable consequences, it is reasonable to suppose that he thinks the administrators he has in mind reason justly in the inference they draw from it. But they do not. The inference involves a quite egregious fallacy. It involves the following step:

If someone accepts p, he will *not* feel justified in doing Y

If someone accepts p, he *will* feel justified in doing Z.

It is, I think, quite obvious that an administrator or anyone else can quite consistently subscribe to the Special Theory and still attach importance to other rights of students and faculty members than can be derived within it. The Special Theory provides no justification whatever for failing to do so.

III SOME ATTACKS ON ACADEMIC FREEDOM

I suggested earlier that one advantage of an axiomatic theory of academic freedom should be that one can consider in relation to its assumptions attempts at justifying infringements of academic freedom. In some cases such attempts will involve rejecting or qualifying those assumptions. They will attempt to establish that some case in question is not one where therefore any rights are being infringed. There are also cases where the axioms are not called in question at all but where it is maintained that it is not possible to respect the rights one person has to academic freedom and at the same time safeguard the rights of others.

The assumptions I have stated are, I think, minimally contentious. And I am not sure how someone would proceed who wanted a round rejection of any of them. Nonetheless they are rather general. It may be objected, for instance to Assumption (A) that, as stated, it cloaks, because of its vagueness, a lot of important issues. Again, it may be objected to Assumption (B) that it does not hold for all cases.

Suppose, for example, an academic gives himself over to investigating the spiritual life of butterflies. His employers dismiss him, not on the ground that he is employed to do something else but on the ground that butterflies have no spiritual life. He might protest that here his academic freedom was being infringed. His employers, he might say, were doctrinairely assuming to be false some belief which his investigations might have shown to have some truth. They might reasonably be able to defend their action by denying that he had any rights of academic freedom in connection with this line of inquiry. To the extent that there is a problem about what would *count* as evidence in favour of saying that butterflies do have a spiritual life, there is a problem about assuming (B) to be applicable in this case and therefore a problem about identifying it as an issue of academic freedom.

There are of course more serious examples where the objectivity of the standards people employ in a particular area of inquiry is held in dispute. One way in which someone's academic freedom can be infringed is where his competence is judged by arbitrary standards. But it is necessary to this being an issue of academic freedom that there are, for that area of inquiry, objective standards by which his competence *could* have been assessed. Someone who claims his rights of academic freedom have been infringed because he repudiates the standards by which he has in fact been assessed cannot afford to be sceptical on this point.

I turn, finally, to the question whether it is possible for the rights of academic freedom to conflict with other rights. If there is such a conflict it would seem necessary to resolve it by an appeal to *utilitarian* considerations. The rights of academic freedom would then be no more indefeasible than are the rights of free expression.

One might attempt to defend a very rarified theory of academic freedom which denies the possibility of such a conflict. No harm can result from inquiry as such since, the argument would go, propositions are causally impotent. The truth can hurt no one. Such an argument, however, overlooks the fact that propositions are believed and harms result often enough from people holding beliefs which would not have resulted had they not held them. Nor can one patch up the theory by a distinction between research and its applications. For it is difficult to see how Assumption (A) could be defended if inquiry never yielded results of practical interest. And in any case the distinction between research and its application has no general validity in practice.

I am not sure that an overall rationale for Assumption (A) can be given. On the one hand I think it would be wrong to demand clear social benefits from every area of inquiry. There is no reason why inquiry should not be prised in itself. On the other hand I find it strange that people should apparently subscribe to the doctrine that *all* knowledge is good in itself. If that were so time would be well enough spent which was devoted to counting the hairs on people's heads or blades of grass on their lawns. Such activities would add to the stock of human knowledge but would generally be regarded as a waste of time from an *academic* point of view. I shall not attempt to identify a position between these two extremes. But I would like to suggest that utilitarian considerations do become relevant and considerations of the intrinsic value of research recede into the background where there is reason to believe that dissemination of its results will have harmful consequences. In these circumstances, it seems to me, it is merely obscurantist to represent the issue between those who favour having the results of the research disseminated and those who favour preventing it as one of *principle*. It need not at all be a question of who believes in academic freedom and who does not. The Special Theory, as I have stated it at least, does not place academic values above all others.

That being said, however, there are no cases where infringements of academic freedom can easily be defended by arguing that it would be harmful to upset a particular belief. Historically, I suppose, there can be few beliefs in whose name academic freedom has more often been attacked than the belief in the literal truth of the Bible. And undoubtedly there have been many who have thought it virtuous to hold this belief and vicious to promote doubt about it. It is possible that some felt that widespread doubt about the literal truth of the Bible would have resulted in a loss of moral standards and a drastic increase in attendant social ills. And this might be regarded as at once a justification for suppressing lines of research or at least publication of their results if they tended to promote such doubt and also a justification for indoctrinating the young with such a belief. Supposing we accepted those moral standards we might think that these people were quite wrong in their diagnosis of the consequences of widespread doubt about the literal truth of the Bible. Again we might believe that the evils of suppression and indoctrination would, on balance, be greater than the evils resulting from widespread doubt. But is it obvious that *if* their diagnosis had been correct their infringements of academic freedom would still have been unjustified?

This brings us to one of the most sensitive areas of contention relating to academic freedom. On the one hand, I think we are all inclined to say that — certainly from the point of view of academic detachment — no value should be given to holding a belief except insofar as that belief is reasonable. Only considerations, that is to say, which bear on the truth or falsity of a belief should be allowed to affect whether or not it is accepted. On the other hand, it is at least arguable that there are beliefs people ought to hold for other reasons and about which scepticism should be discouraged.

One such belief, perhaps, is the belief that races do not

differ genetically in respect of their abilities. A curious
feature of racialism is its ability to thrive on almost any piece
of evidence which points to something like an essential
difference between an out-group and the in-group. Members
of group A who dislike members of group B will *fear* them
the more if they have reason to believe that group B are in
some way genetically superior and *despise* them the more if
they have reason to believe the contrary. Any positive result,
it might be argued, of research into which is superior to
which in respect of any valued ability will encourage racialist
attitudes. This is one case where, perhaps, we cannot avoid
asking what good is supposed to come of such research. We
need to put, as it were, in the balance whatever good that
research might do and the harm we think results from its
publication. On the side of not preventing the research or
free dissemination of its results we must, of course, add
whatever harm we think is involved in this infringement of
academic freedom. Reasonable people may differ in the
conclusions they reach as a result of such an assessment. But
I would not expect them to use their belief in academic
freedom as an excuse for not embarking on it. The Special
Theory provides no such excuse.

14 Academic Freedom: A Reply to Dr Brown

A. PHILLIPS GRIFFITHS

Dr Brown sets out three asumptions which, he argues, lead to the conclusion that certain freedoms should be allowed to academic persons as such, given a certain historical and social context, and allowing that these freedoms may be overridden by other considerations. The case is, briefly, this: Knowledge can be advanced only if objective standards are applied in deciding what counts as its advancement. This is often difficult to decide, but we can use further objective standards to decide who is competent to decide. But those so judged competent by such objective standards must obviously be left free to decide what lines of research they consider profitable and what communications they need to make to others, if they are to advance knowledge.

Any discussion of moral, social, political, professional or other rights is always bedevilled by the immense complication of such notions. The history of the urgent, practical discussions of such matters is rife with example of failures to make important distinctions through failure to notice crucial differences. I might protect myself to at least some extent from this if I set out a few crude distinctions in terms of which I can argue.

There are rights which presuppose no correlative duties in their subjects, but rather in others towards them.

Thus, though I have a right, possessed by all, to express views on the treatment of Boadicea by the Romans, I do not have, in normal circumstances, any duty to do so. On the other hand, I would be wronged if others prevented me from doing so, except in the execution of their duties, such as superintending a quiet reading room. Such are rights of doing what one wants just because one wants to, so long as one's actions do not affect others in such a way as to give rise to rights on their part to prevent one. I shall call these rights *idiosyncratic* rights.

But there are other rights which, while they presuppose no duties correlative in the subject to the specific right concerned, arise out of other duties of the subject. Let us assume that everyone has a duty to contribute to the common good. Generally, what one has a duty to do one has a right to do (I fear I must skate over the exceptions to this); so everyone has a right to contribute to the common good. The duty to contribute to the common good is what has been called indirect or imperfect, in that it demands only that none of one's acts detract from the common good and some contribute to it, not that all one's acts contribute to it. But it is also peculiar in that it does not establish a duty to contribute to any specific aspect of the common good. This is because no one can contribute to every aspect of the common good (being at once a physician, a teacher, a farmer, a professional comedian, a plumber, a priest, etc. etc.,); thus one can have a duty to contribute only to some aspects of the common good, but this does not imply that there are some aspects of the common good rather than others, i.e. some particular aspects of the common good, to which one has a duty to contribute. On the other hand everyone has a duty not to detract from the common good[1], and one does so if one prevents another from contributing to the common

[1] In order not to spend too much time on prolegomena, I am forced to oversimplify. It is for the common good that wives should be concerned for the welfare of their families, and that judges should be concerned with the preservation of public order. Thus the wife must oppose the execution of her husband for a crime, whereas the judge must order the execution. It is thus the duty of each to prevent the effectiveness of the action of the other; thus each in contributing to the common good is attempting to prevent such a contribution on the part of the other, so at once contributing to and detracting from the common good. We can say that while what either or both parties wills to do may not be materially contributory to the common good, what each wills to do is formally so; but I think this would reflect only on the inner goodness of the two parties. However, such difficulties, which are immense, partly arising out of the fact that we have no concrete notion of the common good, can be ignored in so far as I am trying only to establish a terminology.

good. If therefore everyone has a duty not to prevent another from so contributing, everyone has the right, but not everyone the duty, to make a contribution to this or that aspect of the common good. This right, which presupposes no duty in the subject correlative to the specific right, I shall call a *common right*.

Sometimes it is necessary for the common good that what might have been a universal common right or some other right should be denied to all except a specified set of persons. Thus, for example, it is for the common good that children should be subject to direction inappropriate to mature adults. But if we said it was therefore the common right of every adult to direct any child, we would have to face the possibility of widespread and dreadful abuses, as well as subjecting children to maddening confusion. We might therefore decide that a child should be subject only to a small number of persons, and only to those who can be expected to love him: and on this ground limit this right, with respect to any particular child, to its parents. I shall call such a right a *special right*. But notice (and this will become important in my criticism of Brown's position) that, whatever the ground might be for limiting the common right to a specified set of persons, the set must be specified in terms distinct from their mere capacity to exercise the common right, otherwise there is no real limit and we are left with the original common right. Thus, the right to direct children is limited to a set of persons specified as *those who may be expected to love them*; not *anyone who is capable of directing them*, which would be no limit at all on the common right.

It can become, through particular circumstances, an individual's duty not merely to contribute in *some* way to the common good, but to contribute to some *specific* aspect of it. For example, as a contribution to some aspect of the common good (e.g. caring for the sick, maintaining social order, educating children) some person or group of persons may found or sustain some institution specifically for that purpose. Such an institution, as an artificial person, has a duty to pursue that specific aspect of the common good, for if it does not it infringes the comon right of its founders or sustainers in pursuing the common good. Such an institution may need to contract with real persons that they should pursue that specific aspect of the common good with which it is concerned. These then also have a duty to pursue that specific aspect of the common good, for otherwise they will frustrate the purposes of the institution and hence infringe the common rights of its founders. The institution, and its contractual servants, having a duty to pursue a specific aspect of the common good also thereby have a right to do so. I shall call this a *deontic right*. By doing so I do not imply that it is a stronger or even different right from the original common right: calling it a deontic right serves only to draw attention to the fact that there is, through particuar circumstances, a *duty* in the subject correlative to a particular common right.

My view is that everyone has both an *idiosyncratic* and a *common* right to academic freedom; and, in addition, some, including Universities and those contracted to them to contribute to knowledge by teaching and research (whom I shall call 'professors', whether or not they are paid, or how much they are paid e.g. whether they are paid within the 'lecturer' or *'privatdozent'* or 'assistant professor' scales) have a *deontic* right to academic freedom. But since it is my view that there is a universal common right to academic freedom, it follows that I must deny that anyone has a *special* right in this respect: and this is where I disagree with Brown, since he would limit the right to academic freedom to a particular group of persons, namely 'academics' (in his sense of the word). Brown is not to be taken to be implying by this that necessarily and in all circumstances there must be some who do not have this special right. The attribution of a special right implies no such thing: for example if some catastrophe resulted in the disappearance of everyone except licensed surgeons, the right to cut off people's limbs would still be a special right peculiar to surgeons; while the right to direct their children was a special right of Adam's and Eve's even before they had grandchildren.

If the reader finds these last remarks paradoxical, he should remember that a special right comes about when a common right, which inheres in persons as such, is limited to inhere only in persons *under some description*; but that still

leaves it open that under certain circumstances everyone may
fall under the description in question. (Brown makes this
point clear in his example of the universal priesthood.)

Brown generates his special right from his three axiomatic
principles (which I would claim generate a common right) by
the introduction of such a description, namely 'academic'.
This is the description of a person as occupying a certain role.
The notion of an academic role, and with it that of an
academic community is, he says, vague, but not useless for all
that. I agree that it is vague, but not so vague as to escape all
confusion. I shall argue that in so far as it is not confused, it
is useless.

As to the confusion: In introducing the term 'academic'
Brown puts it alongside 'parent', 'teacher', 'magistrate' and
'employer', rather than 'football fan', 'cousin', 'woman' and
'art lover'. All of these terms except 'cousin' and 'woman' are
applied to persons in respect of their engaging in certain
activities. In the case of the first group, sometimes the
activity itself involves the carrying out of some obligation (I
presume an employer, for example, is one who in virtue of
employing is immediately under an obligation to pay his
employees; otherwise he is not an employer but a slave-
owner). While this might not apply to all such terms, it is
surely true in every case that whoever engages in the activity
proper to the term and to whom the term applies immediately becomes subject to a whole set of (positive)
obligations (which may vary from society to society)
regarding the activity. On the other hand there seems to be
no such obligations laid upon a football fan or an art lover
which are not laid on anyone else (football fans are under the
obligation to respect railway property to the same extent and
for the same reasons as everyone else). Roughly, they can
please themselves how they engage in their activity. But is
this not also true with the sorts of activities proper to
academics? Let us take an actual case, that of a musicologist.
When Albert Schweitzer had finished his great work on Bach,
he decided to work as a physician in Africa. Doing so, he
seems to have contributed to the common good more than
most. But every man needs to relax, and perhaps he got very
interested in Buxtehude. Perhaps he could have written a

great book on Buxtehude, indeed perhaps he did and didn't bother to publish. Asked why, he might have replied that his real work was with the sick and he engaged in musicological study no more than was necessary for recreation, and he could not allow the distractions which would result on his publicly engaging in his studies. Surely, everyone would agree Schweitzer had acted within his rights, even if they thought it a pity. A parent must not neglect his children, a teacher fail to give lessons, a magistrate to sit and give judgement, an employer fail to pay his workers or neglect their safety. But what does a musicologist have to do? He can study when he likes, or not as he likes, and he can publish, or not, as he likes (unless perhaps that means that he is a totally useless individual in every other way). To that degree he seems to fall in with the football fan and the art lover.

As to the uselessness: The role is not confined, says Dr Brown, to those on whom it is conferred, as in the role of magistrate. Nor is that of parent, except for the adoptive parent. Nevertheless, there are pretty clear and explicit conventions as to who is a child's parent and on whom the various obligations and rights lie. These do seem to be cases of persons having special rights, but in each case the special rights to do certain things are in respect of activities distinct from the description which defines the group. (Thus employer: special right: *to exact work from another*; description: *one who pays wages*. This (positive) special right may attach to others under a different description: e.g. *slave-owner, spouse*.) But when Brown gives a clear characterisation of a criterion permitting the application of the description 'academic', this requirement is not satisfied. The description under which persons having the special right of academic freedom falls turns out to be 'offering a *bona fide* contribution towards the advancement of knowledge'. But this description is also precisely of what activity a person falling under it has the right to do, such that an interference with it is an infringement of academic freedom.

If what I say is correct, then the introduction of the role of 'academic' so defined can do no work and make no difference to what is anyway a common right. This certainly appears to be so in the case with respect to the only clear example which Brown gives of what he regards as an infringement of the special right of an academic: the refusal by the editor of a learned journal, on doctrinaire grounds alone, to publish a *bona fide* contribution to knowledge written by an 'academic'. If an academic is one who offers a *bona fide* contribution to knowledge, then a refusal to publish a *bona fide* contribution to knowledge written by an academic is no different from a refusal to publish a *bona fide* contribution to knowledge(written by any person).

Contrast Brown's account of the role of an 'academic' with that of a role which clearly and obviously introduces special rights. A man licensed to practice as a surgeon has a right which is denied all others: he can cut people's arms and legs off with their consent. Now, to be licensed he has (one hopes) to prove a certain competence. But it is not the competence itself which confers the right, since if he is struck off for malpractice — e.g. advertising — he loses his right but not his competence. Now I might sometimes be competent to operate on someone, and offer to do so for half the licensed surgeon's fee, with the enthusiastic consent of the impecunious patient. But I still would have no right to do so, nor would my competently doing so save me from conviction if I were prosecuted for mayhem. But if we abolished the licensing of surgeons, and allowed anyone to operate who was able to offer a *bona fide* surgical operation, we would be saying 'everyone has the right to perform surgical operations if he can'. The propriety of performing an operation and the impropriety of interfering with one would have passed from a consideration of *what sort of person is doing it* to a consideration of *what is being done.*

It follows from Brown's third assumption that *anyone* competently pursuing some line of research should not be prevented from doing so or publishing his results, on irrelevant grounds. This is to establish a common right; and I have argued that his introduction of the notion of an academic person cannot serve in any way to establish a special right, or that the right of academic freedom is a special right.

I fear that what I have said so far has been somewhat negative; but I want now to show how certain deontic rights of academic freedom can be generated from the common right, and how in doing so one can deal with certain particular issues.

Let us start with the right, which I claim resides in everybody, of pursuing such research of which they are capable and publishing their results. We must all respect this right, because not to do so is to detract from the common good by damaging the advance of knowledge. To respect this right is, however, to do no more than sit still and let others get on with their enquiries without interference. But there is point in this only if there are quite a number of people who from time to time do engage in such activities; and perhaps if we just sit still and avoid interference, there will not be enough people with the necessary resources to advance knowledge. So some of us, individuals like William of Wykeham and Wolfson, or Governments, decide actively to promote the advancement of knowledge by setting up institutions which will give people the wherewithal, the leisure and the funds, to pursue research and communicate its results. Since the process won't go on for very long unless more people are brought into the endeavour and helped to acquire the necessary competence, these institutions, or at least some of them, will need to undertake teaching. I propose to call any such institution a University, so long as this sort of research and teaching is integral and necessary to its function. Of course many, if not indeed most, Universities also fulfil other, though compatible, functions; while many institutions called universities are not Universities in this sense.

For those appointed by Universities for that purpose — professors — engaging in enquiry and publishing results is a deontic right: not merely the common right which everyone has, but a duty lying on them. Their duty is to the University. The University in laying such a duty on them, and having as its primary function the advancement of knowledge, has a duty to create the conditions in which such advancement is possible: and this includes fostering and protecting the freedom of its members to carry out their duties. It also includes fostering and defending the freedom of anyone so engaged — that is, fostering and defending the common right — since every professor needs as much help as he can get. Everyone has a right to pray, but it would be particularly anomalous if the Church were not the first to comdemn attempts of others to interfere with this activity.

What I am trying to emphasise is this. Professors do not have a special and peculiar right. Rather, they have the same right of academic freedom as everyone else; whereas University authorities have a special and peculiar duty to see that they and others respect it. An attack by University authorities on academic freedom is doubly reprehensible.

For the rest of this paper I shall examine the ways in which from my position certain supposed matters concerning academic freedom should be judged. I find that many of the specific conclusions I draw are very different from those reached by persons usually most vocal in the defence of what they take to be academic freedom. I would regard most of them as the enemies of it. I think this is because if we regard the advancement of knowledge as important enough to set up institutions whose primary function is to promote it, then the needs of such institutions will be considerations we must weigh *against* other prima facie rights which might be claimed, including civil rights. Because many of the defenders of academic freedom are subject to some of the muddles which Brown rightly exposes, what they are often concerned about is not really academic freedom at all, but certain civil rights; and they will defend the exercise of these civil rights even if it militates against the academic function of the University and the academic freedom of its members. Of course, I doubt whether rights of academic freedom could ever totally override any of the important civil rights: but I would hold that they can properly restrict them. People should not be denied the right of effective political judgement, which requires them to engage in certain political activities; but perhaps they should sometimes be denied the right to exercise these rights on University campuses. But more of that specific case later: first I must look at the particular examples mentioned by Dr Brown.

The case which seems uppermost in Brown's mind is the right of an academic not to have an article refused by the editor of a learned journal on merely doctrinaire grounds. This supposes that if the editor of a learned journal follows a doctrinaire policy, he is impeding the advancement of knowledge. But just such a policy might sometimes be considered necessary to the advancement of knowledge. It might be thought that some doctrine or approach to a subject ought to be given as good a run for its money as possible; and some quite respectable journals have been founded to do just that (e.g. *Analysis, Radical Philosophy*). Brown might reply that the founders and editors of these journals were not doctrinaire; they would be prepared to defend their views of the nature of philosophy by giving reasons. But I can't see that this fact, if it is a fact, makes any difference. As far as what gets printed in these journals is concerned, it's all one. And I think that the infrastructure of the pursuit of knowledge has got to be like this: we must submit all our theories to criticism, but there must be people who defend theories so that they are not too readily brushed aside, and who are given time to work out their fruitful implications.

The only other application which Brown makes of his special theory is the case of an academic who gives himself over to investigating the spiritual life of butterflies. This academic's exployers dismiss him, not on the ground that he is employed to do something else but on the ground that butterflies have no spiritual life. Brown says that this can be identified as an issue of academic freedom only if his second principle applies: that is, if the area of his research is one in which there can be objective standards for deciding whether anything is a contribution to knowledge. Deciding this requires we have to decide whether butterflies have a spiritual life, or whether there are any objective standards for deciding this. But I think this makes the case look unnecessarily difficult. For, if the case we are discussing is that of a professor dismissed by a University, considerations relevant to deontic rights come into play. The University has a duty to pursue knowledge by teaching and research. It must appoint people who contract to do that, thus having a *duty* to do that laid on them by the University. It is not a fulfilment of a duty to carry out a certain project to employ an agent who will have the duty of carrying it out unless the agent is able to carry it out. If I announce that I am going to devote myself to virology, my University would have good ground for dimissing me not beause there are no viruses but because I personally am incompetent in that field and would not be able to study viruses. A University is not doing its duty if it merely assures itself that some necessary condition of a professor's carrying out his duties (such as the existence of viruses) is satisfied: it must ensure positively that the professor is able to carry them out. It is the duty of the University to employ only competent professors; to protect in every way possible their freedom to do their duty; and if they later become unable or unwilling to carry out these duties, to remove them from their posts (to use here the words of my own University's Statutes). So if I, acting together with other professors on behalf of the University, had to consider the dismissal of Dr Brown's butterfly psychologist, we would probably ask to see the details of his research programme. He might well turn out to be a Skinnerian behaviourist, and produce a perfectly coherent programme of S—R experiments with butterflies, testing some highly interesting hypothesis. But if he meant what I think Brown meant him to mean by the spiritual life of butterflies, I predict quite confidently that we would recommend dismissal, if we had the courage. To put it differently, difficulties in applying Brown's second principle should not cause difficulties about whom Universities should employ, because it is not that Universities are wrong not to employ people whom they cannot prove are incompetent, but they are wrong to employ people whom they cannot assure themselves are competent.

There is however a rather analogous problem which is more difficult. How does a University decide, if it is not merely a matter of scarce resources, that some new subject will not be pursued or taught within it? It is no good saying that it would be failing in its duty, and committing a wrong analogous to an infringement of academic freedom, only if it refused to accept a subject which had gained the respect of the academc community generally: because 'gaining the respect of the academic community' is to a considerable extent constituted by 'admitted as a proper subject of study by Universities'. It is clearly damaging to the advancement of knowledge and a failure of duty on the part of Universities if proper subjects of academic study are arbitrarily excluded by them. But having said that, I do not know what more to say, except to suggest some institutional arrangements which would be a safeguard. One such arrangement would be to have, all over the world, hundreds of Universities all competing with each other to establish the highest academic reputations and to be in the forefront of intellectual progress, and lots of intellectually lively people who are anxious to reap the material and other rewards offered to those who can help Universities to do this; and lots of journals, doctrinaire and otherwise, in which they can publish their research. Such a system would have the disadvantage that a lot of time and point would be wasted on a great deal of bogus and trendy junk; but one would hope that time would sift out the dross. In such a situation it might still be said that there are a lot of subjects of study finding it impossible to break into the academic establishment. It would be apposite to reply that there are also a lot of burglars finding it impossible to break into people's houses.

Brown points out one important possible ground for limiting academic freedom. It is, where certain research causes scandal, and the harm of that is greater than the harm caused by limiting academic freedom. An example of this would be research into genetically based differences causing scandal by inclining the ignorant towards racialism. Brown says it is no excuse for not trying to assess what causes scandal that such an assessment might justify a restriction of academic freedom. I think that must be right as a general point. But the particular example is far too close to urgent contemporary cases to treat it as a mere fictitious thought-experiment relevant to an abstract general principle. The Universities have a paramount duty to protect academic freedom, and to do so until it is established beyond reasonable doubt that scandal is caused to an extent that this important duty must be overridden. The actual situation is that people have been shouted down and physically attacked as scandal-mongers where there is no objective evidence whatever that their work (in the case of Jensen and Eysenck work explicitly motivated by humanitarian concern) encourages racialism.[2] Universities have often failed to meet their protective duty in this matter. This is not because they have been convinced that academic freedom should be restricted but because they have been inadvertent, lazy, muddle-headed and intimidated.

Is it any infringement of academic freedom if the University authorities interfere with the freedom of professors, students and others to engage in political activities on campus? (By political activities I mean the holding of political meetings to promote the aims of this or that political group, the sort of meetings that might just as well take place in Trafalgar Square or the local Temperance Hall, not the sort of discussions that go on in departments of politics or among friends.) I think Brown would agree that it is not, any more than a refusal to allow Senate House to be used to promote the sales of Mars bars. There might, of course, be other reasons why the University should not interfere. In the first place, no one should interfere with anything anybody wants to do without good reason. But, furthermore, it might promote the academic life of the University to allow and encourage multifarious activities including political ones in which people meet informally, establish fruitful relationships, and increasingly identify their lives with the life of the University and increase their loyalty to it. Again, it might be that any such interference would cause such a reaction that it would bring the academic life of the University to a stop. On the other hand, if, as has certainly often been the case recently, allowing such activities on campus leads to such noise, disturbance and disruption that the proper function of the institution is affected, to the extent that the members of the University concerned with

[2] See Antony Flew, 'The Jensen Uproar', *Philosophy*, Vol. 48, No. 183.

the advancement of knowledge are prevented from fully carrying out their tasks, Universities would be justified in preventing any further political activity on campus whatever; if only they could.

The advantage of having some sort of theory of academic freedom, rather than some incoherent hodge-podge of sentimental slogans, is that it enables one to concentrate on essentials by making clearer what *is* essential rather than peripheral. Otherwise one can with the best will in the world make serious mistakes. I did, when in the days of my youth I went to talk to the University authorities about a meeting which the University Conservative Association proposed to hold with Mr Patrick Wall, M.P., who at that time was regarded as a walking provocation to left-wing violence. It was clear that the University authorities didn't want the meeting held. I was solemnly warned that any damage caused would be charged to the Conservative Association rather than its perpetrators, that the meeting could be allowed only if it were restricted to ticket holders, and so on. On the day, it seemed some administrator had given orders for all the lights to be cut off in the hall. The Union of Students refused loudspeaker facilities to which the Association were entitled, and the left turned up in force to howl the speaker down. I was so outraged by all this harassment from all quarters that I delivered a very angry attack on the University authorities, the Students' Union and the left-wing disruptors, and saw that this attack got into the hands of the local press. What I did in no way improved matters at the University and probably didn't do the University any good in the area. I now think I was almost entirely wrong. What I should have done was try to persuade the Conservatives to hold the meeting in the town (leaving the police to deal with the Vice-Chancellor, the President of the Students' Union, etc., if they tried to interfere with us). Mr Patrick Wall is the kind of sturdy plant whch can sprout anywhere, but it is only in University groves that such tender shoots as philosophy and mathematics can flourish. I say I was almost entirely wong, in that there is still one criticism which might be levelled against the University authorities. If the exercise of civil rights has to be limited on campus for good reason, this should at least be done impartially with regard to all political groups. But of course, it wasn't that the University authorities didn't think it right to treat the left in the same way as the Conservatives, it was simply that they wouldn't dare to do so, given their concern for keeping the institution working, and the fact that the left, unlike the Conservatives, were on the earnest look-out for any excuse to smash things up. As it was, that was held off for a whole year.

University administration is, like every art, the art of the possible. And the very real factors militating against academic freedom are the ones that I should have been worrying about then as well as now.

If a politician like Patrick Wall, or for that matter a professor like Chomsky, is prevented from coming onto the campus to fulminate about this-or-that, it is a sad thing, but no kind of denial of acadmic freedom. On the other hand, if a group of University historians wanted to include in their research seminar an ex-Cabinet Minister who had also once been a don, and who had published works of academic distinction in political theory or constitutional history, then for the University authorities or anyone else to prevent it would be a clear infringement of academic freedom, whether the man concerned were Richard Crossman or Enoch Powell. That the duty of Universities to protect academic freedom is not merely an academic matter for us is shown by the fact that if any group of historians did try to bring Enoch Powell into a British University for such a purpose, they would be prevented fom doing so.

This conference is about philosophy of education, and even if it were possible to claim that among the anecdotage I have offered so far there is a tinge of philosophy, what I have so far said hasn't much to do with education. In discussing academic freedom in the context of Universities, I have considered Universities only in so far as their function is to promote enquiry and research and to teach future enquirers and researchers. Neither of these is a specifically educational function except in the broadest and vaguest sense of the word. But those institutions called universities devote most of their efforts and resources to education. So, of course, do many other institutions — all those polytechnics and art colleges which are Universities, and all primary schools and secondary schools, and those polytechnics and art colleges which are not Universities. Now why should Universities, as well as those as those other institutions, have any concern with education? I suppose the best answer would be some historical explanation. But people might want to give some rationale for it, even if that has nothing to do with why it actually happens. The rationale would presumably be that it is thought that there is some peculiar advantage for people who need higher education, but who are not going to be academics themselves, to be taught by those actively exploring the frontiers of knowledge, rather than by persons well informed in their subjects and specially trained to teach but not devoting time to original research or scholarship. If this is true, it gives a reason for increasing Universities beyond the number which might be thought to be needed for the advancement of knowledge. Nevertheless, if it is thought important, for whatever reason, that the lay public should be educated at universities which really are Universities, then the principles of academic freedom which apply to Universities should also apply to those Universities whose major effort is education, since that effort is not essential but merely accidental to their purpose. For if these principles are denied, then one result will be that it will be at universities which are not Universities that the public are educated. Another result will be that there will be no Universities in Britain, since here all British Universities fall into the class of those whose major effort is educational.

Recently, there has been pressure, not entirely unsuccessful, to give students an effective voice in the decision-making processes of institutions of higher education. There may be a growing conviction that in general people should not only have those civil rights which might give them some, albeit minimal, influence on national and local politics, but that they should have an effective say in any institutions to which they belong and which affect in any serious way what happens to them; and that this applies to educational institutions as much as to industry. As Mr Dick Atkinson has put it: students, with staff, should 'gain control over their joint work situation, so making it relevant to contemporary life'. Whatever we say about other institutions this cannot apply to Universities. Mr Atkinson's formula is in fact a proposal to restrict academic freedom. If academics are to be restricted in their activities to matters which are relevant to contemporary life, then the direction of their research and their publication of it will be constrained by an arbitrary, irrelevant and doctrinaire check, and they will have to proceed not in accordance with the logic of their subjects and the way problems present themselves to them, but according to what Mr Atkinson thinks is important.

I may be being unfair to Mr Atkinson here, and I certainly am if he is one of those who deny, because of the objective role which Universities must play in the third stage of capitalism, that the advancement of knowledge by teaching and research in Universities is not only desirable but possible. Anyone who denies that, ought to reject my whole account (and Brown's). If in fact the whole enterprise of promoting the advancement of knowledge in Universities is digging for fools' gold, then perhaps the only thing those benighted beings who find themselves in Universities can do is to follow Mr Atkinson's advice; or perhaps even better to leave the University and do something worthwhile, meanwhile doing all they can to get rid of those institutions supposed to be Universities from outside rather than from within.

But, sticking to my own presuppositions, I think it is a mistake to give students much power over University matters because whatever benefits there may be for future employees, business men, etc., to receive an education at the hands of professors, the academic aims which are the primary concern of the University are not likely to be of major importance in the interests and values of such students. The academic function of the University tends to be carefully protected from interference by University lay councils; so also it needs to be protected from interference by other lay persons, such as students. The more so, in fact; because one finds that in accepting membership of a University council, lay members do so with the intention of helping the institution to fulfil its purposes as laid down in its Charter; whereas most students have no such concern in engaging in University politics.

I must confess here however that my conclusion is a bit abstract, in that my resolute distinction between what are called universities and Universities protects what I say from having any obvious application to any given institution. Nevertheless, I would claim that the University of Warwick is a university which is also a University, and I believe many other British universities are. But then the question is, ought *all* of these to *be* Universities (particularly when many polytechnics seem hell bent on turning themselves into Universities)? A negative answer might well be given to this question by someone who thought that the needs of thousands of students are not being properly catered for in Universities, but would be better served in other sorts of institution, while the advancement of knowledge by teaching and research could be quite sufficiently served if there were far fewer Universities. I think there would be nothing wrong in principle if such a person were to urge that many existing Universities should change their nature, ceasing to be Universities and becoming institutions of higher education with a different primary aim. But if my conclusion is for this reason a bit abstract, it is not without one important application. If the pressure of students' needs leads, and possibly should rightly lead, to the erosion of the University function of many of the existing Universities, it is important that it should not happen everywhere. We should be open- and clear-minded about this, and instead of crippling every University in the country to some degree, radically change some and at the same time protect the others. Otherwise, unless we create some Universities with no educational responsibilities at all, we may find that the only Universities left in Britain are Birkbeck College and possibly the Open University: since in my experience the students of these institutions have aims and interests which set a high value on the academic for its own sake. On the other hand, there would be no need for such desperate measures if we could feel assured that the 18-year-old school leaver who means to become a salesman, a welfare worker, an engineer or a civil servant when he grows up will receive great benefit from spending three years at a University; so long as we do not ask him to run it.

We sometimes hear of issues supposed to be about

academic freedom, in institutions which nobody would claim to be Universities, such as colleges of arts and crafts, and even schools. Similar issues can arise in Universities, because Universities like other institutions I have mentioned are concerned with education. But I think these issues are quite different from those I have discussed concerning academic freedom, and they should not be confused with them. There is a freedom which does not attach to the professor as such, but to the teacher as such. Moreover I think this is a special, not a common, right. The members of the teaching profession have responsibilities to their pupils: charged with having a concern for them, they should be chosen in part according to whether they do manifest such a concern and have the judgement which its exercise requires. Having the duty to manifest this concern, they must have the freedom to exercise it. People must not, except in the cases where this duty is clearly being neglected or this freedom clearly being abused, come between teacher and pupil any more than they should come between doctor and patient. The teacher has this professional privilege because of his professional responsibilities; it is abused when aims other than concern for the pupil as a pupil — such as sexual aims or political aims — direct his activities. Unless the profession can manage to stick to this as a part of their professional ethics, the privileges of the profession may not long survive. Once the public realises that a large number of teachers are using their privileged position to seduce the bodies and the minds of their pupils, public acquiescence in their independence is likely to be withdrawn. And this truth will out: teachers sometimes fail to realise (some of mine did, and were very surprised when I took my gentle revenge) that what enormities they practice on their victims in private places may be safe enough at the time, but their pupils grow up, or get away, and remember. And professors should realise, even if common decency does not move them, that if they lose their professional standing as teachers they are liable to lose their academic freedom as well.

Finally I would like to discuss another, and I think very important aspect of academic freedom which is rarely referred to, and in general not observed.

I agree with Brown in basing the desirability of many civil rights, not on any utilitarian consequences of allowing free expression, but rather on one's simply finding it objectionable that people should be interfered with in doing whatever they want to do, without good reason. The kind of academic freedom I have been talking about is not justified in this way; it is a common right based on considerations about what is necessary to the advancement of knowledge. Nevertheless I think there is an additional justification of academic freedom, which rests on the same basis as the justification of the civil right of free expression, that is, on the basis of an idiosyncratic right.

Academic activities can be very roughly identified as those concerned with the pursuit of truth and understanding. These activities, like others differently identified such as love-making, religious observance, conversation, sport, and artistic activities, are the objects of natural human inclinations, and things which many human beings value for themselves. The pursuit of truth requires the co-operation of others, and this requires the free exchange of views, conclusions and objections. To prevent, say, an amateur historian from communicating with other historians or indeed anyone who can help him do history, when he wants to do history, is objectionable for at least the same reason that it is objectionable to prevent people playing football or drinking beer, if they want to. But perhaps it is more objectionable, in that one might judge that pursuing history is more serious, more important to the development of the individual and satisfying something deeper in him than playing football or drinking beer; or perhaps not, in which case playing football and drinking beer can be very important.

Now this right, to engage in valued academic activities and to make such communications as are necessary to do so, is one attaching to everybody. One might think that in Britain this right is universally respected: no legal or other constraints prevent anyone who wishes, and who can, taking up history or physics or archaeology. But in an important sense this right is not respected.

Most felicitous human activities require some material or other facilities. Mountain climbing requires access to mountains, art appreciation requires access to paintings, preserving health requires access to doctors and hospitals, and developing academic activities requires access to academics (not necessarily professors, but let us ignore that point). All these facilities are natural or social resources; and if men have a right to pursue these felicitous activities they have a right of access to such resources. Limits on their rights of access constitute property, and in general the system of positive property rights simply consists in limits on the freedom of some to use natural and social resources. Property there must be, though not necessarily private property: access to these resources requires some arrangements. For exampe, one might want to exclude from hospitals those who are not sick, or from mountains those who are. Access to academic resources (by which I mean *academics*) is no longer thought to be rightly limited to those who can afford to pay for it: most people accept that education, including initiation into academic pursuits, should not be the preserve of the wealthy. In theory, one of these limits is that only, though all, people who are capable of academic pursuits should be given access to them. In fact, there are a whole set of quite different limits.

The artificial limits set on access to academic facilities are *idiotic:* so much so that one has only to list them for the point to be made. In order to take up academic pursuits, which require access to academics, one must be about 18 or 19 years old. One must have performed at a certain level, or at any rate have been lucky in being assessed to have so performed, in writing a series of short essays over a period of about two weeks in the June of one's 18th year. One is not allowed to earn one's living: one must be unemployed, though in some cases this is mitigated by the provision of an income at near starvation level. One must, in order to continue having access to the necessary resources, study to pass examinations for a degree. Often one is liable to be turned away unless one survives a series of tests meant to determine that this is what one is doing. This means that for a sixth or more of the time one might spend with academics one is denied this, because at first one is swotting to get through these tests and then afterwards the academics are marking them. It also means that even when one has been given access to the necessary resources, because one is tied to a choice between degree syllabuses one is often forced to study many things one is not interested in and not allowed to study many things one is interested in. On these conditions, one is allowed access for three years, but unless one wants to continue to pursue these delights for money as a full time occupation, one is then made to stop and never allowed to do it again. On the other hand, no very serious commitment to academic pursuits is required, and indeed any long term commitment to academic interests is usually lacking.

I admit of course that these limits are not absolutely rigid, and that a number of people manage to exercise their rights despite them, not only at Birkbeck and the Open University, but also in more conventional establishments. But even if, as I have no ground to hope, the recommendations of the Russell Report are fully implemented, the situation will remain much as I described it. The freedom to learn is not respected.

Rejoinder: Roles and Special Rights

STUART BROWN

Many rights and duties other than the rights of academic freedom attach, on my view, to the role of academic person. One such right connects with the right to free criticism of a theory. And that is the right to have one's criticisms taken as seriously as they deserve. Corresponding to this right on the side of Professor Griffiths I have an obligation to give careful consideration to the objections he makes to my account of academic freedom. Common courtesy requires that I thank him for commenting so attentively and so fairly. If I am not so attentive in my rejoinder it is because replies to replies quickly lose the interest of those not party to the discussion. I shall therefore content myself with trying to show that the case against a Special Theory is not as conclusive as Professor Griffiths' persuasive paper may make it appear. I shall comment briefly on what I take to be his main objection. Then I shall try to show that the rights of academic freedom cannot be isolated, as they are on Griffiths' account, from certain other rights and duties and how these attach jointly to what I call the *role* of 'academic person'. Finally, I shall try to explain why I find Griffiths' account unacceptable and how I would now qualify my own.

THE ALLEGED USELESSNESS OF THE NOTION OF AN 'ACADEMIC', CONCEIVED AS A ROLE

I think that Griffiths is quite right to insist that, where a group of persons (parents, licensed surgeons, or whoever) have special rights, 'the special rights to do certain things are in respect of activities distinct from the description which defines the group'. (p. 226)

243

It seems clear that, if there is a right of way across a particular field, it would be silly to suggest that this is a special right, namely, one attaching only to whose who are able to walk. And I must confess that, in saying that 'anyone who offers a *bona fide* contribution towards the advancement of learning may be regarded as *eo ipso* a member of an academic community' (p. 211), I did not guard myself adequately against the objection he makes. For it looks as though I embrace the (silly) view that the rights of academic freedom are special to just those who are ready and willing to exercise them. Clearly, if that were my view, I should have offered no defence of the thesis that academic freedom is a special right. On the contrary, the argument — by collapsing any real distinction between special and common rights — would offer a sort of confirmation to Griffiths' thesis.

I will not haggle over the justice of Griffiths' interpretation[1] of this passage. It is, however, a *mis*interpretation, and one Griffiths would not have made had he not been searching in my paper for a *formula* which can be used to tell who is an academic person and who is not. When I said that 'anyone who offers a *bona fide* contribution. . .' etc. I was in fact envisaging a limiting case. I do not think there is a formula one can give for identifying academic persons. There are clear-cut cases everyone would agree about — the sort of people universities hire. But these have formal qualifications and, while there may be good reasons for hiring only such persons to teach in universities, there are not such good reasons for barring unqualified persons from academic communities altogether. So one has to be prepared to consider that a layman who, say, finds an invalid argument in *Philosophy* and wants to contribute a piece to that effect, is '*eo ipso* a member of an academic community'. That is the sort of limiting case I had in mind.

I agree with Griffiths entirely in not wishing to say that any member of the population is in principle to be excluded from contributing to advancement of knowledge. I express that agreement by allowing that the role of academic person is

[1] I will observe, however, that the offending clause occurs shortly after I had explained why I thought that Galileo had no right of academic freedom.

one which could be assumed, in principle, by almost anyone. Does it follow that the notion of such a role is useless, as Griffiths suggests? If it did then the argument would apply equally to the notion of parental role. Here again there are the obvious and clear-cut cases, namely, of actual parents looking after their children in the socially-approved way. But there are also the limiting cases. When Mrs Smith asks Miss Jones to bring back her Jimmy from the Play Group and Miss Jones agrees to do so she thereby takes on, for a short time and in a limited way, the role of parent. She acquires for that time certain rights and obligations, e.g. the right to forbid the child to cross the road before she is ready and the obligation to see to it that he doesn't. So the role of parent is just as much open to everyone as is that of academic persons. I do not think it follows from this that the rights must be common rights. Nor does it follow that there is no use for the notion of a parental role. The notion of a role here, as in the case of 'academic person', serves to remind us that there is a cluster of rights and obligations which go together. If we follow Professor Griffiths and abandon the notion of an academic as a role, we will be led to conceive of the right of academic freedom in isolation from certain other rights and obligations. I can best defend the utility of such a notion against Professor Griffiths by showing that he is wrong to try to conceive of the right of academic freedom as an isolated right.

ROLES AS FOCI OF SETS OF SPECIAL RIGHTS AND OBLIGATIONS

Griffiths holds that there are no duties correlative with the right of academic freedom in those who have that right. An amateur musicologist can, as he points out, study when he likes and publish when he likes. Here the contrast is between amateur and professional, not between who is engaging in academic work and who not. But though there are *some* obligations that attach specially to professional academics (i.e. the duty to do some research), there are still some that attach to all academic persons. One such duty, I think, is to foster criticism of their own work and to give that criticism the attention it deserves. This duty seems to me to be correlative with the right of academic persons to make their views known and to have them given the attention they deserve. It could not be maintained that those who neglect such duties forfeit their right of academic freedom. But I think Griffiths is wrong in implying that a theory about the conditions under which knowledge can be advanced will generate rights for people without also generating obligations. Such a theory is indeed rich in its implications for what one might call *the ethics of inquiry* as well, as I have indicated, for the ethic of teaching.

I have mentioned the right to have one's criticisms given the attention they deserve. This has an evident connection with the advancement of knowledge. One kind of refusal to take criticism seriously consists in being doctrinaire. The obligation not to be doctrinaire rests upon the very same persons as those who have the right to have their criticisms given the attention they deserve. Given the social nature of inquiry those who engage in it are subject to what we might term 'the ethics of inquiry'. But the rights they have are not ones they have *in their own persons*, so it is 'ethics' in perhaps an attenuated sense. It is the cause of inquiry which is harmed, if criticism is not taken seriously, rather than an individual, insofar as his 'rights' are identified within the ethics of inquiry. That is one important difference between the right of academic freedom and 'idiosyncratic' rights which Griffiths' account glosses over.

I have talked rather loosely about the 'advancement of knowledge' and 'inquiry'. I have had in mind, of course, the sorts of inquiry carried out in universities and in research establishments. So understood, and distinguished therefore from various sorts of day-to-day inquiry, the number of persons who are competent to engage in it is in practice very limited. Indeed it may be that the number of persons who have any conception of what is involved in inquiry, why communication is important and why being doctrinaire is bad, is limited. And that may be one reason why it is tempting to speak of the *role* of academic person, relative to some socially desirable end.

But, even if it were a role which could be readily assumed by anyone and was understood by almost everyone, there would still be some point in calling it a 'role'. For someone who is seriously engaged in inquiry will, as a dilettante will not, accept certain obligations. The dilettante enjoys the various civil liberties which, as Griffiths and I agree, can readily be extended into academic as well as political controversies. The dilettante cannot be accused of being doctrinaire but neither has he any right of academic freedom to defend. He has no wish to assume the role which would make him liable for the first or eligible for the second.

UTILITARIANISM AND ACADEMIC FREEDOM

In my paper, I now think, there are two strands of reasoning which do not marry well with one another. The broad framework of the 'special' theory I expounded is *utilitarian* in character. Academic freedom is broadly justified by reference to the consequences of respecting it, namely, the advancement of human knowledge. Any rights which could be derived from such a theory could be attributed indifferently to persons in any historical context. Professor Griffiths seems to have recognised, as I did not, that if one pursues this utilitarian approach rigorously then one cannot accept a 'special' theory, at any rate of the form I offered. For roles have a history and the rights which attach to them do not attach to persons without respect to their historical context.

More hangs, therefore, on what is to be said about the treatment of Galileo than I recognised in my paper. I there concluded that, since the role of academic person as later defined did not exist in Galileo's time, Galileo did not have any rights of academic freedom to be infringed. Whereas, on a thorough-going utilitarian account Galileo had the rights and, insofar as attempts were made to prevent him from engaging in academic intercourse, his academic freedom was infringed. At worst, on a utilitarian account, it may appear a little anachronistic to talk about 'academic freedom' in connection with Galileo since he would not have thought about his case in his way. And that of itself would make no difference to whether or not he had the rights.

My view is that, as with freedom of the press, a certain historical background is needed to make academic freedom intelligible. There has to be a *tradition* of using the freedom in a particular way, which comes to be regarded as socially valuable, and there has to be some expectation that it will generally *continue* to be used in that way. That expectation corresponds to obligations on the side of those who embark on newspaper editing or academic work, whether full-time or part-time, professional or amateur. That tradition did not exist in Galileo's day or, at any rate, has not always existed. It seems to me therefore to be wrong to ascribe the rights of academic freedom retrospectively to persons who lived before such a tradition grew up.

The difficulty with a thorough-going utilitarian account is that it is not easy to derive rights and obligations within it. What seems at best to follow within such a theory is that it is right to respect the freedom of others to pursue and publish the results of their research and wrong not to. And that is by no means equivalent to those others having the right to pursue and publish the results of their research without interference. I allude here to a familiar difficulty utilitarians have in making sense of the notion of 'a right' and 'obligation'. For even if, in the particular case, the advancement of knowledge is not hampered by suppressing someone's research, his right to academic freedom has still been infringed. On a thorough-going utilitarian account it is difficult to see why, in such a case, it would be wrong provided there was some general advantage which outweighed the frustration caused to the individual affected.

I agree with Griffiths, then, that if the right of academic freedom could be derived from 'considerations about what is necessary to the advancement of knowledge' it would be a *common* right. But I do not see how a *right* can be derived within such an abstract utilitarian theory. It seems to me that Griffiths' theory only shows that it is, in general, right to respect the academic freedom of anyone else. Some of the right connected with academic freedom could be regarded as following upon the common right of everyone not to be interfered with in whatever he wants to do, without good reason. But not all such rights could be derived in this way. The refusal to publish someone's work, to continue to pay his salary or to finance his research, could *in certain circumstances* constitute an infringement of academic freedom. But none of these could straightforwardly be represented as interference. They need not involve any infringement of civil liberties. Academic freedom does, therefore, need a special rationale to avoid a license being given to those who would disregard it but not interfere with civil liberties.

15 Chairman's Remarks

R. S. PETERS

I have a disinclination, like Burke, to discuss issues in terms of abstract rights — that 'Serbonian bog where armies whole have sunk' — unless the context manifestly makes that type of language appropriate. The language of rights — outside, of course, the legal sphere, is a very specific sort of language within normative discourse. There are countless things that are right and wrong where there is no need to have recourse to the specific language of rights to make the point. It is wrong, for instance, for people to break their promises to us, to tell us lies, and to be cruel to us. But it seems unnecessary to construct a case for enjoying general or special rights in these spheres. Similarly, to take one of Stuart Brown's preoccupations, indoctrination is wrong in that it shows lack of respect for persons. I cannot see that it helps the case to conjure up a general or special right not to be indoctrinated. Indeed recourse to rights, as at several points in this symposium, is often a case of *obscurum per obscurius* — rather like the proliferation, in the recent literature, of 'welfare rights' that are not freedoms. In many cases it would be more straightforward just to say that people ought to have various kinds of provision rather than to create a new class of rights.

But, it might rightly be said, the symposium is about academic freedom and the notion of 'rights' is introduced because, according at least to one well established tradition of thought, rights are freedoms in that they prescribe non-interference with interests. Clarification must therefore concentrate on the interests at stake and the ways in which the options of those whose interests they are are being closed up by constraints for which others can be held responsible.

250

There are further questions about how such freedoms can be justified and the conditions under which they are defeasible with which I cannot concern myself without writing another paper. But at least this preliminary anchoring down operation must be conducted before such further questions are raised. And I am not particularly happy about the way in which either of the symposiasts handles this operation.

Talk of freedoms in particular areas has point or application only when an interest or sphere of activity is threatened in some way. We do not go on about freedom in spheres where no interest is at stake or where others cannot, or cannot be bothered to interfere. In civilised societies special institutions have to be developed, for a variety of reasons, for the advancement and transmission of specialised knowledge and skill. It is possible for the activities which are typical of such 'academic' institutions to be interfered with in various ways, and many people have special reasons for trying their hand at this. So they are resisted by members of such institutions in the name of 'academic freedom'. Obviously, therefore, Stuart Brown is right in a certain obvious sense against Mr Searle; for whether or not an interest becomes erected into a special freedom usually depends upon there being a vociferous class of people whose interests are subject to interference. Members of academic institutions belong to such a class. But if members of the general public were bombarding the editor of *Mind* with articles and being told that they were not eligible to publish them there because they did not belong to an 'academic community' they might well start talking about their academic freedom. But the fact is that few of them, as yet, want to do this, and, to my knowledge, the editor of *Mind* does not and would not refuse publication on such grounds. So 'academic freedom' in this sphere is simply not an issue for the ordinary citizen; it is a form of complaint that lacks both point and application in his case. And if the ordinary citizen began talking about his 'academic freedom' it might be similar to historical talk about 'the priesthood of all believers'. For those who proclaimed this were attacking the notion that a man had to be a special person or occupy a special role to communicate with God. The distinctness of the role of 'priest' *was* lost on such a view just as that of the academic would be challenged by widespread talk by the general public about threats to their academic freedom. They would be challenging all the trappings of training and special office peculiar to the academic which are assumed to be preconditions of publishing in learned journals.

Actually, of course, the case of being denied this sort of outlet for contributions to knowledge is not a paradigm case of the denial of academic freedom, any more than is the tyranny of academic fashions which is a more widespread type of constraint by academics on their fellows. A more palpable type of case is when such a journal is suppressed by a government for being, e.g. too bourgeois, individualistic, or unpatriotic, when a teacher in a school or college is banned by local or central government from teaching certain things, or when research is suppressed which is inconvenient to governments or other vested interests that are in a position to constrain academics. Stuart Brown does not concentrate on such cases. Instead he pursues more detailed questions about the status of research conducted on the assumption that butterflies might have a spiritual life which, from a certain point of view, seems no more absurd than the opposite supposition dominating research on which millions and millions of dollars have spent, namely that human beings are purely mechanical systems. He also, as I have mentioned before, explores the right not to be indoctrinated which he thinks an important aspect of academic freedom. But in so far as this is connected with freedom it is surely much more closely connected with assaults on those subjective conditions without which a man cannot properly be described as a chooser, still less as an autonomous being. It shows lack of respect not just in refusing to treat a man as an agent capable of evaluation and choice but in impairing a man in respects of those capacities without which he could not become a free man.[1] It is not an obvious case of interference with the objective conditions of choice with which academic freedom is usually concerned, which presupposes that a man is a chooser.

[1] See Benn, S. I. and Weinstein, W. 'Being free to act and being a free man', *Mind* Vol. 80, No. 328 (Apr 1971).

Why does Stuart Brown stray into these byways of academic life? Largely because he tries to produce a theory of academic freedom which includes a justification of it. His theory gives rise to objections about the worth of knowledge, objectivity and so on, which he feels obliged to answer. So he concentrates on these details and does not pay sufficient attention to some more obvious issues raised by complaints about infringements of academic freedom. But more of this later.

Phillips Griffiths is equally ambitious, though in a different direction. He invents an ideal academic community in which people seem to understand what the common good is and in which they enjoy 'deontic rights'. But his normative vision makes it difficult to deal with many actual cases of threats to academic freedom. He thinks that academics enjoy a special right to conduct their activities which is consequent on their duty as contractual servants of an institution to pursue a particular aspect of the common good. The authorities of the institution have, in their turn, a duty to prevent others from interfering with this deontic right to academic freedom. What sort of thing, then, are academics saying when they complain of invasions of their academic freedom in countries in which the administrators of schools and universities prescribe syllabuses, books, and teaching methods? In so far as these administrators understand what the 'common good' is they certainly do not include the pursuit of truth in it. That is just something that the wayward academic regards as valuable. How is his protest about his 'academic freedom' to be interpreted in such a situation? Must he have in mind an ideal type of situation such as that portrayed by Phillips Griffiths to give meaning to his protests? Are not many perfectly intelligible complaints about loss of academic freedom less tightly structured than those of members of such an ideal community? And does not the location of this type of talk in an institution in which there is an accepted duty to advance knowledge, on which the right to academic freedom is consequent, confuse the question 'What do we mean by academic freedom?' with the question 'Under what sorts of conditions might we ensure that others would not interfere with this right?' Is not Phillips Griffiths more concerned with an ideal picture of a university and employing it to draw the attention of university authorities to their duties than he is with exploring the messiness of actual claims to academic freedom, which represent much less structured complaints about actual or possible interference with interests and activities?

I cannot see, either, that his portrayal of the various obstacles that lie in the path of those who want to learn has much to do with academic freedom unless a romantic type of story is told, e.g. by an Illich, of countless Emiles eager to learn whose opportunities for so doing are blocked by the guardians of a repressive establishment. Indeed the depressing reality is that so few people want to learn unless they see an obvious pay-off. Maybe their wants have been conditioned by the consumer society. Maybe they are like contented slaves on whose behalf others must protest. But some story of this sort must be told for talk of academic freedom to have much application to their case.

Actually it has more application in a sphere where Phillips Griffiths is reluctant to admit its applicability — that of student protest against the constraints imposed upon them in their actual learning situation by paternalistic professors and headmasters. I do not go along with those who think that academic institutions should be fully 'democratic'.[2] I am well aware, too, that many radicals make such protests without any specific interest in educational institutions as such; they just see them as a convenient starting place for disrupting 'the establishment'. Nevertheless there are genuine protests against certain sorts of decisions being made solely by academics, be they professors or headmasters, where it is difficult to see what rational case there is for them alone making them.

Phillips Griffiths can deal simply with such protests because his concern is mainly with universities and his vision of a university is of a graduate school concerned only with the advancement of knowledge and with the initiation of others to continue it. This vision, of course, has little application to real universities either past or present; for they

---

[2] See Peters, R. S. *Authority, Responsibility and Education*, Ch. 4 (Allen & Unwin, 1973).

are and always have been concerned with general education, with preparing people for professions, and with contributing to the solution of the problems of the communities which finance them. Most people who pass through universities, also, have neither the inclination nor the ability to advance the frontiers of knowledge. The most, in my view, that can be said for Griffiths' ideal is that what makes universities distinctive is that these other purposes should be pursued in a context in which many are dedicated to the advancement of knowledge.

The influence of Griffiths' type of vision is, of course, fairly widespread, especially with the proliferation of single subject honours degrees. It means, in effect, that many university teachers see their students in their own image, as potential succesors to themselves in advancing knowledge. They are reluctant to face the question of what there might be in their subject for the majority of their students who will never step into their shoes. So their students talk incoherently about 'relevance' and complain about constraints erected against their learning what they deem 'significant'. Alternatively they complain about being processed, graded, and labelled in a way which will determine their future in the occupational structure. This raises the difficult and crucial question of what types of knowledge and understanding are central to the development of educated people. It is not necessarily the type of specialised knowledge which university teachers may be interested in developing. It is not obvious, either, that academics should be the sole determiners of what this knowledge should be. For, though they are obviously authorities on matters internal to their subject, they cannot claim the same authority for the importance of their subject, or of particular aspects of it, in the general education of students. There is obviously a case, therefore, in this sphere, for some kind of consultation or joint decision-making, in which students should have some kind of say.

This might be regarded as a marginal case of academic freedom, though it is not thought of as marginal by supporters of the Council for Academic Freedom who argue that it cannot exist without the democratisation of educational institutions — whatever that may mean. I draw attention to it, however, because it raises a similar issue to that raised by the central cases of academic freedom about which there has been very little systematic discussion. In these central cases academics complain about constraints put on research and the curriculum by governments, the general public and students even though increasingly their livelihood depends upon cash provided by such outside bodies. To what extent should the representatives of the people, who vote the cash for the pursuit of this aspect of 'the common good', be entitled to exercise control of how this cash is spent? What rationale exists in the philosophy of education for an ad hoc arrangement like the UGC? And if universities are concerned with education as well as with the advancement of knowledge at what point and in what kinds of contexts should students be allowed to raise fundamental questions to do with 'what knowledge is of most worth' which lie behind their obscure ramblings about 'relevance'? Similarly at the school level what is the rationale for the reluctance of the Secretary of State to legislate about the curriculum — with the notable exception of religious instruction? Is the setting up of the Schools Council an incipient threat, as many think, to the academic freedom of teachers? The *de jure* position of the right to determine the curriculum in English schools is so complicated that headmasters enjoy a great deal of autonomy de facto in this sphere. But why should they rather than the staff collectively or in consultation with governors, parents, and pupils?

Surely the central cases of academic freedom being threatened are when academics complain about interference with their teaching and research by outside individuals and bodies. My complaint against both symposiasts is that, in developing their theories of special and deontic rights, they have failed to discuss fundamental issues centring round the question 'Who should determine the curriculum of schools and universities?' which lie beneath such central cases. This, in my view, is one of the most important questions in the philosophy of education which remains, to date, unexplored in any clear and systematic manner.

Postscript

A. PHILLIPS GRIFFITHS

The difference between Professor Peters and myself is such a gulf, that further discussion on my part would be out of place. His piece and mine must simply lie there side by side. This difference has many aspects, perhaps the most important being our views on what one demands of a philosophical theory, or perhaps even any theory. But the difference which makes further discussion most difficult explains why of course I did not, as he so rightly accuses, discuss his question, 'Who should determine the curriculum of schools and universities?'. 'The separation between Jowett and myself', wrote Mark Pattison, 'consists in a difference upon the fundamental question of University politics – viz. Science and Learning v. School keeping'. The separation between Peters and myself is that I think Pattison's distinction is of the first importance.

I fear, however, that I must make a brief reply, because this volume is likely to be read by people who will be advising candidates for Universities where to apply to read philosophy. Something Professor Peters says could mislead them.

'The influence of Griffiths' type of vision is, of course, widespread, especially with the proliferation of single subject honours degrees', he says. Now I think he means to speak of this vision as one would of a disease: its ravages are not the direct responsibility of its bearer. But I must point out that whatever the general effects of this vision, it has not so affected me. Of the 100 or so students we hope to admit to read philosophy at Warwick in October 1974, eighty will be entering joint degrees with literature, politics, sociology, physics, mathematics or psychology; and these are carefully planned integrated degrees which my colleagues have worked very hard to develop over the last nine years. If these students are anything like those we have now, they will not 'talk incoherently about "relevance" and complain about constraints erected against their learning what they deem "significant".' They will not talk incoherently at all, not even I hope about schools and Universities when we start our joint degree with education in 1975.

Index